Σο ψου ωαντ το δο Εκκλεσια?

..."The glory of this latter Temple shall be greater than the former" Haggai 2:9

by
Doug Krieger

So You Want to do Ekklesia?

So, You Want to Do Ekklesia?

... "The glory of the latter Temple shall be greater than the former" Haggai 2:9

Douglas W. Krieger

TRIBNET PUBLICATIONS
SACRAMENTO, CALIFORNIA

SO, YOU WANT TO DO EKKLESIA?

... "The glory of the latter Temple shall be greater than the former" – Haggai 2:9

TRIBNET PUBLICATIONS
SACRAMENTO, CALIFORNIA
PRINTED IN THE UNITED STATES OF AMERICA

© COPYRIGHT TRIBNET PUBLICATIONS, 2020

SECOND EDITION

ISBN- 9781709695308

Imprint: Independently published

ALL IMAGES FROM WIKIPEDIA COMMONS, PUBLIC DOMAIN UNLESS OTHERWISE NOTED

COVER DESIGN BY DOUGLAS W. KRIEGER

ALL SCRIPTURE TAKEN FROM THE NEW KING JAMES VERSION OF THE BIBLE UNLESS OTHERWISE NOTED

Table of Contents

Table of Figures x

Dedicated to Him Who: xiii

About the Author xv

Author's Introduction xvii

Acknowledgements xxiii

Chapter 1: Who's Controlling This Ekklesia Anyway? 3

    Who's Really In Control? 6

    Hosting An Ekklesia 7

    The "Controlling" Host 8

    The Difference Between Ekklesia and Ministry 9

    Summing Up 14

Chapter 2: How Can the God of Peace Crush Satan Under Your Feet? 15

    Friends, Romans, Countrymen, Lend Me Your Ears 17

    Four Obvious Factions 19

    Paul Knew What's Up with the Saints in Rome 22

    Peculiar Folks—These Four Groups 23

Chapter 3: So, You've Got a Corner on the Truth? 29

    The Lone Ranger 30

    Groupies 32

    The Emperor's New Clothes 36

Chapter 4: An Unfederated Wildfire 41

    The Final Harvest 41

    Filled With The Spirit – Not Spirits 43

    Kill and Eat – No Way – No Partiality!! 44

Uncontrolled Burn – Fires Just Flare Up! 46
The Evangelistic Crusade That Wasn't 47
What Does an Awakening Look Like? 48
The "Court of the Nations/Gentile" – Rev. 11 49
My, How Things Get Organized! 51
Summing It Up 53

Chapter 5: There's Doctrine and Then There's Doctrine 55
Introduction by Doug Krieger: 55
Truth: God and His Eternal Work 56
What Is Not Truth? 59
It's Easy to Be Distracted Away from the Truth 61
Confusion: Doctrine Unites, Doctrine Divides 63

Chapter 6: One by One – Each One of You Has 73
Bring & Share Your Portion of the "Good Land" 76
Discerning the Lord's Body 78
What Do We Have, One by One? 82
God is the God of Variety 84
Perennial "Control Freak" – Alpha Male (or Jezebel) ... 85
We've Got this "Thing" under Control 86
Ending on a "Happy Note" 87

Chapter 7: Balancing Act Between Clergy & Laity – Part 1 89
Clergy Abuse/Exploitation 90
Allow me to quote Renner on this: 91
Congregant Malfeasance – The Laodiceans 92
The "Congregational System" 93
Balance Between "The Work" & the "Congregants" 94
Who's in Control – Why I Left a "Christian Cult" 95

Rejection? "Seems Antioch was Controlling Them" 97
"Work & Ministry" vs. "Ekklesia/Congregants?" 103

Chapter 8: Balancing Act Between Clergy & Laity – Part 2 ...107
If "Each Has"—Then Why Do Some Dominate? 107
Separate the "Gifted" when Needed in the Trenches? ..110
"House Churches" Don't Guarantee Ekklesia 112
Ekklesia isn't Therapy-Intimate Sessions.....................113
Too Big OK – But Keep Ekklesia Intimate 120

Chapter 9: Balancing Act Between Clergy & Laity – Part 3 ...123
What About the Flock-less Shepherds Taking Over?....123
Paul & Barnabas NOT Controlled by Antioch................126
What About Local *Eldership*? 128
The BBQ that got Busted!..131
What About Wolves & "Flockless Shepherds"?............135
Let Paul be our Example 139

Chapter 10: Ekklesia Replicates "Lord's Appointed Times" – Part 1 143
An Introduction to the Topic at Hand: 143
Seven Sacred Feast Days of the Hebrew Calendar.........151
The Feast of Dedication . . . Connecting the Dots 154
King Solomon's Temple Dedication & Haggai's 9/24....154
Feast of Dedication 24/25 Kislev—2,300 Days of Dan. 8157
Haggai's 24/25 Kislev – "Glory of the Latter House" 163

Chapter 11: Ekklesia Replicates "Lord's Appointed Times" – Part 2 169
9/24 Amplified in Latter House Dedication 169
Jesus at Feast of Dedication vs. Antichrist 173

Feast of Tabernacles Tied to Feast of Dedication 175
What is Haggai Really Saying? 177
Is the Seed still in the Barn? 180
Laboring on the "Good Land" = Surplus of Christ 185
He Shall Bear the Glory 188

Chapter 12: This is Not an Ekklesia – Part 1 191

Backseat Drivers? 191
Submit or Else . . . or Else What? 192
We're it – the Overcomers – the Elite! 195
It's US vs. THEM 197
"Jezebel spirit": CONTROL, Control 198
Emotional Dependency Works! 201
Each one has a Revelation? 205
Summing it up… 208

Chapter 13: This is Not an Ekklesia – Part 2 211

How About "Deliverance Ministry?" 214
"Once Saved Always Saved" – "Our Little Click" 216
Christians Suing Their Brothers and Sisters 218
Clump Mentality 219
The Witch Who Broke Up Our Gathering 221
Ekklesia Under Strict Eldership Guidelines 224
"Get out of your Mind" – "Stop thinking" 226
"Hit the Road Jack . . . and Don't you come back!" 229
"Boys will be Boys and Girls will be Girls" 231

Chapter 14: Lord's Supper – Division in the Camp? 237

Traditional Theological Issues on Communion 238
Yes – Divisions in the Body 242

NT Occurrences and Descriptions 243

New Covenant & New Commandment - Implications ... 244

"Ekklesia" Implications at the "Lord's Table" 251

Dividing the Cup in Luke's Gospel? 256

Endnotes to Chapter 14: 259

Chapter 15: The 24 Axioms of Ekklesia *261*

ENDNOTES & INDEXES & PUBLICATIONS ***273***

So, You Want to do Ekklesia?

Table of Figures

FIGURE 1 - MY EKKLESIA VS THE GATES OF HADES 3
FIGURE 2 - I LIKE THIS EKKLESIA, HERB - BECAUSE YOU'RE IN CONTROL! 4
FIGURE 3 - YOU CAN ALL PROPHESY - EVEN INTERRUPT 6
FIGURE 4 - EVERYONE THINKS THEY'RE IN CONTROL 9
FIGURE 5 - LET'S PLAY RECOVERY BINGO 11
FIGURE 6 - IT'S MY WAY OR THE HIGHWAY 12
FIGURE 7 - ANCIENT EATING HABITS DIE SLOWLY 15
FIGURE 8 - ROMANS & BARBARIANS AT WAR - BY LUDOVISI 20
FIGURE 9 - THE COMPLETION GOSPEL BY HON & KRIEGER 27
FIGURE 10 - SO YOU THINK YOUR PART OF THE ELEPHANT IS WHAT? 29
FIGURE 11 - THE LONE RANGER 30
FIGURE 12 - GROUPIES 32
FIGURE 13 - HERE COMES THE "MAN OF GOD" 33
FIGURE 14 - BUT THE KING HAS NO CLOTHES! 37
FIGURE 15 - AN UNFEDEREATED WILDFIRE 41
FIGURE 16 - THE "FINAL HARVEST" 42
FIGURE 17 - THE "WILD FIRE" OF PENTECOST 44
FIGURE 18 - PETER USED TO OPEN THE DOOR TO THE GENTILES 46
FIGURE 19 - MASSIVE EVANGELISTIC CRUSADE 47
FIGURE 20 - FRANK BARTLEMAN'S "ANOTHER WAVE ROLLS IN" 49
FIGURE 21 - THE "COURT OF THE GENTILES" - REV. 11 50
FIGURE 22 - THE "JESUS MOVEMENT" 52
FIGURE 23 - HENRY'S HON'S BOOK: ONE TRUTH 55
FIGURE 24 - LUTHER VS. OFFICIALS ON TRUTH OF SCRIPTURE 57
FIGURE 25 - PONTIUS PILATE VS. JESUS 58
FIGURE 26 - SALVATION ARMY "SPIRITUAL BAPTISM" 60
FIGURE 27 - THE MOUNT OF TRANSFIGURATION 62
FIGURE 28 - DOCTRINES THAT DIVIDE 64
FIGURE 29 - 1 TIMOTHY 6:3-4 67
FIGURE 30 - EPHESIANS 4:4-7; 11-16 69
FIGURE 31 - THAT THEY ALL MAY BE ONE 70
FIGURE 32 - HENRY HON: ONE TRUTH 72
FIGURE 33 - QUOTE FROM HENRY HON 73
FIGURE 34 - "THE JOY OF EARLY CHRISTIANITY" - BY STEVE SIMMS 74
FIGURE 35 - 'I AM NOT A CONTROL FREAK" 76
FIGURE 36 - THE LORD'S FEASTS AKIN TO A HUGE TAILGATE PARTY 77
FIGURE 37 - 1 CORINTHIANS 11:29 78
FIGURE 38 - THE LORD'S SUPPER 80
FIGURE 39 - "ONE BY ONE - EACH ONE HAS" 82

FIGURE 40 - GOD IS THE GOD OF VARIETY	84
FIGURE 41 - "I'M SO IN CONTROL!"	85
FIGURE 42 - EPHESIANS 4:4-7	88
FIGURE 43 - THE CLERGY AND THE LAITY	89
FIGURE 44 - THE RISE OF THE DONES	90
FIGURE 45 - LAODICEA - THE LUKEWARM CHURCH	92
FIGURE 46 - WALLAPALOOZA	94
FIGURE 47 - "I KNOW THE 'GROUND OF UNITY' IS OUT THERE SOMEWHERE"	96
FIGURE 48 - FRANK HANKS - "HOW TO GET KICKED OUT OF A CHURCH"	98
FIGURE 49 - TOXIC CHURCH ENVIRONMENT	100
FIGURE 50 - "THE BORG"	102
FIGURE 51 - EPHESIANS 4:12	104
FIGURE 52 - "I'M IN CHARGE OF THIS EKKLESIA - WHO'D LIKE TO SHARE?"	107
FIGURE 53 - "HOUSE CHURCHES" DON'T GUARANTEE EKKLESIA	112
FIGURE 54 - SOMEONE HAS TO CONTROL CHILDISH FOOD FIGHTS	117
FIGURE 55 - 12,000,000 MEETING AT NIGERIA'S REDEEMER CHURCH OF GOD	120
FIGURE 56 - BEWARE OF WOLVES IN SHEEP'S CLOTHING	123
FIGURE 57 - THE LEVITE PRIEST AND THE "SHRINE OF MICAH"	125
FIGURE 58 - THE BBQ THAT GOT BUSTED	132
FIGURE 59 - WE'RE JUST WAITING FOR THE FLOCKLESS SHEPHERD!	135
FIGURE 60 - ACTS 28:30-31	140
FIGURE 61 - KING SOLOMON - THE "FORMER HOUSE" - G. BONITO	143
FIGURE 62 - THE SEVEN FEAST DAYS & HANUKKAH	147
FIGURE 63 - DOUG KRIEGER'S HEBREW & CHRISTIAN CALENDAR	150
FIGURE 64 - KING SOLOMON'S TEMPLE DEDICATION	155
FIGURE 65 - JUDAH - THE MACCABEE	158
FIGURE 66 - KING SOLOMON DEDICATES THE FIRST TEMPLE	169
FIGURE 67 - GLORY OF THIS LATTER HOUSE - GREATER THAN THE FORMER	170
FIGURE 68 - JOHN 10:24	174
FIGURE 69 - JOSHUA THE HIGH PRIEST CROWNED	184
FIGURE 70 - "MOM, DON'T TELL ME HOW TO DRIVE--I'M IN CONTROL!"	191
FIGURE 71 - KEEP CALM AND SUBMIT TO MY AUTHORITY	192
FIGURE 72 - "SHUT UP AND DO AS YOU'VE BEEN TOLD!"	194
FIGURE 73 - THE ELITE FORCES	196
FIGURE 74 - CIRCLE THE WAGONS	198
FIGURE 75 - JEZEBEL VS. ELIJAH - DR. BREE KEYTON	200
FIGURE 76 - WE ARE "DAS VOLK"	202
FIGURE 77 - THE REVELATION OF JESUS CHRIST	205
FIGURE 78 - SECRET QUEST - THE PATH OF THE CHRISTIAN GNOSTICS	207
FIGURE 79 - GRIEVOUS WOLVES AMONG THE SHEEP	209

FIGURE 80 - CUTTING AWAY AT YOUR CRITICAL THINKING SKILLS	211
FIGURE 81 - YOOU NEED TO BE UNDER MY COVERING	215
FIGURE 82 - THE CHURCH DOES SAVE YOU - ONLY JESUS CAN	217
FIGURE 83 - THE MAN WHO DIDN'T "HEIL HITLER"	220
FIGURE 84 - THE "CHRISTIAN" WITCH	222
FIGURE 85 - SHEEP WHO THINK YOU ARE GOD	226
FIGURE 86 - SHUNNED BY "TRUE BELIEVERS"	229
FIGURE 87 - CONFORMITY IS THE ONLY REAL FASHION CRIME	232
FIGURE 88 - "BEARDED CONFORMITY"	234
FIGURE 89 - THE BODY - THE BLOOD - COMMUNION	237
FIGURE 90 - THE LAST SUPPER - LEONARDO DA VINCI	239
FIGURE 91 - "LOVE REVOLUTION NOW" - BY GAYLORD ENNS	245
FIGURE 92 - THE NEW COVENANT "IN MY BLOOD"	250
FIGURE 93 - "THAT THEY ALL MAY BE PERFECTED IN UNITY"	259
FIGURE 94 - 2 CORINTHIANS 3:2-3	261
FIGURE 95 - THE 24 AXIOMS OF EKKLESIA	265

Dedicated to Him Who:

"... is our peace, who has made both one, and has broken down the middle wall of separation ... to create in Himself one new man from the two, thus making peace" (Eph. 2:14-15).

And to:

My dear Family
Deborah – my beloved for over 50 years
And My Children – Eric, April, and Geoffrey
And all our Grandchildren

And to my dear Friends:

Henry and Sylvia Hon
And to all who desire to
"keep the unity of the Spirit
In the uniting bond of Peace"

So, You Want to do Ekklesia?

About the Author

Douglas W. Krieger is a published author having written or co-authored over 14 volumes, including **The Final Babylon . . . America and the Coming of Antichrist** (with Dene McGriff and S. Douglas Woodward); **SIGNS IN THE HEAVENS and ON THE EARTH...Man's Days Are Numbered...and he is Measured!**; **Blood on the Altar** (co-authored with 11 others); **Uncommon Sense** (co-authored with S. Douglas Woodward); and the two volume set of **THE TWO WITNESSES...I Will Give Authority to My Two Witnesses**—a treatise on Israel and the Church in the Last Days; **Unsealing the End of Days**—A Commentary on Zechariah; **Commonwealth Theology**—An Introduction; **The Testimony of Jesus**—Why the Rapture of the Church Matters; **One in Messiah** with twelve authors—derived from the 2019 Denver Convocation; **The Completion Gospel** with Henry Hon—a Treatise on the book of Romans; **The World in the Bondage of Egypt**—Under the Triumphal Arch of Titus with Chad Schafer; Charts & Graphics by Doug Krieger; and now, **So, You Want to do Ekklesia**.

Doug currently serves on three boards: One Body Life (an international ministry bringing the Body of Christ together in ministry); the Commonwealth of Israel Foundation whose ultimate goal is the publication of a Reference Bible presenting commentary on Scripture: "The Commonwealth of Israel Edition"; and Urban Hope Alliance, based in Sacramento, CA—all three are not-for-profit corporations. Each of these ministries has its own social media (blogs) outreach with conferences and other formats (video, publications, etc.).

Doug has been married to Deborah since 1968, has three married children. For twenty years Doug was in public education as a high school teacher and administrator—he was graduated from both California State University Los Angeles and CSU Sacramento in Education Administration.

His background includes serving as an elder-pastor in Berkeley, California during the Jesus Movement and is a frequent speaker at prophecy conferences during the past decade.

So, You Want to do Ekklesia?

Author's Introduction

THE COMMENCEMENT OF THE TWENTY-FIRST CENTURY HAS WITNESSED THE PERCIPITOUS IMPLOSION OF "CHURCH AS WE KNOW IT."[1] NOT ONLY HAS Christianity's impact decreased in the West—especially the USA—but the growing number of "nones" (non-affiliated) and "dones" (still Christian but wholly unaligned with any denominational affiliation or traditional "church attendance" yet who maintain their "spirituality" and embrace most of the major principles found in Christianity)[2] has rapidly increased.

Whatever we are doing in the "heart of the West" is NOT working—insofar as a vibrant Christian witness concerns . . . notwithstanding the contrary impact that Christians are having throughout the rest of the world in general (outside the West).[3]

This "spiritual phenomena" has wrought an agonizing reappraisal by sundry Christian ecclesiologists as to why these cultural upheavals in the West are having such a seemingly deleterious effect upon the Christian demography. Leading, as far as this author concerns, these challenges facing the "people of God," have been activists, protagonists, and influencers who have, in the main, sought to historically and theologically identify the causes and possible solutions to the aforementioned "decline." Many of these individuals have been involved in what has become known as "organic church" movements.

Individuals such as Frank Viola—and his periodic associate, George Barna (Pagan Christianity, Reimagining Church); Milt Rodriquez (@ Planting 1st Century Style Organic Churches in the 21st Century; e.g., Starting Organic Churches; Christianity Today's article regarding "Organic Church Movement" (2010)[4] – all bear witness to this organic quest.

Solutions abound to the present malaise afflicting Christendom in the West—everything from the revival of the Five-fold Ministry to radical Deliverance (normally, from demonic possession/obsession) with scores of "Discipleship" instruction, "Missional endeavors" with "Purpose-Driven" efforts, along with 24/7 prayer thrown in for good measure. Disappointment abounds—even confusion—when author/speakers like Frank Viola

So, You want to do Ekklesia?

genuinely desire for a more "authentic Christianity" yet leave us pondering the apparent, and purposeful, ambiguity minefields awaiting the seeker of true Christian expression/community:

> There's nothing magical about meeting in a home. And a physical house isn't God's passion, nor is it mine. Never has been. In my earlier books, Pagan Christianity (2008), Reimagining Church (2008), and Finding Organic Church (2009), I point out that there's a monumental difference between a house church and an organic expression of the church.
>
> Some "house churches" (so-called) are organic. Many others are not. George Barna and I make this exact point in Pagan Christianity (p. 240).
>
> Despite the fact that what I've written above has been repeated on this blog, in my books, and on my podcast, some folks continue to benightedly engage in straw-man argumentation by falsely stating that I believe house churches are "the only way to do church." [Cough, #Fail.]
>
> To add to the confusion, over the last several years, the phrase "organic church" has been hijacked to mean 1,001 different things.
>
> So the term "organic" is pretty much meaningless now. For that reason, I hardly ever use it anymore. And so I don't advocate "organic church" in the way that it is so often employed today.
>
> What I advocate is Christ-centered, face-to-face community. And that's what I describe in my earlier books from 2008 and 2009. This means a community that is taking care of one another 24/7 . . . not just twice a week for a meeting. A community that has a shared life together, like an extended family. A community that has been equipped to have open-participatory gatherings where each member shares the riches of Jesus Christ (I'm not talking about anything that resembles a "Bible study," by the way). A community that makes decisions together under the headship of Christ, rather than under a human head. And a community who's (sic.) goal in life is to pursue Jesus Christ and His Eternal Purpose together. Such a

community has been birthed from the apostolic declaration of the explosive gospel of the kingdom. That kind of community, friends, has always been rare on this earth. (House Church vs. Organic Expression [Beyond Evangelical—A Blog by Frank Viola])

Several of the aforementioned writers/influencers were themselves motivated by folks like Gene Edwards or people like Witness Lee—both of whom sought after a more organic expression of the Body of Christ but whose efforts seemed to have bogged down into fratricide and cult-like behavior (although Christian in nature—yet, considered very divisive by scores of well-meaning brethren).

Why is it a somewhat expansive network of "house churches" here in North America (2000-2019) seems to have disintegrated into denominational disarray and/or expressions resembling the "circling of the wagons" wherein insulated believers have little impact upon the unwelcoming world surrounding them? That's my practical awareness . . . and I don't think I'm that far off with such a presumptuous claim.

When ministers within the Body of Christ draw saints "unto themselves" with bombastic claims that they alone are for the true unity of the Body of Christ—BEWARE! In particular at nearly 80 years of age, I have had the obtuse privilege (if you can call it that) of witnessing scores of "enlightened brethren" riveted upon the unity and expression of that unity within the Body of Christ, yet find it impossible to labor together with their peers; consequently, these "leaders" reflect a distasteful elitism ("I am of Christ"—1 Cor. 1:12) wherein an overweening sense of their own propriety afflicts them . . . leading, many times, to dishonesty, even bombast which is nothing more than egomania somehow admired by those with weaker ego!

So, with all these somewhat lackluster results why not throw in the proverbial towel and simply admit it'll be "like this" until the Second Coming—notwithstanding all the Biblical injunctions to "press the battle" ever forward?

So, You want to do Ekklesia?

A very good friend of mine for the past nearly 60 years has given me additional encouragement to "quit tilting at windmills" and simply come to grips that rampant apostasy and Laodicean-style compromise is the harbinger to the pending "Tribulation" in any event—*"Give it up Krieger—it is what it is . . . someone has to control this 'thing' called the CHURCH . . . and don't you know that those who do so are imperfect beings bent on 'whose God is their belly' with those who manage to survive with pure hearts and clean hands normally are the ones most have stepped on in making sure they don't survive their own successes in ministry anyway?"*

So, with encouragement like this—who needs another book on organic communities of believers or Body Life? Honestly, sometimes I feel like Tom Edison whose 1,000+ experiments in creating the electric light bulb should have brought him into utter despair. Notwithstanding, the man was obsessed with discovering what would work until a simple carbon-filament lamp in a vacuum did the trick!

Yes, this text will waft from heady theological constructs to simple solutions, from the comedic to complicated ecclesiastical imbroglios. Purposefully, I have taken graphic license to keep the reader engaged (besides, I like illustrations to enhance the content).

Somehow with the acceleration of these "organic Body Life" experimentations taking place during the past twenty years, one could safely surmise "Surely, we've learned a thing or two!" What to do and not do—indeed, virtually all the epistles were written (and frankly, most of the Bible) because of human frailty, error, fault and just plain sin—while showing us that God is still in control and *"Jesus is the same, yesterday, today and forever!"*

Have we arrived? Have I got the answer to this maelstrom of ecclesiological consternation? Am I confident that when Jesus said: *"I will build my Ekklesia, and the gates of hades will not prevail against it"*—that He's going to wait until this generation (which is really arriving at the end of "man's days") to affect the prophetic fulfillment: *"The glory of the latter Temple shall be greater than the former?"* Why not "finish my course" with one last dash to the ribbon? If the Lord will grant me His grace to see John 17 come in fullness—to arrive at what you will find in this text known as *"the Completion or Fullness of the blessing of the Gospel of Christ"*—then why not!

I truly pray this at times "folksy" effort to persuade you to keep pressing the battle for the *"unity of the faith and of the knowledge of the Son of God, unto a perfect man"* (Eph. 4:13) will inspire you to *ENDEAVOR to keep the unity of the Spirit in the uniting bond of peace* (Eph. 4:3). Do we who seek the Lord have an alternative? Not really, if we claim to mean business for the Master. *"Woe is me if I do not preach the gospel"* (1 Cor. 9:16); and, as you will see, the Gospel of the Grace of God and the Gospel of Peace is the "completion of the Gospel" and the two constitute the "Gospel of the Kingdom" . . . may you be blessed and may the Holy Spirit stir in your spirit the same desire of our Lord:

> *"I in them, and You in Me; that they may be perfected into one, and that the world may know that You have sent Me, and have loved them as You have loved Me"* (John 17:23).

Douglas W. Krieger
November 2019

So, You want to do Ekklesia?

Acknowledgements

THERE ARE SCORES OF DEAR BRETHREN UPON WHOSE SHOULDERS I STAND IN PUTTING INTO WORDS THESE CONCERNS REGARDING THE BUILDING of His Ekklesia.

Sometimes "thick" and sometimes "thin"—but definitely there to inspire and guide in this quest for the Ekklesia whom *"Christ also loved ... and gave Himself for her, that He might set it apart and cleanse her with the washing of water by the word, that He might present her to Himself a glorious Ekklesia, not having spot or wrinkle or any such thing, but that she should be holy and without blemish"* (Eph. 5:25-27).

In this journey I have been blessed, not only by the encouragement of my family members, but by the likes of Henry and Sylvia Hon, who of late during the last several years, after a long hiatus, have enlightened me so much on matters of "Ekklesia" to which heretofore I had virtually abandoned in vision and practice—so "done" was I ... but the patient was revived having a "near death" experience but brought back to life through vision and now practice of ONE BODY LIFE!

Our little "band of brothers" (and sisters) in Sacramento and the Bay Area—of whom are Rod and Kendra Brace, Turia Davis, Hal Townsend, Scott McCarroll, John Polli and our beloved Nigerian brethren, especially Femi (Churchman) Adebayo, along with Dayo, Dr. Tobih, and Ola Abraham—all have contributed.

Without the encouragement of brethren who have seen the bringing together into the One New Man under the banner of the *"Commonwealth of Israel"* (Eph. 2:12) as the true expression of His Ekklesia, I could not have written this volume—of whom are Dr. Gavin Finley, Dr. Doug Hamp, Chris Steinle and many others who are discovering the meaning of the "United Kingdom of David" (aka, *"The Tabernacle of David"*—Acts 15; Amos 9).

Again, reinforcements to press the battle have faithfully come from my two "best friends" in the Faith—Dene McGriff and Doug Shearer and their spouses, Carol and Sita. Finally, that enthusiastic remnant who gather weekly—ever probing the depths of the Savior's infinite love through mutual sharing at His Table, His "inheritance in the saints—the unsearchable riches of Christ!"

So, You want to do Ekklesia?

So, You want to do Ekklesia?

. . . . . .

"The glory of the latter Temple shall be greater than the former"

(Haggai 2:9)

So, You Want to do Ekklesia?

Chapter 1:
Who's Controlling This Ekklesia Anyway?

Figure 1 - MY EKKLESIA vs THE GATES OF HADES

"I will build My EKKLESIA and the Gates of Hades shall not prevail against it"

(Matthew 16:18)

DOESN'T IT SEEM A BIT ODD THAT EKKLESIA IS SOMEHOW TIED TO "CRUSHING SATAN'S HEAD?" WELL, IT'S EITHER THIS OR SOMEONE ELSE IS in control... let me explain.

I know, the title to this first chapter sounds negative—it is in a "positive sounding way!" However, when you or your little group of controllers (*forgive me if I sound like I'm using a 2X4 to get your attention—I mean well*) tries to manipulate a gathering of God's people who are desiring to have a free and open fellowship—all the while Satan is having a "heyday!" How's that? IF SOMEONE(S) DOESN'T CONTROL what's going down in this meeting—it'll all become confused and wolves (aka, flock-less shepherds) will come in and try to "take over" the meeting in any event, right? And, that's why we need to "control this thing!"

So, You want to do Ekklesia?

So, casually but intentionally, you come together in someone's home or business or public building (e.g., social hall, dorm lounge, etc.) to pray, read God's Word together, worship through song and praise, and share testimonies about your experiences with Christ—but someone HAS TO LEAD the meeting, otherwise, it will go awry or will be prone for someone to rise up and dominate the conversation, the exchange.

Have you ever been in an Ekklesia-style gathering where 1 Corinthians 11-14 is actually practiced—I mean, without the Pastor's notes, or some pre-ordained program (aka, the infamous AGENDA—going down "item by item" 'til all is covered)?

And, FORBID, if all the saints present don't share at least something! I mean, really, why come to a "participatory meeting" and then just sit there like you're in some "church pew" stuffing yourself with another sermon . . . most of us, at best, are just used to some minimal participation (like praise and worship) and then we sit there and take it all in . . . so, this is just the same but on a smaller scale, right?

Figure 2 - I LIKE THIS EKKLESIA, HERB - BECAUSE YOU'RE IN CONTROL!

It's all good to get everyone "in on the action" but how does that look? I've been in some gatherings in which a strong personality type (usually a man) will so dominate the conversation—either talking about his own experiences, or trying to get everyone to "function" the way he sees fit—that in actuality the entire gathering turns into "his ministry."

Now follow me here... I'm not against someone having a ministry or even a time of ministry somewhere during an "ekklesia-style" gathering where, *"There are diversities of gifts, but the same Spirit... There are differences of ministries, but the same Lord... there are diversities of activities, but it is the same God who works all in all"*... and where there are *"the manifestation(s) of the Spirit... given to each one for the profit of all"* (1 Cor. 12:4-7) but, again, what does that look like?

In 1 Corinthians 14:26-33 it is abundantly clear: EACH OF YOU HAS... something to build up the Body of Christ; to wit:

"How is it then, brethren? Whenever you come together, **each of you has** *a psalm, has a teaching, has a tongue, has a revelation, has an interpretation. Let all things be done for edification. If anyone speaks in a tongue, let there be two or at the most three, each in turn, and let one interpret. But if there is no interpreter, let him keep silent in the EKKLESIA* (not "church" as in a "church building") *and let him speak to himself and to God. Let two or three prophets speak, and let the others judge. But if anything is revealed to another who sits by, let the first keep silent. For* **YOU CAN ALL PROPHESY ONE BY ONE**, *that all may learn and all may be encouraged. And the spirits of the prophets are subject to the prophets. For God is not the author of confusion but of peace, as in all the churches* (again, "ekklesia" plural form) *of the saints* (1 Cor. 14:26-33).

Consequently, it appears that such a gathering of God's people—and, by the way, 1 Corinthians 11-14 is nigh the only detailed account of what goes on in an "ekklesia-style gathering"—is immensely participatory, extremely engaging... as YOU COME TO JOIN IN and contribute your portion whatever is your gifting. It's

So, You want to do Ekklesia?

a CONTRIBUTING environment. Yes, there's undoubtedly some "give and take" but it's mostly giving, not taking.

> "Two or three prophets should speak, and the others should weigh carefully what is said. And if a revelation comes to someone who is sitting down, the first speaker should stop. For you can all prophesy in turn so that everyone may be instructed and encouraged. The spirits of prophets are subject to the control of prophets." 1 Corinthians 14:29-32

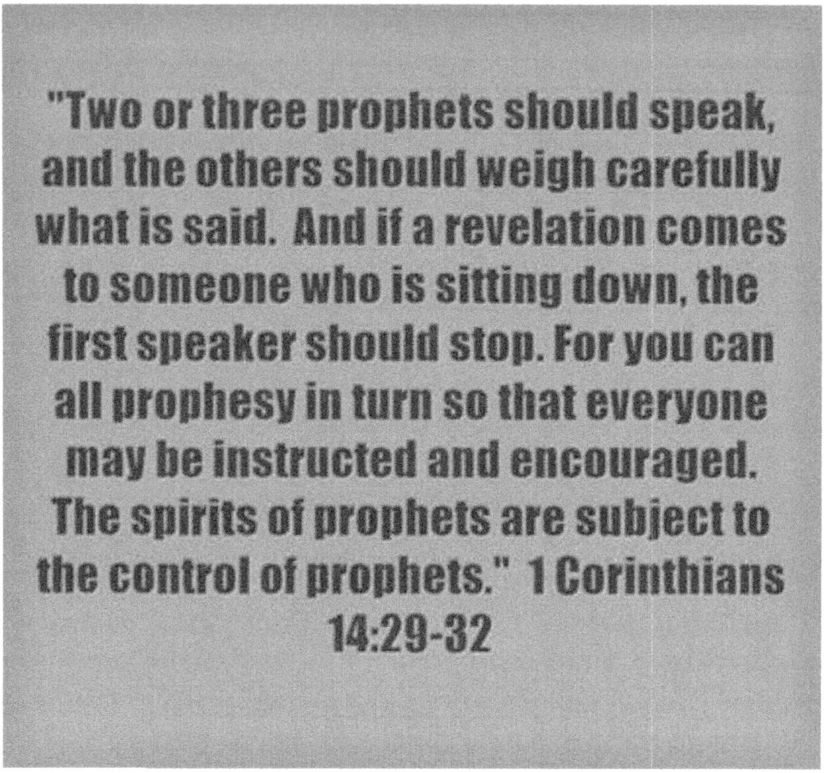

Figure 3 - YOU CAN ALL PROPHESY - EVEN INTERRUPT

Consequently, it appears that such a gathering of God's people as seen in 1 Corinthians 11-14 is nigh the only detailed account of what goes on in an "ekklesia-style gathering" is immensely participatory, extremely engaging . . . as YOU COME TO JOIN IN and contribute your portion whatever is your gifting. It's a CONTRIBUTING environment. Yes, there's undoubtedly some "give and take" but it's mostly giving, not taking.

Who's Really in Control?

But who's in control of such an environment? The only folks who seem to be involved in any form of "control" are known as those "*who are approved*" or those considered "*genuine*" (1 Cor. 11:19):

"*For there must also be factions among you* (viz., *"it is NECESSARY there must also be factions among you"*), *that THOSE WHO ARE GENUINE may be made manifest among you*" (1 Cor. 11:19).

Obviously, these "genuine ones" are not factious (although factions are required, expected, even some would say, mandatory—this "grouping" of saints is NOT homogeneous—there are differences among them, most certainly) nor divisive (although there are divisions among the saints)—so these brethren "manifest" when these factions become "factious" and those in various "divided camps" become divisive in a gathering. In other words, these folks are mature enough to "keep the peace" among diverse brethren—they practice what Paul said:

"Endeavoring to keep the unity of the Spirit in the bond of peace" (Eph. 4:3). *Clarke's Commentary on the Bible* states:

"The apostle guards them against this, and shows them that they should intensely labor (for so the word **σπουδαζειν** implies) to promote and preserve peace and unity. By the unity of the Spirit we are to understand, not only a spiritual unity, but also a unity of sentiments, desires, and affections, such as is worthy of and springs from the Spirit of God. By the bond of peace we are to understand a peace or union, where the interests of all parties are concentrated, cemented, and sealed; the Spirit of God being the seal upon this knot."

Hosting An Ekklesia

We find in Romans 16:23 . . . a chapter in which Paul calls out around 36 saints who are encouraged to "meet and greet" one another (not optional, by the way, but mandatory if you wish to practice true ekklesia in a community) . . . but Paul draws attention to brother Gaius: *"My host and the host of the whole ekklesia."*

So, You want to do Ekklesia?

Here, the word "host" is the same term used elsewhere but interpreted as "entertaining strangers" with "host" being associated more with "strangers" or someone with whom the "host" is unfamiliar (***xenos*** or ξένος—Strong's G#3581—also translated as "alien"—"guest"—"strange" or "strangers"). However, in Romans 16:23 we find that the only time the word ***xenos*** is translated as "host" or "hosting" is used here. Thus, by implication, the host is entertaining strangers.

So, having strangers over to one's home—the person who is "hosting"—is the norm . . . the "more strangers, the merrier."

The "Controlling" Host

There's no such thing as a "controlling host" if you wish to host an ekklesia. NO—not when it comes to the ekklesia. In a way, it may be that the stranger coming into the host's habitat has no idea who is hosting the gathering. I've seen some hosts who are so "in the background" that you'd never know they were hosting the ekklesia—so gracious are they! Finally, folks start asking where the utensils are located—ah, yes, this must be this guy's place because he/she knows where everything is located (but, even then, you're not certain who is hosting).

Meanwhile, Mr. Controller, is apt to call the meeting to order—even though he's not even hosting the ekklesia; as in:

"O.K.—It's time to pray over this meal—So-and-so, You pray, but make it short, we're all hungry around here!" This, of course, can be "manifested" in any number of ways—the idea is: "I'm in control of this affair and you need to know this from the get-go!" This is especially true if the person hosting is likewise controlling!

No one wants to offend a controlling host; however, this makes it more difficult for true "Spirit spontaneity" in the gathering. Is it the same one who leads off in prayer, praise and worship, some form of speaking every time? Even with the best of intentions, the "controller" can become the "control freak" of the gathering—telling and/or even commanding people to share, pray, or whatever the "expression" takes—in sum and substance, it becomes "his/her meeting"—but NOT the meeting of the ekklesia,

Who's Controlling This Ekklesia Anyway?

the gathering of the saints. In essence, it is really NOT an ekklesia, it is the "controller's ministry." Listen up, I'm not talking about someone leading a Bible Study group—that's an entirely different environment—sure, we're all members of the Lord's Ekklesia; however, having an "ekklesia-style gathering" is totally different than someone conducting a Bible study!

Figure 4 - EVERYONE THINKS THEY'RE IN CONTROL

The Difference Between Ekklesia and Ministry

I know, this is a "biggie"—because most "churches" today are, in the main, expressions, not of ekklesia, but of sundry "ministries" where one normally is NOT interrupted—but in an ekklesia, ***"If anything is revealed to another who sits by, let the first keep silent"***—sure sounds like someone is being interrupted and all the more when Paul substantiates that remark by the following verse: ***"For you can all prophesy one by one, that all may learn and all may be encouraged"*** (1 Cor. 14:31).

But it doesn't sound like the person interrupting is being "enlightened" by the "controller"—as in, "Wait, before Alice finishes sharing, maybe Joyce has a word to share."

So, You want to do Ekklesia?

I've seen "controllers"—again, with all good intentions—interrupt someone in a "teaching-style prayer" (You know: *"Dear Lord, we know that we're not all that loving but we should be, so keep speaking to us out of 1 Corinthians 13 and telling us that the greatest of these is LOVE or we are going to miss the mark altogether, etc."*) by saying: *"Brother, try not to preach when praying, just talk to the Lord—He doesn't need to hear your preaching, and neither do we—we need to hear your prayer."* No kidding . . . and there's more; as in someone sharing a testimony which *kinda* drones on until the "controller" speaks forth:

"So, brother XYZ, what's the point, get to the point, we don't have all day around here"—perhaps said in jest, but "words matter" don't they? Hopefully, the "peace makers" manifest here—but it won't be easy, when folks who are trying to practice ekklesia "participate" in this fashion with a "controlling overlord."

Or, how about this one:

"We've heard from everyone in the room except Bill—Bill, isn't it time for you to spill the beans—like, what's really going on in your life, Bill?"

This is when the controller, unbeknownst to himself and perhaps most in the gathering, has turned the "session" into a "recovery group" therapy or counseling session with everyone (especially, the controller) giving "sound advice" on what to do and not to do for Bill.

Now, Bill, Sue or Joyce may need a little "fellowship" (aka, sound advice) but is the ekklesia the normative place where such advice and/or fellowship is given? 1 Corinthians 11-14 doesn't give great detail to such "counseling sessions" during an ekklesia but it does give wide leeway to the saints CONTRIBUTING spiritual experiences either in song, psalms, prophesying, testimony, prayer, worship, praise, etc.

Ministers—in the "ekklesia" (and that is the operative word used in 1 Corinthians 12:28) who are "God-appointed": *"First apostles, second prophets, third teachers, after that miracles, then gifts of healings, helps, administrations, varieties of tongues"* are apt to "take over" a gathering because they are "apt to teach" or "preach" on occasion—because that's who they are! And, that is precisely why in an "ekklesia environment" 1 Corinthians 13—the chapter on LOVE—is so desperately needed—indeed, Paul sums up after his exquisite chapter on love with 1 Corinthians 14:32-33:

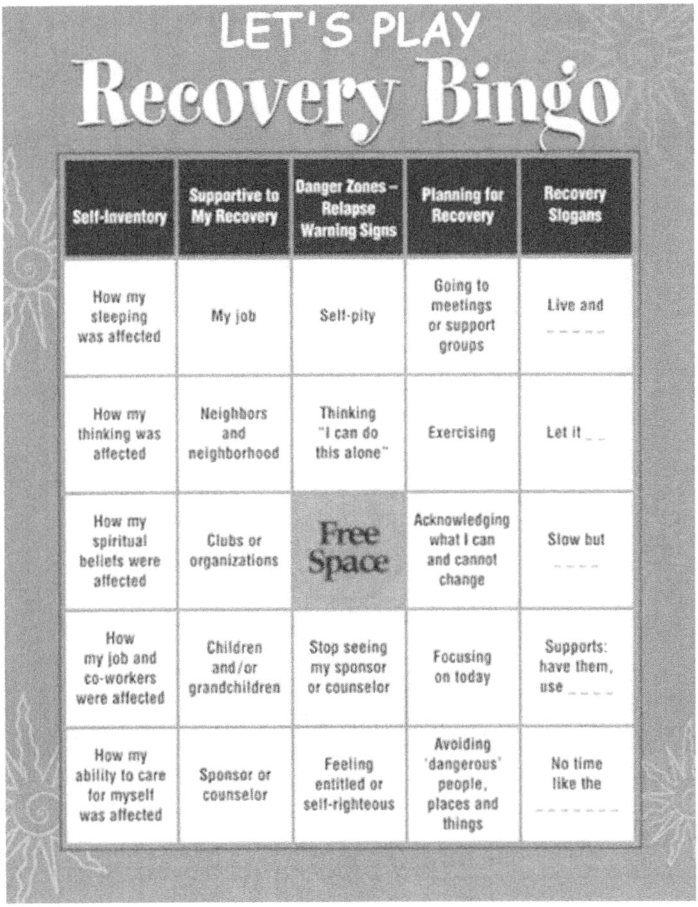

LET'S PLAY Recovery Bingo

Self-Inventory	Supportive to My Recovery	Danger Zones – Relapse Warning Signs	Planning for Recovery	Recovery Slogans
How my sleeping was affected	My job	Self-pity	Going to meetings or support groups	Live and _ _ _ _
How my thinking was affected	Neighbors and neighborhood	Thinking "I can do this alone"	Exercising	Let it _ _
How my spiritual beliefs were affected	Clubs or organizations	Free Space	Acknowledging what I can and cannot change	Slow but _ _ _ _
How my job and co-workers were affected	Children and/or grandchildren	Stop seeing my sponsor or counselor	Focusing on today	Supports: have them, use _ _ _ _
How my ability to care for myself was affected	Sponsor or counselor	Feeling entitled or self-righteous	Avoiding 'dangerous' people, places and things	No time like the _ _ _ _ _

Figure 5 - LET'S PLAY RECOVERY BINGO

"And the spirits of the prophets are subject to the prophets. For God is not the author of confusion but of peace, as in all the ekklesia of the saints."

Frankly, by "controllers" doing "their thing" is nothing more than CONFUSION and "not of peace." Yes, there is a pseudo-peace when someone(s) is/are in control but the *"spirits of the prophets are subject to the prophets"* and NOT subject to the controller(s). Unless and until we can cultivate an atmosphere where the Holy Spirit, working with the *"spirits of the prophets"* is in control, there will be no real ekklesia among the saints.

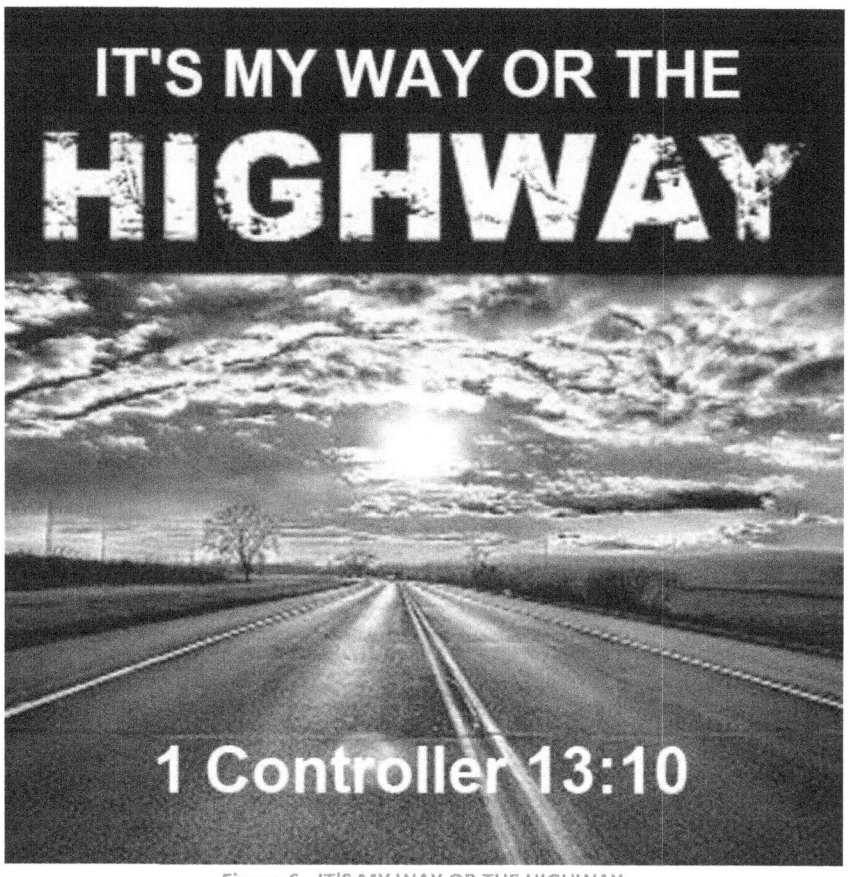

Figure 6 - IT'S MY WAY OR THE HIGHWAY

It is plain: ***"For you can all prophesy one by one, that all may learn and all may be encouraged."*** But if all are under the control of the controller—even when all are participating—they are still NOT prophetically engaged . . . manipulated, but not prophetically engaged!

Gifted apostles, prophets, teachers, evangelists (even)—those ordained and/or "God-given" to the ekklesia on a "spiritual plain"—and even those who on a "natural plain" (e.g., school teachers, administrators, entrepreneurs, managers, etc.) have God-given and/or natural tendencies to "take charge" of an ekklesia—yes, everyone may be participating—but there is NO FREEDOM OF THE SPIRIT—you may have a ministry "going down" but you don't have an ekklesia going up!

One more thing—a "controlling environment" may not be so overt—but the same results endure. The "controlling authority" is simply more clever at controlling how the "meeting" goes down; and, normally, it's in accordance with the particular gifting of the controller. For example, if the "controller" has the gift of prophecy, he'll normally lead the gathering in that vein of thinking—with everyone, eventually, either awaiting a prophecy (aka, a "prophetic word" or "word of wisdom") or "speaking into one another's life" the way the "prophetic controller" who's setting up the environment wants the saints in that meeting to practice.

Let's say we come together and those "take charge" brethren (who may or may not be hosting) find the grace to "restrain" their instincts with just a "little encouragement" for the group; and then, wait to see how things go. They know that they are capable of "controlling the environment" and, therefore, realize they need to take "a low profile" in order for the saints to become more activated, spontaneous.

So, what I'm suggesting is this: Indeed, the controlling brother(s) or sister(s) may ignite the gathering, but then once it's up and running—and the saints know it's normative to "function" or "prophesy"—then, the "take charge" person simply needs to become just another member of the group and allow the Holy Spirit to take charge of His people!

If during the course of a gathering someone becomes factious or overbearing or "out of order" (droning on forever types)—then the "take charge" brother or sister may have to step in to encourage the person to allow others to participate—however, it would be better if others actually "do the honors"—that way, the "controller" allows others to participate when something "gets out of control"—then, those attending are not just "pew sitters" but actual "stake holders" in the gathering.

Summing Up

This initial chapter on **WHO'S CONTROLLING THIS EKKLESIA ANYWAY?** . . . one can only imagine, there are so many different environments where ekklesia-style gatherings enthusiastically "takeoff" and then degenerate into the same individuals showing up week after week with no new people coming to the gathering—thus, a "group mentality" evolves, "comfort sets in" and then everything turns stale. Hosting "strangers" is the norm—it's difficult to keep that in view!

Finally, should we abandon any and all efforts at *"endeavoring to keep the unity of the Spirit in the uniting bond of peace"*—or EXCLUDE from our gathering such controlling influences/individuals? No, we should endeavor to keep the unity of the Spirit in the uniting bond of peace—that's precisely why Paul said:

"And be kind to one another, tenderhearted, forgiving one another, even as God in Christ forgave you" (Eph. 4:32). And, that's why, 1 Corinthians 13 is smack dab in the middle of this "ekklesia experience"—for without "the greatest of these"—which is love—there will be no ekklesia coming together to uplift our Lord Jesus Christ!

Know this, Satan hates the Ekklesia our Lord is building. Why? Because the *"gates of Hades will not prevail against it"* and *"the God of peace will crush Satan under your feet shortly"* (Matt. 16:18; Rom. 16:20)—and that's why this "hill" is worth fighting over! Don't despair—this is what the Lord, the Holy Spirit, desires for His people!

Chapter 2:
How Can the God of Peace Crush Satan Under Your Feet?

Figure 7 - ANCIENT EATING HABITS DIE SLOWLY

IT SEEMS SOMEWHAT OXYMORONIC TO SUGGEST, AS DOES ROMANS 16:20 THE "GOD OF PEACE" HAS ANYTHING TO DO WITH SHORTLY CRUSHING SATAN under the feet of the saints. The saints in the capitol of Rome well-understood what CRUSHING was all about—since Nero was then Emperor when Paul wrote his epistle to the Romans—well, let's just put it this way, Satan was a very tangible commodity at the time . . . but why attach the "God of Peace" to such a stark contrast?

Better yet, why does Paul insert such a statement at the close of his otherwise brilliant and deeply enlightening overview of the entire Christian life, let alone link his insights *"according to the revelation of the mystery kept secret since the world began but*

So, You want to do Ekklesia?

now made manifest, and by the PROPHETIC SCRIPTURES made known to all nations" (Romans 16:25).

Obviously, Paul did not disclose these revelations to these believers in Rome in a vacuum—he based his entire treatise, including crushing Satan under the feet of the saints in Rome by the God of Peace, upon the **prophetic Scriptures** which he recites vociferously throughout his letter.

We've examined Romans 16:1-27 at length on occasion through the insightful writings of Henry Hon, who suggests that Paul's "greeting" of the saints was an "imperative" form of speech—not a suggestion as in: *"Say 'hi' to Olympas, if you get a chance."* No, *"You in Rome, go and greet Olympas."* Indeed, the *"churches of Christ greet you"* from a distance, *"but you folks in Rome need to go on over and not only greet Olympas, but while you're at it, 'greet all the saints who are with them'"* (Philologus, Julia, Nereus and his sister, et al). In all—and it's a bit difficult to calculate—however, I've identified some 36 individuals (even "his sister"—Romans 16:15) and found there are 9 women and 27 men who are identifiable for a total of 36 individuals—that's a whole lot of greeting. But, and as Hon brings out, it's far more than just saying "hi" on Paul's behalf—and more than just going over and meeting Priscilla and Aquila, along with greeting the "ekklesia" in their house. It's actually RECEIVING one another *"in a manner worthy of the saints and assisting her in whatever business she* (Phoebe) *has need of you"* (Romans 16:1-5). You're getting involved—it's one thing to say *"hi"* and a quick *"goodbye"* but altogether another matter when you begin **RECEIVING** one another.

Again, it behooves us to connect the dots. In Romans 15:7 it appears Paul was putting some finishing touches to his exposition by stating: *"Therefore* **RECEIVE** *one another, just as Christ also* **RECEIVED** *us/you, to the glory of God."* Well, now, that kind of "receiving" is far and away beyond the pale of congeniality. How Christ receives us all to the glory of God wherein *"that the Gentiles/Nations might glorify God for His mercy"* (Read: Romans 15:7-13 to grasp the profundity of Christ receiving the

Gentiles to the glory of God.)—this is a superlative expression of the mercy and grace of God to all who would believe!

Therefore, this receiving of Phoebe which Paul introduces at the commencement of Romans 16:1-27, strikes a tone far and beyond a superficial *"say 'hi' from me"* but is the very "receiving" Christ wrought on behalf of the Gentiles whereupon the nations would glorify God! All barriers were broken down—just as Paul announced to the Ephesian saints:

> *"For He Himself is our PEACE, who has made both one, and has broken down the middle wall of separation, having abolished in His flesh the enmity, that is, the law of commandments contained in ordinances, so as to create in Himself ONE NEW MAN from the two, thus making PEACE . . . And He came and preached PEACE to you who were afar off and to those who were near"* (Eph. 1:14-18).

So what Paul was saying: *"Just as God for Christ's sake has received us Gentiles to the glory of God and to glorify God, you do the same—start RECEIVING one another, it will glorify God!"* Not to put words into Paul's mouth—no need—however, that's the gist of what he was saying and that's what he meant by meeting and greeting one another in Rome! Unconditional, all barriers having been abolished by His cross—it's a "no holds bar" receiving, meeting and greeting one another, just as God, for Christ's sake, has received us!

Friends, Romans, Countrymen, Lend Me Your Ears

William Shakespeare in his "Julius Caesar" captures some of the diverse population in Rome spoken by Marc Antony, who concluded his salutation with: *"I come to bury Caesar, not to praise him."* Now, Rome was indeed a hodgepodge of nationalities—primarily, however, and in accordance with the names so mentioned by Paul in Romans 16:1-27, she (Rome) consisted of Roman citizens, Jews, Greeks, and a rather nameless bunch of swarthy barbarians—you know, the obscure worker bees (aka slaves, some of whom had gained a degree of freedom and could actually own

So, You want to do Ekklesia?

property—alas! What gratuity for their indentured efforts!). In the film, **The Gladiator**, these, in the main, barbarians kept the masses at bay by "entertaining them to death." Trafficking in the bodies and souls of men is really nothing new—we humans have been at it for millennia.

We have no record any apostle had physically been to Rome prior to Paul's letter, which appears to have been written cir. A.D. 56 (Paul was converted cir. A.D. 35)—no doubt "visitors from Rome" (Acts 2:10) became believers in Jesus and carried back to Rome the "good news" of salvation . . . that's how the faith spread to Rome. Therefore, when Paul writes in Romans 1:7 "To *all who are in Rome, beloved of God, called to be saints*" he does not address his letter to any leadership among them but directly TO ALL WHO ARE IN ROME—CALLED TO BE SAINTS. This is as "general" as it gets—Paul lumps all those in Rome who were "*called to be saints*" into one group. It appears Paul was beheaded under the reign of Emperor Nero (who reigned from 54 A.D. to 68 A.D.—13 years); so, when Paul wrote Romans (especially, Romans 13:1-14 regarding the believers' relationship to civil authorities) Nero was in full sway. Paul's beheading, as a Roman citizen, took place in 68 A.D. (Nero committed suicide on June 9, 68 B.C. with, most likely, Paul beheaded by Nero at the same time—see Bible Study @ https://www.biblestudy.org/question/sauldie.html)

Paul's generality stops there. What we can ascertain from his writing of Romans 1-8 is the "Romans Road" where he, after formally greeting the saints in Rome, moves from man's sinful state of affairs, and under God's wrath through to justification by faith, unto sanctification of the believer, and thence to the believer's ultimate glorification of the body; in other words, from divine hostility to Peace with God (individual). Indeed, Romans 8 concludes with this divinely sweeping generosity:

> "*For I am persuaded that neither death nor life, nor angels nor principalities nor powers, nor things present nor things to come, nor height nor depth, nor any other created thing, shall be able to separate us from the love of God which is in Christ Jesus our Lord*" (Rom. 8:38-39).

That should have wrapped things up—but, no, now that YOU have Peace with God—how about you having peace with your brethren? That's where the latter half of Romans comes in: Chapters 9 through 16. Paul spends, quite frankly, an extraordinary effort in disclosing the GOSPEL OF PEACE (Romans 9-16) after revealing the Gospel of the Grace of God in Romans 1-8. There is absolutely no question this "divine disparity" is illuminated in the book of Romans—if so, then why have so very few declared its demarcation—especially, having anything to do with the FULL MESSAGE OF THE GOSPEL?

Could it be that we Christians have simply compartmentalized Romans 9-11 as having to deal with the "Jewish issue" and then moved on to further disclosures of "sanctification" as we present our bodies a living sacrifice by not allowing the world to squeeze us into its own mold (Romans 12)? Having accomplished the fete in Romans 12 we somehow need, now, to rise above political entanglement by heeding Paul's injunctions in Romans 13 and from there move on to "body life" as per Romans 14-15 and then consider Paul's final chapter as little more than, as Hon says, *"credits at the end of a movie"* (you know, that's where you get up and begin to walk out the door).

This treatment of Romans 9-16 is, sadly, how most of us have viewed Romans—hardly a stereoscopic overview of what Paul was really trying to illuminate via the Holy Spirit through the PROPHETIC SCRIPTURES (Rom. 16:26).

So, let's get a bit real here. Rome's diverse population, again, could cluster by nationality; by ethnic persuasion—mainly, Roman citizenry, Greeks, Jews and the ubiquitous barbarians pouring into the capitol via conquest and consequent labor exploitation (slavery). The most profound problem facing the "saints in Rome" would have been their predisposition to "keep to themselves" in these various groupings.

Four Obvious Factions

ROMANS: These were the conquerors—the guys in control, the management, the bureaucrats, the architects, the law givers. If philosophers came from the Greeks, and the Prophets came from the Hebrews, the lawgivers came from the Romans. The Romans were allegedly founded by Romulus in 753 B.C. and persisted from the monarchy, through the Republic, unto some form of Empire (West and East) until the Fall of Trebizond in the summer of 1461 A.D.—over 2,100 years—these guys weren't fooling around when it came to controlling things. In comparison, we in the USA may have the oldest Constitution (232 years: 1787 A.D. until 2019 A.D.) but Rome's ability to manage affairs far exceeds our own—and in point of fact, our entire system of law and a host of other bureaucratic and general civilization is permeated by Roman influence.

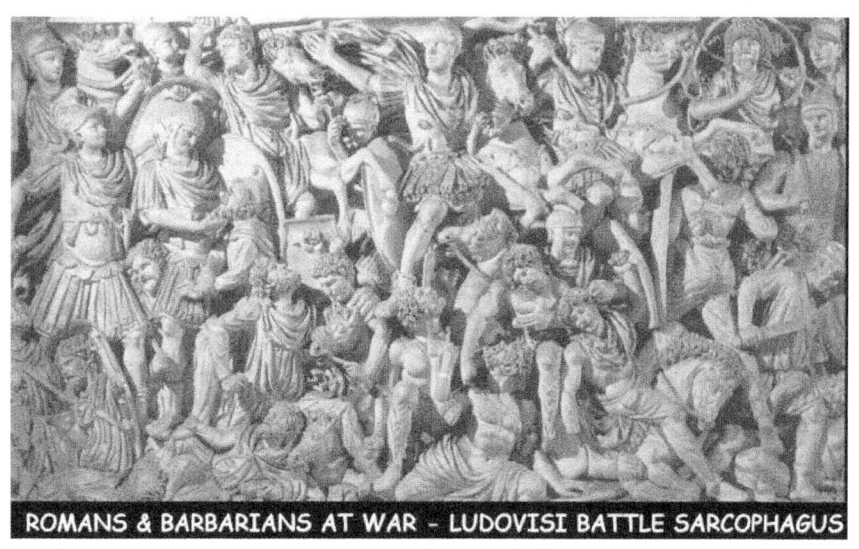

Figure 8 - ROMANS & BARBARIANS AT WAR - BY LUDOVISI

GREEKS: This group in the Roman capitol was undoubtedly connected to Greek culture. Actually, the Greeks greatly influenced the Romans . . . and they were quite proud of that fact . . . everything from architecture to ekklesia. Likewise, being philosophers, they were the studious bunch—Paul said it this way: *"The Jews demand a sign and the Greeks seek after wisdom"* (1 Cor. 1:22). When Paul proclaimed the gospel on Mars Hill in Athens, most responded in this manner:

"And when they heard of the resurrection of the dead, some mocked, while others said, 'We will hear you again on this matter.'" (Acts 17:32)

And, why not hear more of this matter?

"And they took him (Paul) *and brought him to Areopagus* (Mars Hill), *saying, 'May we know what this new doctrine is of which you speak? For you are bringing some strange things to our ears. Therefore we want to know what these things mean"* (Acts 17:19-20).

Yes, we want to KNOW—for the Greeks seek after wisdom . . . *"For ALL THE ATHENIANS and the foreigners who were there spent their time in nothing else but either to tell or to hear some new thing"* (Acts 17:21).

JEWS: In sum, *"the Jews* **demand** (not just "require") *a sign"* (1 Cor. 1:22). Matthew 12:38 and John 2:18 echo this persistent characteristic: *"What SIGN do You show us, since You do these things?"* Or: *"Then some of the scribes and Pharisees answered, saying, 'Teacher, we want to see a SIGN from You"* (Matt. 12:38). Something miraculous akin to the opening of the Red Sea will do—or raising someone from the dead, "tongues of fire" atop some heads might do in a pinch—but it must be supernatural, beyond any knowledge these Greeks contemplate—that's for sure!

BARBARIANS: This motley crew found itself in Rome under some degree of protest—as in *"I've been conquered and now must work for virtually nothing."* This hapless lot was, in the main, slightly disrespected, not only by their Roman conquerors, but most certainly by the cultured Greeks and enlightened Jews. Their clothing (virtually rags and animal skins, furs, and what not) and their eating habits—atrocious! If they didn't camp out in their servants' quarters, they wondered the streets and alleys of Rome being exploited at every level of debauchery. What an awful subjugation was theirs! They were hardly able to communicate in a society which deem language (Latin, Greek or

Hebrew/Aramaic) to be a mandatory expression of a civilized individual. Alas! **Barbarians** befit their breed! It's not that this sector of Roman society kept to themselves—nobody wanted them around in the first place—they bordered on the leprous and their habits, well, in a nutshell: uncouth and, besides, they stank! But, they're needed to keep "our well-oiled machine" trucking—but it's not easy to train them aside from tearing down things and carving out highways and the like; you know, menial tasks that don't require much intelligence nor skill—just good ole hard labor stuff will do.

Paul Knew What's Up with the Saints in Rome

Paul knew from his statement in Romans 15:29:

"But I know that when I come to you, I shall come in the fullness (lit. "completion") ***of the blessing of the gospel of Christ."***

You see, Paul was preaching a COMPLETION GOSPEL—not just the Gospel of the Grace of God (Acts 20:24; Rom 1:1, 9, 15-16; 2:16)—it was the Gospel of Peace (Romans 10:15-16; 15:16, 19-20, 29; 16:25). Paul wanted to eventually come to Rome but in a way whereby the "*completion of the blessing of the gospel of Christ*" would be manifested among the saints—wherein they would "*strive together*" and whereby when he did arrive, he would "*be refreshed together with you . . . now the GOD OF PEACE be with you all. Amen*" (Romans 15:29-33—excerpts).

Paul was intentional—yes, he had an agenda for this "receiving, meeting and greeting" of the saints in Rome. These cultural groups were more than obvious obstacles to the unity of the Body of Christ in Rome. Yes, these were factions of the most profound order—then again, as Hon states: **FACTIONS ARE NECESSARY** in the assembly, the ekklesia as per 1 Corinthians 11:19: "*For there must also be factions among you.*"

But why? "*. . . that those who are approved* [lit. "genuine"] *may be recognized* [lit. manifest, evident] *among you*" (1 Cor. 11:19b). How are you Romans going to have such factions if you persist in your exclusive "Jewish believers only" demanding SIGNS & WONDERS—studious Greeks who "rightly divide the Word of Truth"—Roman bureaucratic "decently and in order" group—ANYTHING GOES Barbarian group? Factions are necessary (Note: I didn't say being "factious" or "divisive" was necessary—it's NOT.).

Peculiar Folks—These Four Groups

Have you ever noticed how today's **Romans** in an assembly are normally the ones who, after a "meeting goes south," are the ones who blame its demise on "poor organization"—to wit: *"Well, Ann, the reason why we're not seeing any improvement around here has everything to do with a lack of organization—things just don't happen spontaneously, you know, you have to plan things out and do so methodically, like an engineer"*—well, let's cut to the chase here—like ROMANS are wont to do. *"So, get out of my way, Ann, and let me handle this thing!"*

The **Greeks**, on the other hand, when whatever is stressed out in the assembly, simply wish to STUDY THE PROBLEM—sometimes "to death." They border on bureaucracy, like the Romans, but if the "thing" is never resolved, they'll just keep on researching and studying the problem—and are quite happy in doing so; although, everyone else is utterly frustrated by their "ever learning but never coming to the knowledge of the truth of the matter." Something sounds a bit "out of alignment" (doctrinally)—thus, the discerning Greeks will *"hear more of this later"* and continue to *"rightly divide the Word of Truth"* until it's virtually in shreds! Everything has been deciphered to the uttermost. Not much gets done (Romans) but we sure figured it out!

Meanwhile, the ***Jews***—somewhat Pentecostal, one might presume—have little flare for organization (that took place centuries ago on the Mount—besides we have the entire Law)—further study, however, will do . . . but that's why SIGNS, WONDERS and SUPERNATURAL gifts are desperately needed to get the saints excited about true Christianity or a little Messianic movement here and there. "You can study your Scripture all you want (Greeks) but you ought to show up at a DELIVERANCE

So, You want to do Ekklesia?

MEETING where the 'real gospel' is preached and folks are delivered, healed, and are, in general, being struck by the Spirit until they're laid out on the floor! Get out of your brain (aka mind)—and get into the *signs and wonders*—that's where the real action is!"

Barbarians: The name alone ought to tell you what these guys are up to! If you want to destroy the equilibrium of a meeting—just invite a bunch of barbarians. Given an inch, they'll take a mile. Off goes the mouth to announce *"the whole thing needs to be buried"*—let's just allow the "spirit" to move. The question is: What "spirit?" Barbarians are apt to just get up and wander around—you're lucky if they even found where the meeting was in the first place—and, when there—if there are not enough "bells and whistles"—consider their wanderings an expression of the failure of your gathering and/or of the preacher's boring sermon. They may have "never heard this before" but that doesn't matter—they would rather be heard and seen, than to hear and see anyone. You might think they're "high maintenance"—they are, but they have no idea they are and could care less if you think they are! Oddly enough, they get along fine together—why? Because there's no rules and regulations—when you get tired of whatever, just move on and set up a new camp to keep the nomadic flavor of the group alive. Don't dare try to pin them down—Romans have tried; but duly noted, it was, after all the attempts of acculturation, it was the Barbarian hoards who conquered Rome! So, who knew?

Now, with that somewhat humorous elucidation—can you even fathom what Paul knew what was happening in Rome. Not only was there this immense schism between Jew and Gentile ([Romans 9-11](#)) but these little cultural clusters were unhinged in the natural—believe me, Paul needed an additional eight chapters to deal with this quagmire of conflicting souls.

Therefore, it was not out of the ordinary to see Jews desiring to "hang out" with Jews; Romans with Romans, Greeks with Greeks and Barbarians just hanging out wherever they could. Now, here comes upbeat and fully confident Paul celebrating when he arrives that he'll be witnessing the COMPLETION

GOSPEL—the GOSPEL OF PEACE—in which not only are all kinds of folks in Rome receiving the Gospel of the Grace of God—but the nations (Grk. ethnos) in Rome are now witnessing how Christ alone is bringing all these disparate groups together in Him alone! How? By going on over to the ekklesia which meets in the home of Aquila and Priscilla—not at the mega St. Peter's Basilica.

It's time for some Pentecostals to meet some hard-shell Baptists and for some sedate Anglicans to meet up with some Redeemer Church of God folks (you brethren in Nigeria know who I'm talking about). No, your little "comfort zone" comprised of studious Greeks are not really all that comfortable hanging out with a bunch of Barbarians—and the combinations *ad nausea, ad infinitude.* You have to ask yourself: How is it that in 56 A.D.—six years before Paul found himself in Rome—that he knew by name so many brothers and sisters in Rome? Stop wondering. Paul probably met a whole lot of these folks during his travels—he kept tabs on folks. Paul, himself, ceaselessly met and greeted saints all the time—so should we—that's what the ekklesia is all about.

Furthermore, these factions should find themselves together lifting up the Lord Jesus, giving opportunity for sundry differences to be resolved by the God of Peace by those GENUINE brethren who rise up in their midst to maintain the unity of the Spirit in the uniting bond of peace. I know, it's just so nice to be with "brethren who see things as you see 'um"—but, guess what, that is NOT the "**Normal Christian Ekklesia Life**." It is necessary, yea mandatory, for scholarly types to gather together with ditch diggers—for the poor to be with the rich—for the college educated to be with those who never completed high school—for we are ALL ONE IN CHRIST.

This Gospel of Peace has everything to do with Romans 14; to wit:

> *"For the kingdom of God is not eating and drinking, but righteousness and PEACE and joy in the Holy Spirit. For he who serves Christ in these things is acceptable to God and* **approved** (same word as "genuine" as found in 1 Cor. 11:19— *"they that are approved"*) *by men. Therefore let us pursue*

So, You want to do Ekklesia?

> *the things which MAKE FOR PEACE and the things by which one may edify another . . . Now may the God of patience and comfort grant you to be like-minded toward one another, according to Christ Jesus, that you may with ONE MIND and ONE MOUTH glorify the God and Father of our Lord Jesus Christ"* (Romans 14:17-19; 15:5-6).

I know, we all like our "associations"—as in "Bikers for Christ" or **Mensa International** types with high IQs—you're right, these people need to find salvation—but only the Spirit of God can make them of one mind and one mouth glorifying God!

And remember this: **Even a turtle must stick out his neck to make a move!**

> *"There is neither Jew nor Greek, there is neither slave nor free, there is neither male nor female; for you are all one in Christ Jesus . . . where there is neither Greek nor Jew, circumcised nor uncircumcised, barbarian, Scythian, slave nor free, but Christ is all and in all . . . for there is no distinction between Jew and Greek, for the same Lord over all is rich to all who call upon Him . . . for by one Spirit we were all baptized into one body—whether Jews or Greeks, whether slaves or free—and have all been made to drink into one Spirit..."* (Gal. 3:28; Col. 3:11; Rom. 10:12; 1 Corinthians 12:13).

Oh, and by the way, the Barbarians will be pleased to know this is how the GOD OF PEACE will CRUSH SATAN under our feet shortly! (THE COMPLETION GOSPEL is available @ https://www.amazon.com/Completion-Gospel-Crushing-Satan-Glorifying/dp/1092419586

Figure 9 - THE COMPLETION GOSPEL BY HON & KRIEGER

So, You want to do Ekklesia?

Chapter 3:
So, You've Got a Corner on the Truth?

EACH HAS A CORNER OF THE TRUTH

Figure 10 - SO YOU THINK YOUR PART OF THE ELEPHANT IS WHAT?

YOU'VE HEARD BLINDFOLDED PEOPLE TRYING TO FIGURE OUT BY HOLDING PARTS OF AN ELEPHANT WHAT THEY'RE TOUCHING. RIGHT, IT'S THE TASSEL on the end of a curtain! Then the fellow holding the elephant's trunk thinks it's a large fire hose. The guy holding the leg thinks it's a Dutch Elm tree, etc. Each one thinks he's got it figured out—after all, he's got a "corner on the truth"—so he's got the "whole thing" figured out.

How does this kind of attitude affect an ekklesia when the "whole ekklesia" comes together (1 Cor. 11:17-18) or what are the implications of a gifted minister—apostle, prophet, evangelist, pastor, teacher—who thinks that the truth (aka, "the message") he/she has is so incredible that, in point of fact (in their heads) no one else "sees it?" "The truth resides with ME!" Normally, when one takes hold of the elephant, they usually assume that their part is the sum of all the parts and anyone else in the Ekklesia simply doesn't have the "thing" figured out . . . in other words, "*I don't*

So, You want to do Ekklesia?

need 'lesser revelations' when I've got the goods in the first place!"

Indeed, this person, and those he may have overly influenced or hoodwinked into believing he actually is the purveyor of supernatural revelation (which no one else has seen—well, "they" see bits, parts and pieces, but "TRULY, I SEE IT ALL") undoubtedly suffers from an overweening sense of his own propriety. Notwithstanding, he believes he's got it all figured out—he knows for certain it's definitely a fire hose! He does NOT suffer from a lack of self-esteem. In point of fact, this presumptuous member of the Body of Messiah (and he is a member; notwithstanding, a superduper member in his own eyes) hasn't quite discovered **EACH OF YOU HAS**:

> *"How is it then, brethren? Whenever you come together,* ***each of you has*** *a psalm, has a teaching, has a tongue, has a revelation, has an interpretation. Let all things be done for edification"* (1 Cor. 14:26).

The Lone Ranger

Figure 11 - THE LONE RANGER

Have you ever been to a "Christian Conference" where all sorts of speakers share their insights from their experiences with the Lord from Scripture, or minister from their gift given to them by the Head of the Body? Sure, you have. I just returned from a marvelous conference which had nearly 30 speakers for the 450 attendees—a veritable gospel smorgasbord; and, along with the incredible fellowship—well, a weekend of refreshment in the presence of the Lord.

And, what was so incredible about this gathering on Lake Erie near Cleveland was the diverse aspects from the Word, testimony and the prayer and fellowship of the saints. Everyone was encouraged to search the Scriptures—do their own research to "see if these things be so"—I really appreciated that.

Now, I've been to some such confabs and noticed (not at this one) that some invited speakers had little interest in hearing anyone else but themselves! They may have sat in one or at the most two other sessions—but why do so when YOUR MINISTRY is so important, so full of revelation, and so necessary that you can't stop talking about it straight through the entire one-two-three-four-day conference. Instead of listening to someone else—they busy about propagating their own revelation or vision or exercising their own "spiritual gift." If you were to ask them if they heard anything at the conference, they would probably give a very generic answer as in: *It was great—everyone's response to MY MESSAGE informed me they were listening*!

As long as everyone's lining up with what "I have to share"—"Well, what can I say, the others just missed out if they weren't tuning in to ME—as in the form of the 'Lord's Oracle.'" Who needs a posse when you've got the Lone Ranger?

Yes, and normally, the guy can't find the time of day to listen to anyone because he's got the corner on the truth—and if he feigns to listen, it's just to get the other guy's attention so he can insert his own "truth" into the conversation—how sad.

Groupies

Figure 12 - GROUPIES

Eventually, he's got his whole group—his sphere of influence—totally on board with his "corner of truth" which is the "whole truth, and nothing but the truth, so help that man!"

Charismatic leaders—be they Bible expositors or Worship Leaders—tend to develop a "following." Now, I'm not saying this is wrong—but "*I am of Paul, I am of Apollos, I am of Cephas, or I am of Christ*" (1 Cor. 1:12) doesn't auger well when it comes to Ekklesia-style gatherings. You see, when **EACH ONE HAS** is a little different than "All members of the Body are equal—some are more equal than others!"

What's tough on a "minister" is when an Ekklesia convenes and the minister has to "sit in on" a corporate, participatory, engaging, contributing environment wholly centered on everyone sharing for the common good—for building up the Body in love. Forbid! He may have to "wait his turn" because he's found himself in an Ekklesia! Notwithstanding, it may be that a lot of those participating might be considered his "groupies" but at the Ekklesia—there's ROOM FOR EVERYONE!

Still, it's not easy for a "gifted brother/sister" to hear various "factions" in an Ekklesia proclaim their insights—be it a *"psalm, a teaching, a tongue, a revelation, an interpretation"* when "I have a corner on the truth!"

Figure 13 - HERE COMES THE "MAN OF GOD"

Normally, as well, such "truth possessors" have an extremely difficult time giving credit, where credit is due. They have a habit of plagiarizing—coming up with "truths which they claim are their own" but really, they're at best "borrowing" or flat-out stealing the work/research of others without giving due consideration regarding the source of their "revelations."

I once was in the office of a person I initially considered extremely spiritual, charismatic, and most definitely, a mature "man of God." To most observers, he was "deep"—and I mean "God's man on the earth today"—speaking as the Oracle of God. He had a vast library which I viewed—indicating he was well researched in many top evangelical writings and certainly, so I observed, some of the most spiritual ones. I remarked how impressed I was about his library. He paused and proceeded to inform me with profound sincerity with these words: "Brother Doug, you don't have to read any of these books, just **The Spirit of Christ** by Andrew Murray—all the rest are unnecessary."

I thought to myself: "Wow, just *The Spirit of Christ*" and, of course, this man's writings and someday I would be as deep as he! Looking back, it was like "burn all your religious writings and

So, You want to do Ekklesia?

just follow me"—almost like forget everything and read Mao's little *"Red Book"* or burn it all and read Hitler's *Mein Kampf*!

Others, at times, boast by saying: "All I read is the Bible, you don't need anything else—it just muddies the waters—just the opinions of men. You should do exactly what I do." For some inexplicable reason it all vaguely sounds like: *"I am of Christ"* (1 Cor. 1:12).

I should have known then regarding this "Spiritual Man" that his spirituality was based on his inflated view of himself. He didn't need the insights of others—he was "his own man" and didn't need other brethren to shed further light upon his own revelations.

I know, I'm bouncing between MINISTRY and EKKLESIA—there is a difference here. Ministry IS by definition a fairly structured affair. Remember when Paul preached into the wee hours of the evening and Eutychus fell off the ledge—having fallen asleep—then Paul raised him from the dead (Acts 20:9)! You can get away with such a "ministry" (even if you consider it a major dialogue) but that wouldn't do well in an Ekklesia environment. Bringing your preachment to an Ekklesia where *"you can all prophesy one by one, that all may learn, and all may be encouraged"* does not resemble in the least a Eutychus encounter!

I would be remiss in not stating that far too often a gifted minister will take occasion to gather an Ekklesia and then at its close take opportunity to share—normally, consistently, wherein his ministry predominates at the expense of the Ekklesia coming together. Why not? Isn't it fine and dandy to have such ministry after and/or before or during such a gathering of an Ekklesia? Frankly, no it isn't. Taking advantage of the saints in this manner is just that—taking advantage to project your own gifting. Do it on your own time—not at the time of a "general assembly." I know, sounds legal, but what's worse—to manipulate the people of God for your own "ministerial aggrandizement" or allowing the saints maximum time in lifting up the Lord Jesus Christ where "all can prophesy?"

But let's get back to the self-absorbed minister—sorry, he's still trying to figure out a way to insert himself into this discussion. How interesting, and spiritually debilitating it is, when some ministers, akin to the doings of the Lone Ranger, have so few peers with whom they can share, let's say, the pulpit. In Philippians 1:27 we read:

"Only let your conduct be worthy of the gospel of Christ, so that whether I come and see you or am absent, I may hear of your affairs, that you stand fast in one spirit, with one mind striving together (lit. *"teaming up") for the faith of the gospel."*

The Church in Philippi (Phil. 1:1) had "issues" (shall we say) wherein at least two dear sisters, servants of the Lord, were at odds with one another. Yep, Euodia and Syntyche were at loggerheads—so Paul IMPLORED THEM to be of *"the same mind in the Lord"* (Phil. 4:2). They were wrestling, alright, but with one another, and were not acting like a "tag team" as the essence of the Greek text suggests in Philippians 1:27: *"Teaming up for the faith of the gospel."* If they had been, then the rest would follow: *"And in nothing terrified by your adversaries, which to them is an evident token of their perdition, but to you of salvation, and that from God"* (Phil. 1:28).

By "fighting the battle in the Body" (not fighting on your own), these two sisters in the Lord could have pounded their common foe—but instead, they were off the mark fighting one another!

Nearly a half century ago I met a "Man of God" who was so overwhelmingly impressive, he rarely, if ever, was found "sharing the pulpit" with anyone who could have been considered "contemporary" with him. The strength of one's ministry is not in the singularity of it but in its ability to collaborate with other ministers of the Lord. Likewise, the ability of that ministry's leadership to "blend into an Ekklesia-style gathering" demonstrates, even more, the strength of that minister(s) in *equipping the saints for the work of the ministry* (Eph. 4:12).

Did this brother (and he was certainly a brother in Christ) have opportunity to co-labor with contemporaries—many of whom saw the "elephant" differently from his particular insight/vision? He most definitely had such opportunity; and, initially, he did (when he started his ministry) share with co-equals. But he considered himself a "master builder" and not in need of anyone else to "share his ministry." That was, actually, not the issue—a minister has a ministry—that is most definite . . . but that minister is "spiritually obligated" to "team up" with other ministers in the faith of the gospel lest he be overwhelmed by the foe and find himself isolated from the greater Body of Christ.

How tragic it has been when so many outstanding evangelists, prophets, pastors and teachers, and even those in position of apostolic leadership, find themselves without proper "covering"—by that I mean, with brethren who see the overall plan and purpose of the Almighty a bit differently than they do? Again, and again these brethren find themselves vulnerable and unable to co-labor with other ministries—and, when they are tempted, they have no one with whom they can trust nor be in fellowship to sustain themselves from the overwhelming flood.

Sure, they may have a board of directors—normally, a "rubber stamp-style" board. Or, quite possibly, they find themselves in some kind of denominational structure with a Board of Deacons or some kind of "system of responsibility" designed to "keep tabs" on the minister—but far too often such "coverings" are simply "window dressing" and have little, if any, true accountability . . . so the "Man of God" is utterly "exposed" when he/she could have received gracious help from fellow ministers, saints, those who truly cared for his/her soul.

The Emperor's New Clothes

Far too often such a minister of the gospel surrounds himself with YES MEN who simply reinforce the minister's excesses. He's NOT in fellowship with them, per se, but simply "uses" them as a sounding board of sorts to reinforce his control over those to whom he ministers. He feigns "balance" but, actually, he's in total control of "his little ministry"—simply manipulating the pawns on his customized chessboard.

Figure 14 - BUT THE KING HAS NO CLOTHES!

When crisis hits—and his failure is crudely exposed (usually some inappropriate financial dealing)—he seeks refuge in his "inner circle" who will "take the rap" on his behalf with a mealymouth declaration which goes something like this: "We should have warned our beloved brother of the dangers of his actions—instead we kept our mouths shut and now we have endangered the *ministry*" (whatever that's supposed to mean). Indeed, if they would have warned their brother, he would have ejected them from his "inner circle" or he would have scolded them for intruding on his bombastic image—DARE YOU INSULT MY MANAGEMENT SKILLS!

Alas! These YES MEN think they serve God's purposes by "covering" their brother who has convinced them that the revelations enveloping his ministry are so superior to anything else "out there" that if they were to go elsewhere they would in essence be leaving "God's final move on the earth today!" HOW COULD THEY?

Normally, such stupidity and/or leadership intimidation has, at its core, some derangement that is financially or morally off the chart—it is, tragically, allowed to fester until scores of innocent believers are damaged by such "ministerial control mechanisms." I don't need to prolong this diatribe—in that so many

So, You want to do Ekklesia?

large (e.g., the Roman Catholic Church) or smaller ministries have been afflicted by these incessant "cover-ups" all done in the name of "protecting the ministry."

This is NOT how it's supposed to work—unless and until we are of one mind and spirit through Paul's injunction in Philippians 2:1-8 neither a true gathering of the Ekklesia, nor the fruitful results of a God-ordained ministry, will manifest!

> *"Let this mind be in you which was also in Christ Jesus, who, being in the form of God, did not consider it robbery to be equal with God, but made Himself of no reputation, taking the form of a bondservant, and coming in the likeness of men. And being found in appearance as a man, He humbled Himself and became obedient to the point of death, even the death of the cross."*

Brethren, as Paul implored these two sisters—why can't we implore one another to be of the same mind and spirit—TEAMING UP for the faith of the gospel at the close of this age? Yet, far too often "gifted brethren" who appear to have a successful ministry, only reveal their own inadequacies and insecurities when they insist on holding their own "followers/groupies" far too close to themselves—suffocating the release of additional ministries which should have been the case if these gifted ones were truly "equipping the saints for the work of the ministry."

ONE BODY LIFE ministry does not have all the answers—we believe in tone and in practice we are striving together for the faith of the gospel—but we could and have been known to be "insufficient for these things" for:

> ... *"Such confidence before God is ours through Christ. Not that we are competent in ourselves to claim that anything comes from us, but our competence comes from God. And He has qualified us as ministers of a New Covenant, not of the letter but of the Spirit; for the letter kills, but the Spirit gives life....*(2 Cor. 3:4-6).

Know this, "For now we see in a mirror, dimly, but then face to face. Now I know in part, but then I shall know just as I also am known" (1 Cor. 13:12).

May the Holy Spirit grant us greater insight *"when the whole Ekklesia comes together"* as we "team up" as ministers for the faith of the gospel!

So You want to do Ekklesia?

Chapter 4:
An Unfederated Wildfire

Figure 15 - AN UNFEREATED WILDFIRE

I HATE TO ENTITLE THIS CHAPTER ON EKKLESIA "ANOTHER IN THE SERIES" BECAUSE IT SOUNDS LIKE I'M ORGANIZING THIS THING, WHEN IN POINT OF FACT this "series is anything but antithetical to that phrase when it comes to the Ekklesia—perhaps it's as close to something done "*decently and in order*" (1 Cor. 14:40) but that's as far as it goes!

On occasion I've asked my associate, Henry Hon: "*Is this 'Ekklesia business' just another movement 'in a series' of revivals that starts out as 'times of refreshing may come from the presence of the Lord'* (Acts 3:20)—*then matures, gets 'organized'—'institutionalized'—and then fizzles out as per normal? Kinda burns itself out?*"

The Final Harvest

Many of us speak in terms of a "great end-times' revival"—a FINAL HARVEST of souls—the "latter-day rain"—that final burst of Holy Ghost outpouring that shakes the foundations of the world and brings forth His REMNANT in the spirit of Elijah, the prophet who would be sent forth upon the earth before that "*great and dreadful*

So, You want to do Ekklesia?

day of the Lord" (Mal. 4:5)—YES! We're looking with John, the Revelator, when we hear:

> *"Then I looked, and behold, a white cloud, and on the cloud sat One like the Son of Man, having on His head a golden crown, and in His hand a SHARP SICKLE. And another angel came out of the temple, crying with a loud voice to Him who sat on the cloud, 'Thrust in Your sickle and reap, for the time has come for You to reap, for the harvest of the earth is ripe.' So He who sat on the cloud thrust in His sickle on the earth, and the earth was reaped"* (Rev. 14:14-16).

Figure 16 - THE "FINAL HARVEST"

Now, many of us view Revelation 14:14-16 as the final end-time's harvest of souls to be gathered into the Kingdom of His Dear Son—with Revelation 14:17-20 seen as "another angel" who gathered "*the clusters of the vine of the earth, for her grapes are fully ripe*" to be cast "*into the great winepress of the wrath of God*"—the one harvest unto eternal life and glory and the other just the opposite, into the winepress of the wrath of God.

I know, sounds like I'm off on one of my numerous rabbit trails—but I assure you, I'm not. What does revival look like? Well, a lot like the Son of Man reaping the final harvest of the earth!

An Unfederated Wildfire

When the early Ekklesia "took off" it was a "mighty, rushing wind" with *"tongues of fire"* appearing over the heads of 120 disciples of Jesus in the Upper Room—they began to speak in other languages (Acts 2:4). Folks outside heard the SOUND and then heard them speaking in all the languages who had gathered from around the Roman Empire to Jerusalem's feast days and heard in their own languages *"the wonderful works of God"* (Acts 2.11).

Filled With The Spirit – Not Spirits

But, keeping with the theme of an uncontrolled burn (viz., a "wildfire"): *"Others mocking said, 'They are full of wine'"* (otherwise known as DRUNK). (Acts 2:13). Now, most drunks I've known or met don't seem to have their "act together"—slurred speech, with some being very talkative and somewhat delirious—hardly the epitome of a "controlled burn" (if you would).

So, the early Ekklesia, you know, the one Jesus said in Matthew 16:18 . . . *"I will build My Ekklesia, and the gates of Hades shall not prevail against it"* . . . seemed to be akin to a bunch of out of control drunks (according to the folks viewing this from around the world gathered in Jerusalem during the Feast of Weeks [aka, Pentecost]).

I like Peter's retort to this drunken charge: *"For these are not drunk as you suppose"* . . . since it's only 9:00 A.M. in the morning! (Acts 2:15). Don't you love it? The first evangelistic outburst of the Ekklesia Jesus was building was accused of BEING a bunch of drunks spouting off in other languages declaring the *"wonderful works of God"*—I know, seems a bit incongruous—but don't be surprised if, during the final end-time's harvest things get OUT OF CONTROL!

Then Peter, after making it plain he and the others were not drunk (although, I've witnessed some drunks at 9 A.M.), launched into Joel 2:28-32 and the rest is history.

So, You want to do Ekklesia?

> Suddenly there came a sound from heaven as of mighty wind. And they were filled with the holy spirit
> -Acts 2:2

Figure 17 - THE "WILD FIRE" OF PENTECOST

Kill and Eat – No Way – No Partiality!!

The spontaneity of things in the early Ekklesia took a radical turn when Peter was told three times to *"kill and eat"* a rather unkosher meal full of *"four-footed animals, wild beasts, creeping things, and birds of the air"* (Acts 10:12)—of course, Peter was in a trance-like state when he heard the Almighty declare: *"Rise, Peter; kill and eat"* . . . with Peter's repeated reply: *"Not so, Lord! For I have never eaten anything common or unclean."*

But God was setting Peter up to preach the gospel to the House of Cornelius in Caesarea. Think about it. You can't get any more Gentile than that: Caesar (Caesarea) with an "Italian Band" and a Roman Centurion controlling a repressive Roman Regiment—good grief, WHAT WAS GOD THINKING!

Interestingly enough, this Cornelius fellow was a very devout man who had been praying and fasting (go figure) and about the same time of the day (the Ninth Hour, or 3:00 P.M.—Acts 10:30) that our Lord cried out: *IT IS FINISHED* (Matt. 27:45-50) . . . now I ask you: Did not our Savior die for the sins of the world—not just the sins of the Jews? Sounds like there is a connection of these

An Unfederated Wildfire

NINTH hours—His crucifixion and the answer to the prayer of Cornelius at the ninth hour.

In any event, Peter put it this way—as "things" were getting *out of control*:

> *"Then he* (Peter) *said to them* (the Gentiles gathered together by Cornelius), *'You know how unlawful it is for a Jewish man to keep company with or go to one of another nation. But God has shown me that I should not call any man common or unclean'"* . . . then later, after Peter asked Cornelius why Cornelius sent for him in the first place, uttered a most profound out-of-control statement: *"In truth I perceive that God shows NO PARTIALITY . . . But in every nation whoever fears Him and works righteousness is accepted by Him . . . the word which God sent to the sons of Israel,* **PREACHING PEACE THROUGH JESUS CHRIST***—He is Lord of all."* (Acts 10:28, 34-36).

Could it be this is the PEACE spoken about in Ephesians 2:14-18? *"For He Himself is our PEACE, who has made* (viz., Jew and Gentile/the Nations), *BOTH ONE, and has broken down the middle wall of separation."*

Listen up, the emphasis here was not necessarily the Gospel of the Grace of God (Acts 20:24) unto repentance—which it was most definitely so preached by Peter and they of the household of Cornelius did repent of their sins and turn to the Lord Jesus for salvation (Acts 11:17)—no, the emphasis was upon the breakdown of the MIDDLE WALL OF SEPARATION between Jew and Gentile . . . two of the most separated peoples on the planet! (Ref. Acts 10:34-36; Eph. 2:14-18)

Thus, the Gospel of Salvation was directly tied to the Gospel of Peace! *NO PARTIALITY . . . "For there is no distinction between Jew and Greek, for the same Lord over all is rich unto all who call upon Him"* (Rom. 10:12; Acts 3:25; Gal. 2:6; Eph. 6:9; 1 Peter 1:17).

Got it? When things are out of control THERE IS NO PARTIALITY. You don't get to pick and choose who you want to show up at an Ekklesia-style *"I will build My Ekklesia"* gathering! (Matt. 16:18; 1 Cor. 14:23). There's no distinction, no partiality—stop calling so-

and-so common and unclean when God Almighty has declared everyone CLEAN—folks, it's time to KILL AND EAT.

Uncontrolled Burn – Fires Just Flare Up!

Figure 18 - PETER USED TO OPEN THE DOOR TO THE GENTILES

Furthermore, during an uncontrolled burn, fires tend to "flare up" out of nowhere! And just as you think you got this whole thing under control—while giving a most dynamic, even Spirit-filled sermon—you are rudely interrupted as sparks break out and the Holy Spirit *"fell upon all those who heard the word . . . and those of the circumcision* (aka, Jews) *who believed were astonished, as many as came with Peter, because the gift of the Holy Spirit had been poured out on the Nations also"* (Acts 10:44-45).

How dare the Holy Spirit interrupt Peter's amazing sermon! That's what happens in an uncontrolled burn—big time—for this time the whole place is set ablaze . . . not just our little compartmentalized elite, or those with whom we're sort of "used to"—those least expected to respond, do so, and we're left with: I had no idea so-and-so would ever find the Lord! Imagine, Holy Ghost revival striking the Catholic Church or a bunch of Russian Orthodox believers—it can and has happened—notwithstanding what impossibility you might conjecture!

The Evangelistic Crusade That Wasn't

Well, that's what happens when the Son of Man intends to thrust in His sickle to reap the harvest of the earth. Meanwhile, however, we're desperately about trying to crank up the most recent evangelistic crusade—pouring over countless organizational meetings and lots of money to pull it off . . . thinking, even with "organized prayer and fasting" we'll be able to see the "fruits of our labor."

Recently, in my own backyard, an immense effort was made wherein local pastors and earnest Christian workers in the gospel, sought out and succeeded in bringing a famous evangelist to our area for a huge "evangelistic crusade"—a one-day rally that would turn our town upside down (and that's saying a whole lot for this California stronghold of bureaucratic tax and spend, liberal bastion—just sayin').

Figure 19 - MASSIVE EVANGELISTIC CRUSADE

Well, virtually an entire year went into the planning of the effort—over 300 churches were engaged in some way. Lots of concerts, extraneous endeavors were put in place with sundry tents, things to do for the kids, special music, prayer rallies, counseling

So, You want to do Ekklesia?

trainings—you name it, we're PREPARED! Only problem was this: On the day of the "Great Crusade" it was 106F (scores were treated for heat stroke) . . . no kidding, couldn't wait to get out of that place.

Tens of thousands of dollars were spent to pull this off. In all, a whooping six people found Jesus! Oh, I'm sure, a lot more went down at that gathering, but that was the final tally. One could speculate: We organized that "thing" to death. Yes, one soul is indeed worthy of all our efforts—but I think you're getting the picture here, right?

What Does an Awakening Look Like?

Getting back to our Ekklesia issues . . . what does that look like or what doesn't it look like? Well, in past AWAKENINGS and/or REVIVALS or MOVES OF GOD upon the earth (even the early Ekklesia)—things sort of "fall apart" and get institutionalized very quickly. Look at the "Early Church"—by the time John, the Beloved, passed from this earthly clod around 100 A.D. things had gotten more and more institutionalized (aka, DEAD) until 325 A.D. when Emperor Constantine utterly institutionalized the Roman Catholic Church leading to the so-called Dark Ages.

We bogged down into ceremony, rituals, basilicas, hierarchical systems, utter separation of Jew and Gentile (OT Feast Days were replaced with quasi-pagan, do-over Christian holidays), relics, *"having a form of godliness but denying the power thereof"* (2 Tim. 3:5)—in sum: DEAD RELIGION.

Honestly, I don't think my distant relative, Martin Luther (I being a direct descendant) had any idea he would be creating the Lutheran State Church(es)—but he did—then when "sparks broke out" and new fires (Anabaptist) raged, Luther found himself and his "followers" trying to put out these uncontrolled burns with the fire hoses of "Reformational persecution."

Frank Bartleman in his book, *Another Wave Rolls In*, talks about the wave that rolls in and then rolls back into the ocean fighting the new, on-coming wave. Bartleman talks about the "wave of the Holy Spirit" in the Pentecostal early days and how the "organized Church" resisted, even persecuted those who partook of this fresh move of the Holy Spirit—that's just the way it is.

Figure 20 - FRANK BARTLEMAN'S "ANOTHER WAVE ROLLS IN"

The "Court of the Nations/Gentile" – Rev. 11

Let's take the message of Revelation 11 in which those in the "court of the Gentiles" shall persecute (trample asunder) the Holy City for 42 months: *"But leave out the court which is outside the temple, and do not measure it, for it has been given to the Gentiles [aka, "Nations"]. And they [those in that court] will tread the Holy City underfoot for forty-two months."* (vs. 2).

This novelty of the "Court of the Nations" was set up to appease the sect of the Sadducees (the liberals of their day) at the Temple in Jerusalem. Uncircumcised Gentiles who were devout could at least make it up to the Temple Mount but could NOT offer up a sacrifice

So, You want to do Ekklesia?

at the Altar unless they were willing to be circumcised then and there—YOU FIRST!

In point of fact, those unwilling to go "all the way" were defacto compromisers and would be seen "on that day" trampling asunder those who've gone "all the way"—the "worshipers at the altar" who readily constitute the Holy City ultimately descending from the heavens in Revelation 21. Be that as it may, you get the idea, some of the worst "persecutors" of God's people will be "*those of your own household*" (Matt. 10:36) . . . all the while they're thinking they are doing God a service in harassing His remnant!

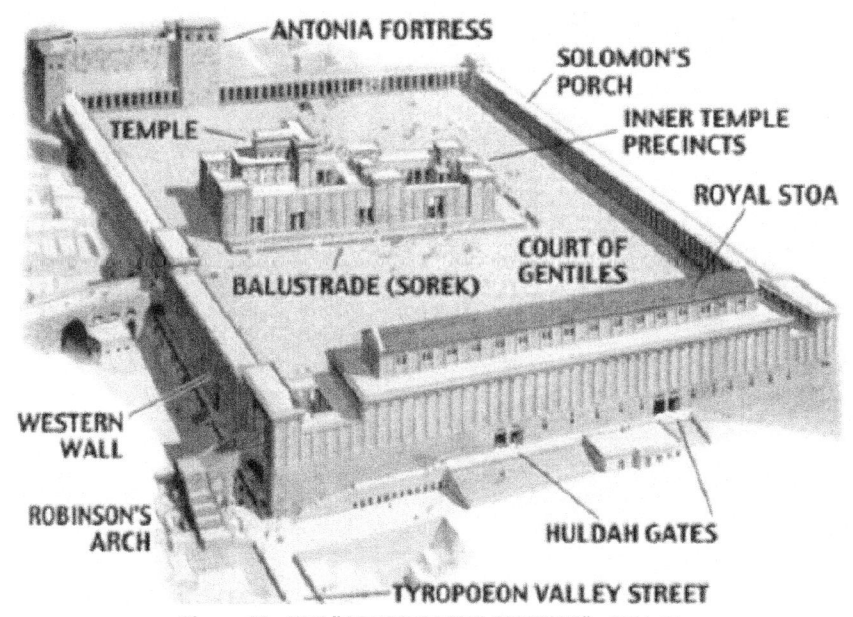

Figure 21 - THE "COURT OF THE GENTILES" - REV. 11

Rarely will you find an atheist in a foxhole under fire—rarely will you find division in the Ekklesia under persecution. I don't know about you, but frankly, believers who have "gone through it"—perhaps been tossed out of "several churches" (normally, because you just don't fit in all that well) or who have found themselves in some sort of "Christian cult" where they thought they were the "only game in town"—only to find they weren't but were actually highly sectarian and divisive (who knew?)—and then found themselves "disfellowshipped" from "the group" and "walking about the streets of confusion" for a time (still might be) . . . well, if that describes your

An Unfederated Wildfire

"journey"—sounds like you might be suspect to join in the Ekklesia where there's NO PARTIALITY and where KILL and EAT is the norm—where "divine interruptions" mess with your sermons (outstanding though the delivery be).

Sincerely, and I mean this with all reverence, you're probably not worth your salt unless you've gone through these bouts of exclusivity and ejection! Not that you must—but you'd be surprised how tenderized meat is when smashed with a metal mallet.

Yes, we praise God for all His moves throughout the centuries—Lutheranism, Presbyterianism, Anglicanism, Anabaptists, Christian Church, Church of Christ, Methodism, Baptists, Plymouth Brethren, Pentecostalism, Charismatics, Jesus Movement—you name it, God's been in it—but given our propensity to corral the herd, or control the burn, we find ourselves, once again, stomping on the Holy City from our well-organized Court of the Gentiles. I know that bites, but folks, once you think you "got it all together"—well, that's the beginning of the end—here comes another wave, and in all likelihood you'll miss it and wind up persecuting that wave because it appears to be messing with your own!

My, How Things Get Organized!

Seriously, attempting to "federate" or make His Ekklesia a "controlled burn" is akin to organizing that which never was intended to be organized. You can burn down a church, but you can't burn down the Ekklesia—we're NOT an organization nor a federated bunch of little *Ekklesias* organized into some kind of ecumenical movement.

Could I? Yes, the Jesus Movement took off in the late '60s and early '70s—initially, it was wholly unorganized—yet, the Spirit of God was "moving upon the waters"—upon the forest—and fires were breaking out all over the place.

"Christian communes" were a-happening, it was hard, nigh impossible, to distinguish it or extinguish it. Yes, it was full of hippies, old and new believers—we weren't concerned about what denomination you were in . . . all we cared about is ARE YOU WITH JESUS? That's all we need to know!

Figure 22 - THE "JESUS MOVEMENT"

Then as the Jesus Movement "matured" some in the denominations realized they had to get a handle on it or join it in some form—new associations were formed (e.g., Calvary Chapel, Gospel Outreach)... new "independent churches" were birthed, and, even new "Christian cults" were started by dynamic leaders "in total control."

Some of us were gathered together near Santa Rosa, California by the hundreds (perhaps 2,000)—from all kinds of "Jesus People" types. Yes, sundry ministries, various emphases, but all under Christ, the Head of His One Body. We invited some "deep brethren" to address us—fellowship with us—they proceeded to inform us that what "you have" is wonderful but there's a problem: "You're not under authority." In other words: WE WERE OUT OF CONTROL.

It was over—any semblance of a "Jesus Movement" died that day—the sheep were scattered. Sure, once in a great while we gather and talk about "the good old days when we"... but if we weren't going to come "under authority"—under some form of "discipleship"—then, we were just in some form of rebellion and OUT THE DOOR YOU GO!

There were, and still are, some true apostles of the Lord who were and still are able to raise up "ekklesia" but know how to keep their hands off it and allow the saints, equipping them, to exercise their gifts for the "*work of the ministry*" in the "*building up of the*

An Unfederated Wildfire

Body of Christ" ... but that's so rare, so very rare. No, if it gets out of control, the fire might rage on!

Were those final days of the Jesus Movement federated? Only in the most informal fashion—but even then, we were vulnerable for another "organized entity" to do us much harm. You see, if we would have maintained our GORILLA WARFARE tactics, we would have caused the enemy of our souls, much destruction. We were "teaming up" with other ministries *"and in nothing terrified by our adversaries, which to them was an evident token of their perdition* [destruction] *but to you of salvation and that from God"* (Phil. 1:27).

Summing It Up

The EKKLESIA is organic—it's not designed to be organized by man, but under the headship of Him Who is the Head of the Body. Once we try to "organize it"—it's the sounding of the death nil. Yes, God's people desperately need to come together—ekklesia needs to occur—ministries need to team up—but above and beyond that don't think for a minute God's Spirit can be contained in your little framework? It can't.

So You want to do Ekklesia?

Chapter 5:
There's Doctrine and Then There's Doctrine

Figure 23 - HENRY'S HON'S BOOK: ONE TRUTH

Introduction by Doug Krieger:

IN HENRY HON'S TEXT, ***ONE TRUTH*** (THE SECOND IN HIS TRILOGY: ***ONE EKKLESIA***; ***ONE TRUTH***; ***ONE IN LIFE & GLORY***), HE DISCUSSES ONE OF THE MORE prickly issues which incessantly divide Christians from each other: **DOCTRINAL DISPUTES**.

For example, an ardent believer can be all over the eschatological map when it comes to the "final days" or *end of the age*. One can believe in a pre-tribulational rapture; another a mid-tribulational rapture, and still another in a post-tribulational rapture—yet, another in no tribulation period (70th Week yet future); or, for that matter, no rapture at all. Thus, the Body of Christ is divided via doctrine. Hon may have resolved these most difficult "Christian doctrinal issues" by bringing the Body of Christ into embracing the "doctrine of Christ" (Heb. 6:1; 2 John 1:9) by distinguishing two Greek words for "doctrine" having very different emphases. (Read the article here as Hon amplifies.)

So, You want to do Ekklesia?

The same goes for "Truth" vs "Truth"—here, Jesus said: *You search the Scriptures, for in them you think you have eternal life; and these are they which testify of Me. But you are not willing to come to Me that you may have life* (John 5:39-40). Jesus said: "*I am the way, the truth and the life*" (John 14:6); yet, Pontius Pilot was starring Christ right in the face inquiring: "*What is truth?*"

Hon's insights on these issues of doctrine vs doctrine and truth vs truth are most profound—and, I believe it leads us to "make the main thing, the main thing" wherein the Centrality of Christ for all believers is the key to "*keeping the unity in the Spirit, in the uniting bond of peace*" (Eph. 4:3). The following are excerpts from ***One Truth*** and constitute a most profound TRUTH which, unfortunately, escapes most believers in Christ:

HENRY HON
(used by permission)

Truth: God and His Eternal Work

In the New Testament, the word *truth* is always used in the singular. It is never *truths* plural. Secularly, the expression "truths" is used and preferred. Due to this influence, even Christians would use the plural rather than the singular truth. To people of the world, there are many truths, such as many ways to enlightenment. In other words, truth in the secular world is relative—not absolute (i.e., "truth" is in the eye of the beholder).

Therefore, one person's truth can be different from another. This kind of thinking has also impacted Christians so they can have conflicting truths. Conflicting and contrary truths have led to divisions and sectarianism. Therefore, it is critical to recognize in the divine revelation within Scriptures: There is only one truth. Since there is a unique truth in this universe, all believers are one in the truth.

This may sound to some ears rather simplistic; however, as we examine the consequences of multiple truths, the profound nature of truth or reality will become more than clear to us.

There's Doctrine and Then There's Doctrine

Figure 24 - LUTHER VS. OFFICIALS ON TRUTH OF SCRIPTURE

Just as God is one and three (Father, Son, and Spirit) simultaneously, truth is one with multiple facets. The more Christians understand and appreciate these facets, the more grounded and established they will become in walking in truth (3 John 1:4).

Let's briefly consider the major items of the truth.

First and foremost, God is truth. *"In the beginning was the Word and the Word was with God, and the Word was God . . . and the Word became flesh . . . full of grace and truth"* (John 1:1, 14).

Second, Jesus Christ who is God in the flesh is truth. Truth was revealed in Jesus Christ. Jesus said, *"I am the truth"* (John 14:6), and Paul declared "the truth is in Jesus" (Eph. 4:21).

Third, the Spirit is truth. The Scriptures declare the Spirit of truth (John 14:17, 15:26, 16:13; 1 John 4:6); this Spirit is Truth (1 John 5:6). The Spirit of Truth guides believers into all truth by declaring and infusing the reality of all Who the Father and the Son are into believers (John 16:13–15).

Fourth, all that the Father, the Son, and the Spirit have accomplished in the New Covenant for His eternal purpose is truth. This includes the death of Jesus Christ on the cross, His resurrection, His ascension and enthronement, and His work of redemption for the forgiveness of sins, justification, sanctification, the believers' regeneration (new birth) and glorification. Therefore, the person of the Triune God dwelling bodily in Jesus Christ (Col. 2:9) and His work of redemption and regeneration is the Word of truth—that is, the gospel of salvation. It is through believing the truth people are saved and sealed by the indwelling Spirit (Eph. 1:13). It is in truth God and humanity are joined and unified together to be the Lord's ekklesia, His body—the new man spoken of in Ephesians 2:15. This is God's eternal purpose: A corporate entity, ultimately the New Jerusalem, created and built up into maturity in truth (Eph. 4:24).

Finally, the Word as recorded in the Bible is truth. The Bible conveys the truth, and truth is understood when the Word is made real to a person. The Word, the logos, speaks to people and communicates to their reasoning. When the Word is received, understood, and becomes real in a person, then it is truth. That is why people need to know and come to the full knowledge of the truth (2 Tim. 2:25, 3:7; 1 Tim. 2:4). For example, the Bible says Jesus Christ is God who became man, died for mankind's sin and was resurrected on the third day. Many unbelievers have heard this, but it is not truth or real to them. One day as they consider this word, they will hopefully open their heart and connect with Jesus through faith. At that very moment, the Spirit of Truth will enter them and make the word of God they heard real; they will understand with a living knowledge, and then, that will be truth to them because they have encountered the truth!

The sum of New Testament revelation of the truth is rich and deep. It is God in Jesus Christ as the Spirit with all that they have accomplished for man and in man, which includes the eternal purpose of God's ekklesia (assembly) fulfilled in Jesus Christ. Therefore, truth is God Himself, with His life, nature, and essence, intrinsically joined with humanity. The truth is eternal (2 John 1:2). Anything which is temporal and has no effect in eternity is not truth.

This entire book, **_ONE TRUTH_**, is dedicated to exploring the various facets and items of the truth as outlined above.

Figure 25 - PONTIUS PILATE VS. JESUS

What Is Not Truth?

Jesus prayed in John 17 for believers to be made one through the truth. Thus, anything which divides believers—things over which Christians argue becoming sectarian—is not truth. Most Christian groups agree truth is what was outlined above. Any doctrines not defined as truth are non-essential. What has divided Christians include doctrines (Grk: *Didaskalia* which will be defined later), various Christian practices, or human causes. Christians have been divided, have fought over, and have rejected each other over some of the most ridiculous items such as musical style in worship, whether women should have their head covered, whether the rapture is pre, mid, or post-tribulation, methods of baptism, and even methods of leadership. Some of these items are tantamount to the rise and fall of denominations—if you're not pre-trib you're deceived, maybe not even saved!

There are literally thousands of such things which have divided Christians; yet, the truth remains the same. A believer who has a growing understanding of the truth stays anchored in the truth and will not be distracted by positioning themselves in non-essentials; they will remain one with all believers.

The tactic of the enemy (Satan) is to use men and women—specifically Christian men and women—to elevate non-essential doctrines and practices thereby forming groups and churches around those doctrines. For example, a major dividing doctrinal point among Christians is centered on the debate over predestination or free will. Churches have been grouped together on one side or the other. Both sides can show supporting Bible verses and speak of how their doctrine is better for Christians, but the fact is, neither of those doctrines died for humankind or was resurrected!

Nowhere in the Scriptures does it say in order to receive eternal life a person needs to believe in one of these doctrines. Ultimately, it does not matter in eternity which doctrine is correct. Therefore, neither doctrine is truth, and certainly not worth dividing over. Whether a person espouses one side or the other, or even both, is not a problem unless it becomes a condition for fellowship—and a rejection of those with contrary views.

So, You want to do Ekklesia?

Another major point of division is whether the Holy Spirit is still doing works of power as in the days of the early apostles, or if these works of power have ceased. Again, using the definition of truth above, this belief is not truth either way. A person who is established in the truth will be able to have fellowship and receive believers no matter what their doctrinal position or preference is. Those who are not standing in truth may be so biased with their personal doctrinal stance they end up taking an extreme position. For example, some may not acknowledge a genuine miraculous healing today can be from God; others may belittle believers for not receiving any manifestation of the Holy Spirit.

Practices are much more common than doctrinal differences in dividing believers. For example, the moment a person believes in Christ and receives salvation, this person is regenerated in Christ; this is biblical truth. It is faith which brings a person into Christ. Baptism is a physical symbol declaring the truth of being in Christ. Every believer agrees with the truth that faith uniquely brings a person into Jesus Christ; however, many sectarian groups have formed over the physical symbol of baptism. Some insist on water baptism, while others insist baptism must be by immersion and not by sprinkling. Still others within the same immersion camp insist the following phrase has to be recited at baptism: "In the name of the Father and of the Son, and of the Holy Spirit." Others insist the wording should be: "In the name of Jesus Christ."

Figure 26 - SALVATION ARMY "SPIRITUAL BAPTISM"

All the above are various ways to practice baptism, but not the truth of being immersed into Jesus Christ, the Triune God. Different teachings on baptism use different scriptural verses as their foundation, and many believers are helped by their way of baptism. However, it is against the truth to use any of these practices to build up an entire sectarian group hindering believers in that group from accepting and fellowshipping with other believers if they do not hold to the same practice

It's Easy to Be Distracted Away from the Truth

At this juncture, let's consider the story in Matthew 17 because it shows how easily and quickly the Lord's disciples forgot the revelation they received just eight days earlier. Here, Jesus brought a few of His disciples up to a high mountain. Peter was included—one who recently received the revelation concerning Jesus being the Christ, the Son of God (Matthew 16). On this mountain, Jesus was transfigured before them; He became shining as the sun. Together with this glorious Jesus were Moses and Elijah, also standing there conversing with Jesus. Peter grew excited and immediately said they should make three tabernacles, one for each of them. Moses represented the Law given by God, since Moses gave the Law (John 1:17); therefore, many times the Law was associated with Moses throughout the Bible. After Moses, the major prophet who performed many miraculous works was Elijah. He was the only prophet prominently named in the New Testament, twenty-nine times; therefore, Elijah represents the prophets with God's supernatural power.

When encountering all three, Peter viewed them the same, giving them "equal honors": Jesus, Moses, and Elijah. Since he wanted to build three tabernacles, one for each, this demonstrated Peter considered them with equal standing, requiring equal reverence. Suddenly, the Father spoke from a cloud and said, "This is my beloved Son, hear Him." The disciples fell in fear of such a voice. When Jesus came to lift them up, and when they looked up, they saw "no one, but Jesus alone." Both Moses and Elijah were gone; only Jesus was left for them to behold.

So, You want to do Ekklesia?

Figure 27 - THE MOUNT OF TRANSFIGURATION

This is the experience of most Christians. They are saved by a wonderful revelation concerning Jesus being the Christ, the Son of the Living God. Then they immediately view the law and so many other items on an equal level as Jesus. "Now that Jesus saved me," they think, "I have to learn these doctrines, keep these laws, pursue these spiritual gifts, do these works, and on and on." Even though Jesus is the shining One, from their perspective, Jesus is now just another item among a long list of things. No, no, no! Another revelation is needed after believing—there is no one else other than Jesus. It is not Jesus plus this and that. It is Jesus Himself alone!

It is unfortunate when most believers study the Bible, they consider it elementary to stay focused on Jesus Christ. There is a thought "deeper truth" is how to behave as a Christian, understand the end times, learn self-denial, obtain a special gift from God, or many other topics. Some think, "I already know Jesus Christ died and resurrected; let's learn about all the other Biblical matters." One can study, know, and discuss many topics in the Bible; yes, it is advisable to thoroughly read the Bible from cover to cover, but a mature believer is one who can only be satisfied with the excellence of the knowledge of Jesus Christ (Phil. 3:8–15). Those items which expand upon Him are focused on the "knowledge of the Son of God."

A mature believer is one who has lost the taste for all peripheral topics other than Jesus Christ, and His pursuit of the truth is to see and know how Jesus Christ's person and work is revealed upon the pages of the Bible. There is a recognition and appreciation Jesus is unsearchable and unlimited in His riches; therefore, it is an eternal pursuit to come to the full knowledge of the Son of God. In fact, Jesus is INCOMPARABLE!

Confusion: Doctrine Unites, Doctrine Divides

The matter of Biblical "doctrine" or "teaching" has also been a great source of division in the Body of Christ . . . let me explain. These two words *"doctrine"* and *"teaching"* can be used interchangeably. It simply means "that which is taught" (Vine's). There is a doctrine which is essential and unites and there are many doctrines causing division. Which is which?

The Bible is full of doctrines, unless you do not read the Bible, but if you do, it is unavoidable to pick up all sorts of doctrines. Believers are encouraged to study the Bible in order to be taught by various doctrines. Some have such a strong emphasis in learning doctrines with a desire to resolve all seemingly contradicting ideas in the Bible; consequently, they formulate and organize these various doctrines into a more uniformed and cohesive arrangement for easier understanding. That body of doctrine is what can be defined as "systematic theology."

The difficulty is this: There are literally thousands of teachings in the Bible ranging from the mysterious and heavenly concerning the person and nature of God . . . to the mundane and earthly such as what one should wear and eat. The more students of the Bible desire to teach and live according to the doctrines in Scripture, the more conflict they discover—interpretations widely vary.

Therefore, Christians are inclined to simplify doctrine by asking: "Just tell me the right doctrine to believe and live by." Depending on personality and influence, some will emphasize one side of conflicting teachings while others will highlight the other side. For example, the Bible does not actually have a doctrine of the Trinity.

So, You want to do Ekklesia?

Sometimes it refers to God in the singular and at other times it speaks of God in the plural, specifically: Father, Son and Holy Spirit. Some can then emphasize their teaching on the side of God being one, while others on the side of three persons within the "Godhead." This has caused great divisions in the past.

Figure 28 - DOCTRINES THAT DIVIDE

Salvation by faith or works can also have conflicting verses. Some will cite why believers are saved by grace, not by works (Eph. 2:8-9), while others will cite "faith without works is dead" (James 2:20). This is the same for whether salvation is eternally secure or whether a believer can lose their salvation. This has been a major divider among Christians for hundreds of years—right up to the present. Beyond these major theological doctrines, there are hundreds or thousands more concerning church practices, methods of prayer, end times, Christian blessings and even life-style doctrines such as marriage, diet, clothing, music, etc.

Due to the many doctrines throughout the Bible, many divisions and factions have been formed among Christians. Additionally, the misuse of Biblical doctrines has placed many people into bondage. They feel if they do not follow and abide by the teachings in the Bible then they are breaking God's laws and are thereby susceptible to God's judgment.

Reacting to how Christians have used doctrines to divide and oppress God's people, numerous believers begin to devalue and even belittle doctrine. They may say something like: "We don't need doctrines; we just need the Spirit." Or, "Doctrines kill and divide." Or, "Studying the Bible is not necessary, it's the Spirit that gives life." They have pitted the experiences of the Spirit against the understanding of the Bible; yet, that is in and of itself their doctrine. Ironically, Christians pushing-back on this "no-doctrine" teaching respond by doubling-down, emphasizing all controversies can be explained with intensive study and "cutting-straight" (e.g., "rightly dividing") Scriptures. It seems constant arguments over doctrines in the Scripture are unavoidable and unending. Those who clamor for "sound doctrine" warn us to beware of those who deprecate the same.

The English word for "*doctrine*" or "*teaching*" comes from two different Greek words. The two Greek words are used differently and have two distinct meanings, but since they are both translated as "*doctrine*" in English, the exact meaning of each is lost. It is a source of confusion for English readers when these two Greek words are not clearly delineated. It would be a great help for believers to understand "*doctrine*" which they need to embrace as truth, and those doctrines which are flexible in application so as not to divide nor be oppressed by them.

The two Greek words translated to "*doctrine*" or "*teaching*" are: *Didachē* (Strong's #1322) and *Didaskalia* (Strong's #1319). According to Biblehub.com, *Didachē* means: Established teaching, especially a "summarized" body of respected teaching (viewed as reliable, time-honored). However, *Didaskalia* means: Applied teaching; systematic theology; Christian doctrine (teaching) as it especially extends to its necessary lifestyle (applications).

Didachē is used 30 times in the New Testament and 25 out of the 30 times refers to the doctrine spoken by Jesus (Matt 7:28, Luke 4:32); the doctrine of Jesus Christ (2 John 1:9-10); and, the doctrine of the apostles (Acts 2:42, 5:28). The other five times are used negatively (Heb. 13:9)—specifically, doctrines of: the Pharisees (Matt. 16:12), Balaam (Rev. 2:14), Nicolaitans (Rev. 2:15), and Jezebel (Rev. 2:24). Both the positive doctrines relating to Jesus Christ or the damaging ones are consistently time-honored and reliable for acceptance or rejection. There are no situations where the doctrine of Jesus Christ should be rejected, or the doctrine of Jezebel should be accepted.

The constant and eternally profitable doctrine (*Didachē*) represents the teaching concerning the person and work of Jesus Christ. It is this fundamental doctrine wherein the truth of the New Testament is found. It teaches people to know God, Jesus Christ, the Holy Spirit, the entire work of Christ from incarnation, human living, death, resurrection, ascension, the outpouring of the Spirit, regeneration of His people unto the building up of His ekklesia, the assembly, His Body until His bodily return in glory. This is the doctrine all believers should speak (1 Cor. 14:6); and from which Christian teachers should not deviate (Rom. 16:17). The above usages fit the definition of a "summarized body of respected teaching (viewed as reliable, time-honored)."

Didaskalia, on the other hand, is used 21 times. It refers to applied-teaching, application to Christian lifestyle with a view to systematizing theology. Therefore, this kind of doctrine instead of being "time-honored" is more contemporaneous. It seeks influence on the hearer's lifestyle. The effect on the hearer can be positive: leading them toward seeking and living a well-pleasing life before the Lord Jesus. However, it could also be negative: leading them away from the Lord toward self-efforts and bondages. Whether positive or negative, those influenced believe the source of this doctrine is divine or Scriptural—sound Biblical teaching.

On the positive side, we are told this teaching (*didaskalia*) of Scripture is for learning, providing us patience, comfort, and giving hope through difficulties in conflicting situations (Rom. 15:4). The Scriptures also provide doctrine (*didaskalia*), corrections, and instruction in righteousness. When one comes to the Scripture for Spiritual breath (life-sustaining), he/she receives the proper "*doctrine*" to be instructed to live and work in an evil generation (2 Tim. 3:16). How we apply Scriptures becomes the doctrine which governs how we live and act as Christians from day to day (2 Tim. 3:10).

Therefore, ministers of the Word should do their best to apply Scriptures in a way that is healthy or sound. When it comes to applying Scripture to a lifestyle, one can imagine all these various approaches. Thus, Paul stressed it needs to be healthy (1 Tim. 1:10; 2

Tim. 4:3; Titus 1:9; 2:1). "Healthy" points to life and growth, not merely behavior. When applying Scriptures, it needs to be in a way leading people to grow in their spiritual life.

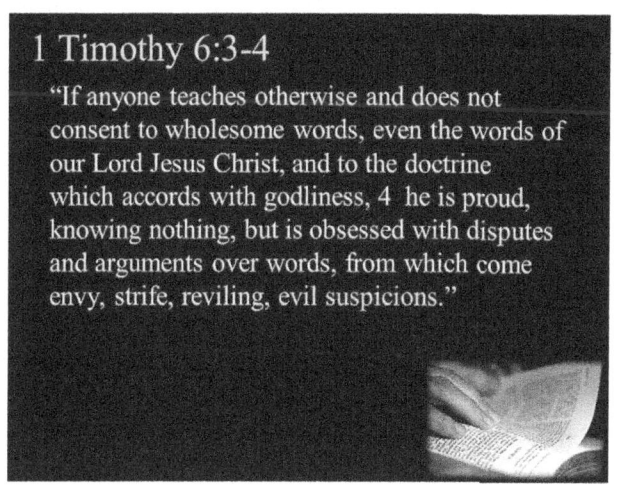

> **1 Timothy 6:3-4**
> "If anyone teaches otherwise and does not consent to wholesome words, even the words of our Lord Jesus Christ, and to the doctrine which accords with godliness, 4 he is proud, knowing nothing, but is obsessed with disputes and arguments over words, from which come envy, strife, reviling, evil suspicions."

Figure 29 - 1 TIMOTHY 6:3-4

It is by this strengthening and growing through the indwelling life of Christ believers are transformed. It is through life-transformation the daily life of believers is truly affected. The Christian life should not be governed by a set of rules; rather, it should be by God's eternal life within each believer. Healthy doctrine (*didaskalia*) is applying Scripture in a way leading the hearer to turn to Jesus Christ, so His life will cause the believer to grow and be transformed from within. Nevertheless, applying Scriptures improperly can also have a very harmful effect—the opposite of applying them in a healthy manner:

"And in vain they worship Me, Teaching [as] doctrines [didaskalia] the commandments of men."
– Matthew 15:9 NKJV

"In order that we may be no longer babes, tossed and carried about by every wind of that teaching [didaskalia] in the sleight of men, in unprincipled cunning with a view to systematized error . . ."
– Ephesians 4:14 DBY

So, You want to do Ekklesia?

In Matthew 15, when Jesus condemned the Pharisees, their teaching was about tithing. They were not teaching something sinful, such as lying or stealing. They were teaching something according to God's command: tithing—giving something to God. However, in their application of God's law concerning tithing, they negated another one which is to honor one's father and mother. This doctrine of *"If anyone tells his father or his mother, 'what you would have gained from me is given to God'"* became a commandment of men. It sounded so spiritual and Scriptural, but it was also in direct disobedience to another one of God's commands: honor your father and mother.

The Scriptures are full of seemingly competing and contrary ideas. When a person applies only one set of verses and negates conflicting verses, the doctrine derived by a one-sided application, no matter how Scriptural, is of man and not of God.

In Ephesians 4:14, the doctrines which were like a wind blowing young believers about can be assumed to be doctrines from the Bible. These differing emphases in applying Scripture became a wind to toss and carry immature believers from one side to another. Bible teachers can use their cunning ways of interpretation to come up with doctrines in support of their sectarian systems. Babes are blown about, captured into such a system by doctrines (*didaskalia*) or "systematized error."

Even doctrine (*didaskalia*) of demons as described in 1 Tim. 4:1-3 were not related to idolatry or some other sinful act; rather, they can be traced to applying scriptural and spiritual references. Didn't Paul say it is better for a man not to marry, so he can be pleasing to the Lord (1 Cor. 7:1, 8, 32)? A doctrine to forbid marriage is just a codifying of a portion of Scripture to help believers to love the Lord without entanglement. As far as abstaining from foods, isn't this also Scriptural and spiritual? Jesus Himself spoke of fasting (Matt. 6:16)—believers in Acts also fasted (Acts 13:2-3; 14:23). Demons merely formulated a doctrine by applying Scripture to regulate a Christian lifestyle.

Today, doctrines (*didaskalia*) which are causing arguments and divisions are mostly focused on how Scriptures are applied. It is not over the doctrine (*didache*) of Jesus Christ. Understanding and appreciating the doctrine of Jesus Christ as the truth brings believers into oneness. Attempting to systematize the Bible correctly among certain Christian lifestyles continues to segregate and divide believers. One desiring to serve the Lord needs to be grounded on and enriched by the doctrine of Jesus Christ with all His unsearchable riches, and simultaneously, be able to apply the appropriate Scriptures to a person in need with a particular condition.

Ephesians 4:4-7, 11-16

- ¹⁴We must no longer be children, tossed to and fro and blown about by every wind of doctrine, by people's trickery, by their craftiness in deceitful scheming. ¹⁵But speaking the truth in love, we must grow up in every way into him who is the head, into Christ,

Figure 30 - EPHESIANS 4:4-7; 11-16

For example, if a person's doctrine (*didaskalia*) is "once saved, always saved" or "saved by grace" alone, then that person cannot apply verses such as Philippians 2:12 "*work out your own salvation with fear and trembling*" in order to help a believer who is lackadaisical in his pursuit of the Lord. Likewise, if a person's doctrine is "you can lose your salvation," there will be another list of verses concerning the security of the believer's salvation which will not be used for comforting one who is under condemnation due to willfully sinning. Rather, a person who is fortified with the doctrine (*didache*) of Jesus Christ will be able to apply all verses without negating any. A healthy word can be spoken based on the need of the person at any specific time. This healthy word will turn the hearer to Jesus, strengthen his or her faith to pursue and serve the Lord. We're not talking about "situational ethics"—we're sharing the riches of Jesus Christ!

There are many more examples of doctrinal (*didaskalia*) applications: head covering for women, the exercise of miraculous gifts,

So, You want to do Ekklesia?

name and claim, modesty, choice or life, social equality, prosperity and health by faith, repentance and many more teachings in the Bible that can be applied to Christian living and practice. Some of these teachings have no doubt helped many believers; therefore, it is precious to them. However, according to the definition given to *didaskalia*, all these doctrinal applications are not truth at their core. Although these kinds of applications have helped many, they have also stumbled many. They have become a source of division and confusion if applied "religiously" in order to compel a certain lifestyle or Christian practice.

Figure 31 - THAT THEY ALL MAY BE ONE

Therefore, it is crucial for those desiring to answer the Lord's Prayer for the oneness of His people to understand these two different kinds of doctrine. On the one hand, we need to be those who keep mining the unsearchable riches of Jesus Christ so the doctrine (*didache*) of Jesus Christ becomes fuller and deeper for our enjoyment and our ministry to people. Satan's strategy is designed to distract believers from focusing on and knowing Jesus Christ.

On the other hand, we need to be wary of Satan's other tactic: motivating ministers to emphasize Biblical doctrines (*didaskalia*) to the point of divisiveness whereby these "healthy teachings" turn into unhealthy food. Instead of teachers divisively tossing believers around by every wind of doctrine, what is needed are teachers who can apply Scriptures to a person in need at the right moment to bring individuals back into fellowship with Jesus for the building up of His One Body. Jesus alone is precious.

"Sound doctrine builds up the Body of Christ." Know this: the doctrine (*didache*) of Jesus Christ is always beneficial for building up; whereas spiritual discernment is needed when applying doctrine (*didaskalia*) to a person's lifestyle. Ministers are needed to equip the saints, so all believers can speak the doctrine of Jesus Christ, which is the knowledge of the Son of God, producing the Perfect Man (Eph. 4:13). This will build up the Body of Christ into one ekklesia.

What will be covered in the following chapters are major points affecting the general understanding of the truth. This is what would be considered as the doctrine (*didache*) of Jesus Christ or the apostles' teachings (*didache*). These chapters will not focus on the various doctrines (*didaskalia*) in their sundry applications: the how, when, and to whom teachings of the Scriptures are applied. The application of teachings is where divisions and factions have been generated. Even disagreements concerning so-called deeper and richer points of truth, such as the Triune nature of God, should never break fellowship. Only the essential faith which brings salvation determines whether one is in fellowship with Jesus Christ. This saving faith is the only item for which believers should contend.

For a fuller disclosure regarding ONE TRUTH – please secure Henry Hon's ONE TRUTH @ https://www.amazon.com/One-Truth-Liberating-Nourishing-Unifying/dp/1732556326

So, You want to do Ekklesia?

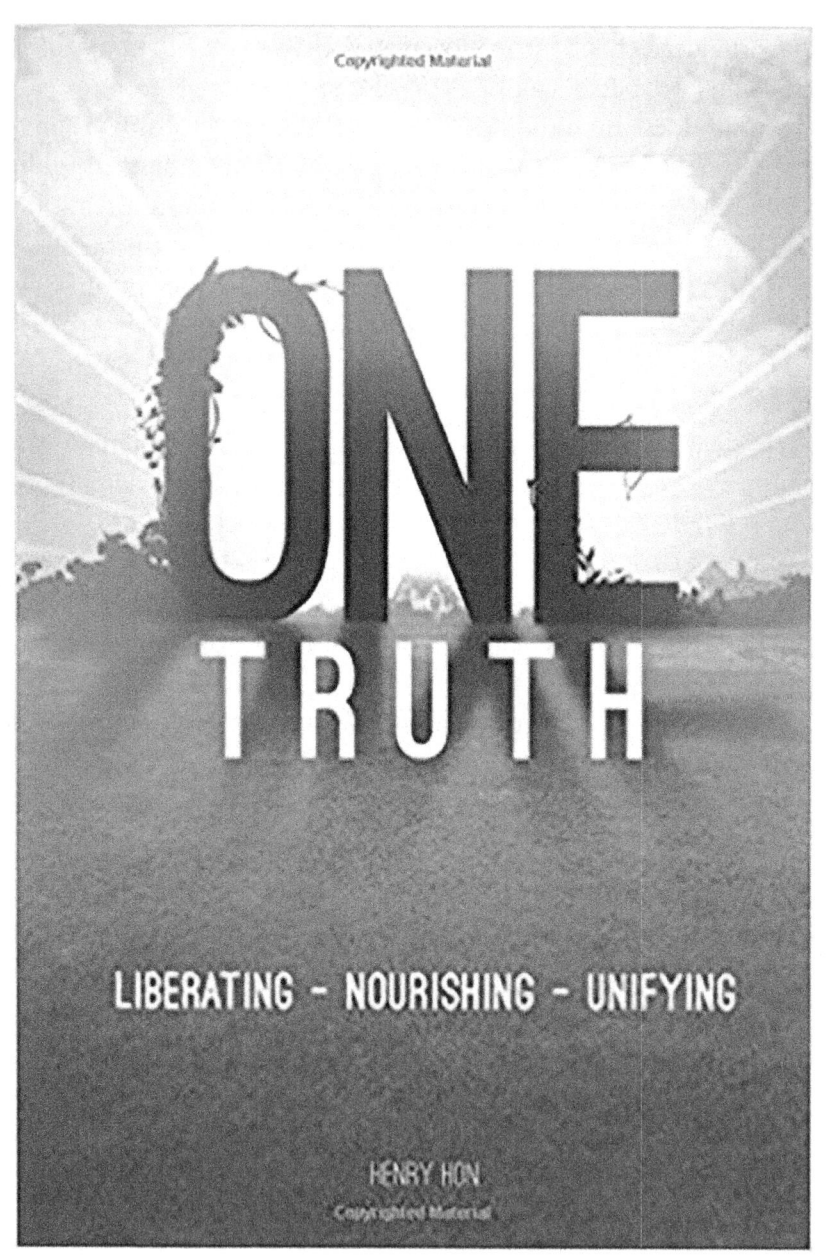

Figure 32 - HENRY HON: ONE TRUTH

Chapter 6:
One by One – Each One of You Has

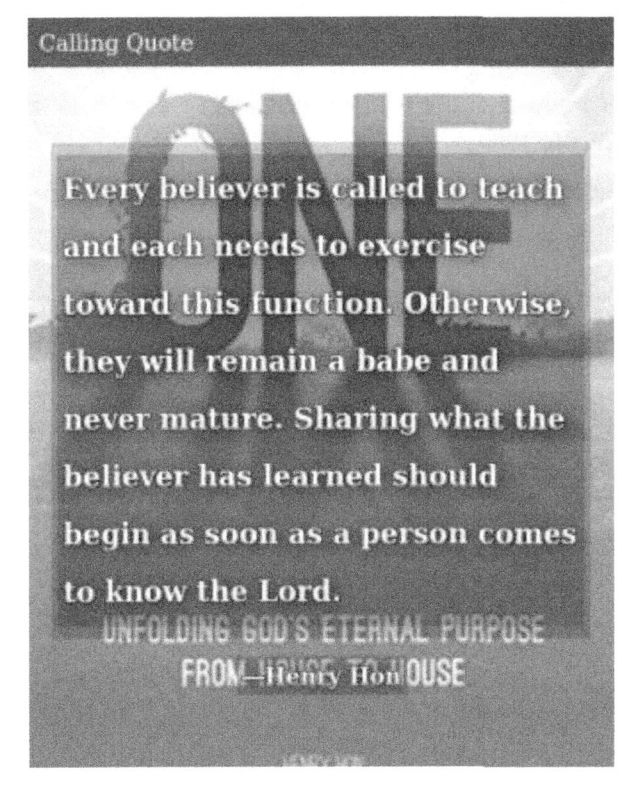

> **Calling Quote**
>
> Every believer is called to teach and each needs to exercise toward this function. Otherwise, they will remain a babe and never mature. Sharing what the believer has learned should begin as soon as a person comes to know the Lord.
>
> —Henry Hon

Figure 33 - QUOTE FROM HENRY HON

IN THIS CHAPTER ON THE EKKLESIA'S PRACTICE I'M HITTING ON A VERY SENSITIVE ASPECT OF *"HOW IS IT THEN, BRETHREN? IF THE WHOLE EKKLESIA COMES together in one place?"* since we are encouraged to so gather (1 Cor. 14:23, 26).

This little "mix and match" of Scripture strikes at the core of our traditional and very familiar "controlled environments." In the main, when Christians gather "as per normal"—aka, the "pulpit-pew" or "ministry" models—prevail. Don't get me wrong here—ministry and ministers are affirmatively spoken of in New Testament passages—but that is NOT our topic here. Just as so-called "gifted ones" given by the Head of His One Body are to *"equip the saints to do the work of the ministry"* (Eph. 4:12) . . .

73

So, You want to do Ekklesia?

even so, "general members" of the Body of Messiah are enjoined to activate under the guidance of the Holy Spirit; to wit:

> *"Therefore if the WHOLE EKKLESIA come together in one place . . . if ALL PROPHESY, and an unbeliever or an uninformed person comes in, he is CONVINCED BY ALL, he is CONVICTED BY ALL . . . so, falling down on his face, he will worship God and report that God is truly AMONG YOU."* (1 Cor. 14:23)

Oh, and by the way, that "uninformed" or "unbeliever" showed up at a Lord's Table, you know, the saints were "breaking bread"— having communion and this person shows up who eventually exclaims: *GOD IS TRULY AMONG YOU*—and with that: *"He will worship God!"*

Figure 34 - "THE JOY OF EARLY CHRISTIANITY" - BY STEVE SIMMS

Are you following here? *WHOLE EKKLESIA, ALL PROPHESY, CONVINCED BY ALL, CONVICTED BY ALL, AMONG YOU*—you see, everyone in the Ekklesia is in on it! This is "corporate evangelism" right in the midst of the Ekklesia. There's no "big shot evangelist" giving an invitation—as much as that may be effective at times—no, this is the Ekklesia, the *"called out ones"* doing the evangelism. How? By ALL prophesying.

Now, we're not talking about everyone predicting California fires and earthquakes (even a clock is right twice a day around 12:00) . . . we're talking about how each member of the Body is apt to share their portion of the Lord in their lives in an Ekklesia-style gathering . . . and ALL means ALL, as in EVERYONE when the whole Ekklesia comes together.

So:

"How is it then, brethren? WHENEVER you come together, EACH OF YOU HAS a psalm, has a teaching, has a tongue, has a revelation, has an interpretation. Let all things be done for building up ("edification") (1 Cor. 14:26).

Forgive me—did you get that? EACH OF YOU HAS and if *YOU HAS*, then *YOUs* better get that out in the assembled and do so with others as in *"let there be two or at the most three, each in turn, and let one interpret . . . let two or three prophets speak"* (NOTE: You're not the only guy who's a prophet when the "whole Ekklesia" comes together.). Are we getting the picture here? This is NOT the "big time minister" doing his/her thing but the Body edifying one another by twos and threes. And, if you're not going to have "interpretation" of your tongue going on—better to "keep silent" and *"if anything is revealed to another who sits by, let the first keep silent"* when it comes to revelation.

Now, I know you're thinking, especially you pastors and teachers, WE'VE GOT TO KEEP THIS THING UNDER WRAPS lest it get out of control. But the apostle Paul is adamant:

"For you can all prophesy ONE BY ONE, that ALL may learn and ALL may be encouraged" (1 Cor. 14:31) . . . *"and the spirits of the prophets are subject to the prophets"* (1 Cor. 14:32).

Figure 35 - 'I AM NOT A CONTROL FREAK"

Whoops! You may have read that: ". . . the spirits of those prophesying are subject to overlord-style prophets who are controlling those who are prophesying"—now, come on now, that's NOT what it says! Clearly, you may have a stupendous gift as a prophet but STOP CONTROLLING those who are testifying/prophesying in the Ekklesia, where . . . the *"spirits of those prophets"* are subject, not to YOU (the big shot prophet) but to the very spirit of the one who is prophesying! I wish I could be more emphatic . . . but doesn't every good orchestra have a Conductor? True, but it's spelled with a capital "C"—take note, as in **G**od!

Bring & Share Your Portion of the "Good Land"

Yes, ONE BY ONE, and EACH ONE OF YOU HAS, and YOU CAN ALL PROPHESY! During the "feast days" described in Scripture, the children of Israel brought the produce and livestock of their labors off the land to offer to the Lord and to share with one another.

Really, these gatherings were like a huge "tail-gate party"—a massive BBQ where everyone shared the "bounty of the Good Land" with one another. Somehow, we've got the notion that everything was a "whole burnt offering" and there was no BBQ—nonsense—there was both and all brought, and all enjoyed these massive feast days. Isaiah 25:6 displays exactly what the Almighty is

One by One – Each One of You Has

preparing for us—why would it be any different today (well, on a smaller scale, of course):

> "In Jerusalem, the LORD of Heaven's Armies will spread a wonderful feast for all the people of the world. It will be a delicious banquet with clear, well-aged wine and choice meat." (NLT)

Figure 36 - THE LORD'S FEASTS AKIN TO A HUGE TAILGATE PARTY

But can you imagine the Ekklesia in Corinth was having what appears to be a "weekly banquet"—as well—but it wasn't to celebrate the Lord's Supper (1 Cor. 11:20-22) . . . *"for in eating, each one takes his own supper ahead of others; and one is hungry and another is drunk"* . . . WHAT! Yeah, you can stop right there: WHAT!

Shaming those who have nothing (1 Cor. 11:22) isn't a celebration of the Lord's Supper . . . there should be food and drink for everyone . . . not just for a bunch of "fat cat" selfish guzzlers (aka, "It's all about ME, isn't it?").

This "Lord's Table" is supposed to be a celebration and marvelous remembrance that we are "breaking the bread" of His ONE BODY; and drinking the CUP OF THE NEW COVENANT in His blood! (I Cor. 11:25) . . . I know, we remember Him, and we think of our sin covered by His precious blood—BUT WHAT ABOUT REMEMBERING HIS ONE BODY? What about the New Covenant in which "Jew and Gentile" have been made ONE through the blood of His cross?

Discerning the Lord's Body

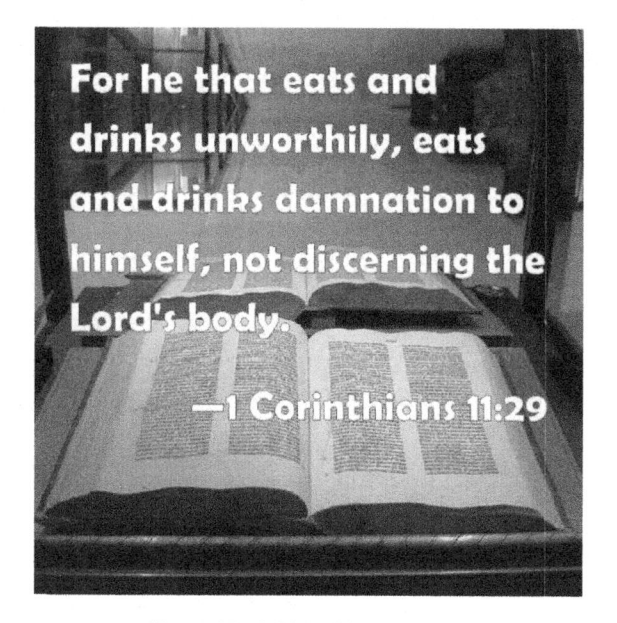

> For he that eats and drinks unworthily, eats and drinks damnation to himself, not discerning the Lord's body.
> —1 Corinthians 11:29

Figure 37 - 1 CORINTHIANS 11:29

But since "it's all about me, isn't it?" mindset—then, it's all about your sinful condition and you analyzing what a wretch you are as you meditate on your peculiar sins and ask the Lord to forgive you once again . . . while having little or no consciousness of anyone else at that Table, but you! Forbid, you'd ever consider *"discerning the Lord's Body"* as in: "Lord, forgive me for not forgiving my brother or sister . . . Lord, I've not really reconciled with brother so-and-so—FORGIVE ME—O Lord, may I discern, not my own condition . . . not my own belly . . . but may I "wait for one another" and "discern Your One Body" more than "It's all about me, isn't it?"

You see, when we come together as the Ekklesia, there's got to be this sense of His One Body and how we're "*members one of another*" (Rom. 12:5)—and, more so, we're not the "only game in town"—that is, what about our "little Ekklesia's" relationship with others in town? Could it be (probably is) we're totally unconscious that there are others outside "our little group" who are just as vitally connected to the One Body as we are? Are we at peace and even in fellowship (if at all possible) with them? Have we, as Paul commends: "*Greet the Ekklesia that is in their house*" (Romans 16:5). (Oh, and by the way, there's normally plenty of houses in most towns and some have God's people in them!)

Paul says that if we do not "*discern the Lord's Body . . . FOR THIS REASON many are weak and sick among you, and many ARE DEAD!*" (1 Cor. 11:29-30). Wow! This business where "it's all about me, isn't it?" vs. "*discerning the Lord's Body*" can be a horrific disconnect to the point that our "little body of believers" is sick, sick, sick! Even DEAD! We're praying for healing, but healing is starring us right in the face when we've got all these hang-ups with other members of His Body.

Remember Jesus' Own words:

"Therefore if you bring your gift to the altar, and there remember that your brother has something against you, leave your gift there before the altar, and go your way. First be reconciled to your brother, and then come and offer your gift." (Matt. 5:23-24)

How about a "table meeting" where we get right with one another—let's not make it some kind of a ceremony or show-off of our humility, but how can we sit there with grievances toward one another and toward other brethren not even in our midst—we're proclaiming the Lord's One Body, all the while we've got these divisions on-going!

Brethren, we've got to become "Body conscious" rather than "me conscious"—I know, you've never seen a drunk at the Lord's Supper, right? Believe me, there's a whole lot more "drunks" at the Communion Table than you may surmise and a whole lot

So, You want to do Ekklesia?

more gobbling up the goodies, stuffing ourselves because we're so used to practicing *"whose god is their belly"* Christianity (or we chow down all the food before the table and have nothing to SHARE with anyone else when we arrive; and, again, some of us arrive drunk) . . . and a whole lot more of us are sick as a result . . . some are even DEAD! *"Them's* tough words," aren't they? But that's how serious it is *"when the whole Ekklesia comes together."*

When we view one of the rare insights into an "Ekklesia in action" in the New Testament, as seen in 1 Cor. 11-14, we get a wholesome glimpse at selfish behavior vs. caring for one another behavior. Having a "big bash" of a gathering does not for a vibrant Ekklesia make. Sharing your substance, sharing your experiences of Christ with others; forgiving your brothers and sisters in true reconciliation vs. "woe is me, I'm such a sinner" complex is how the Body of Christ is discerned. Remember, "this do in remembrance of Me" is NOT a therapy session where you get to vent your on-going crisis week after week. Maybe you should consider laying THAT at the altar and celebrate the fact your problems pale into oblivion compared to everyone else—besides, this gathering is to celebrate the New Covenant in His Blood! Trying to "get right with yourself" should be laid aside as you "try to get right with your brother or sister"—just sayin'.

Figure 38 - THE LORD'S SUPPER

Let me be frank: THE LORD'S TABLE, the "Communion" (whatever you wish to call it) has everything to do with the New Covenant, which in turn not only testifies to you having Peace with God, but has within this "Blood Covenant" the words:

"For He Himself is OUR PEACE, who has made both one, and has broken down the middle wall of separation . . . so as to create in Himself ONE NEW MAN from the two, thus MAKING PEACE, and that He might reconcile them both to God in ONE BODY through the cross, thereby putting to death the enmity . . . and He came and PREACHED PEACE to you who were afar off and to those who were near . . . for through Him we BOTH have access by ONE SPIRIT to the Father" (Eph. 2:14-18).

That's right—PEACE with one another. The Communion Table not only reminds us of His death and resurrection and coming again in glory (*'til He come*) but testifies to the UNIVERSE we are ONE BODY—we have peace with one another through the "blood of the cross!"

Let it sink into the depths of your soul: YOU HAVE PEACE WITH GOD and **PEACE WITH ONE ANOTHER** through the blood of His cross? Celebrate it! And, if you're struggling with the pragmatics of that peace with God and with your other brethren—then RESET, go back to the major tenets of the New Covenant in His blood and get it right before "God and man!" *"This IS the blood of the New Covenant!"* We cannot do this on our own . . . it takes the "whole Ekklesia" to "pull it off"—show me how you can reconcile yourself to your brother or sister up in some wilderness in a monk-like state—an "isolation ward" is NOT the experience of the Body of Christ—that Table loudly proclaims to us all, to the world, and to principalities and powers in high places: WE ARE ONE BODY—we refuse to be a sickly body but cry out to God Almighty that we boldly affirm we are truly ONE with God and with ALL HIS PEOPLE!

And, for you DOCTRINAIRES (for "I are one") we got some real issues with folks who don't see "eye-to-eye" with our interpretation of the Scripture, now, don't we? I just had a conference with some believers—many of whom say the Bible's cosmology conforms to a "flat earth". . . . and these bros. are serious! Well, that *ain't* even on my radar . . . and I can't even go there, even if I tried! Enough folks think I'm a little off the chart anyway (no pun intended). But for four days I "broke bread" with some of the most precious brethren I've had the good fortune to ever meet and greet! Why do we let these "doctrines" become so divisive and allow factions to develop—"*Let each be fully convinced in his own mind.*" . . . "*Receive one who is weak in the faith, but not to disputes over doubtful things*" (Romans 14:5, 1)? A flat or globed earth never saved anyone—a Person did, and I think you know His Name!

What Do We Have, One by One?

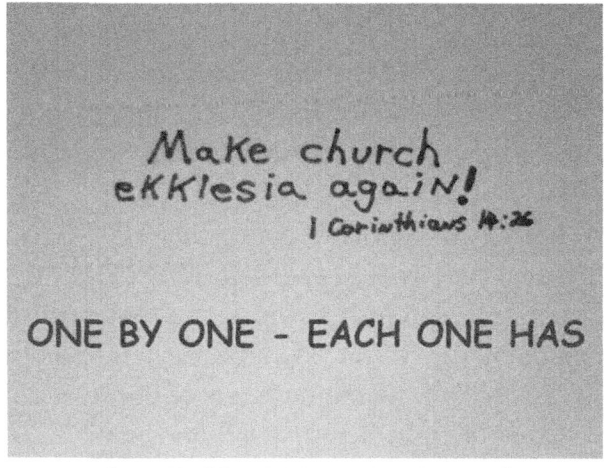

Figure 39 - "ONE BY ONE - EACH ONE HAS"

First of all, if we don't recognize that everyone in the Ekklesia HAS and that whatever each one has is supposed to be shared with the "whole Ekklesia"—one by one and preferably in twos and threes—then right out the chute we have a problem. Why? Because if you think some have more than others—then, you're probably looking for someone's ministry, not BODY MINISTRY where a whole lot of folks are sharing, not just some charismatic leader-type brother or sister with or without a whole string of credentials, even experience, behind their name! Once you think that brother so and so is NOT qualified—well, as they say: Kiss that Ekklesia GOOD-BYE!

You say: But every time sister Betty "shares" it's always (in your eyes) some "superficial" whatever—a little tidbit from the Scripture or something in her life where Jesus shows up somehow—and she drones on and on about it. Well, congratulations, sounds like you and Betty need to "discern the Body"—You, because you're looking down your nose at little sister Betty, and Betty needs to be more "Body conscious" because it sounds like others have little tidbits to share, not just Betty?

As big a mess as the Church in Corinth was—they still ALL HAVE/HAD; and, as chaotic their meetings were (drunks included), they were still encouraged to prophesy ONE BY ONE and to do so "decently and in order" because *"God is not the author of disorder but of PEACE"* (1 Cor. 14:40, 33); and don't think this was focused only on the Ekklesia in Corinth but *"as in all the Ekklesia of the saints"* (1 Cor. 14:33).

What we have here, and since I hail from the US Army, is known as SOP: Standard Operating Procedures . . . all "units" (all Ekklesia) should operate like this. Listen up: *"God is NOT the author of confusion"*—this is NOT a drunken brawl (sorry to keep bringing up these drunks, but Corinth had issues here—there was plenty of confusion)—only the God of ORDER and PEACE could keep these saints together—center on Christ, His New Covenant, New Commandment, where His love pours out through one another—His reconciliation through the Cross—so that when they came together, here's what happened:

"Each of you has a psalm, has a teaching, has a tongue, has a revelation, has an interpretation" . . . brethren, this IS the Body of Christ where there's allotments, diversity, differences, activities that differ:

> *"There are **allotments** of gifts, but the same Spirit. There are **differences** of ministries, but the same Lord. And there are **diversities** of activities, but it is the same God who works all things in . . . but the administration of the Spirit is given to each one for the profit of all"* (1 Cor. 12:4-7).

So, You want to do Ekklesia?

So, at the Ekklesia God is "working all things in"—yes, into a beautiful tapestry of sundry allotments of gifts, different ministries are going on, diverse activities are taking place, everyone has an allotment (just like the children of Israel were given various allotments in the Good Land upon which to labor)—there's NO SEPARATION, but there's a whole lot of MANIFESTATIONS—get used to variety big time!

You know what Einstein once said: Doing the same thing over and over and expecting different results is the definition of insanity—THAT'S CONFUSION—just look at the overabundance of variety in creation: THAT'S GOD! Sure, the way most "communion services" go down looks like we've got it altogether—sort of a "private affair" made public—nothing confusing going on here . . . so we think . . . we're in, we're out, and no harm was done . . . I did my part, some others showed up, but little, if any, expression of the Oneness of the Body of Christ—because nearly everyone kept their mouth shut (except when we took "the elements"), except the priest, the minister, the deacon or whoever was serving us communion, the table, the mass.

God is the God of Variety

Figure 40 - GOD IS THE GOD OF VARIETY

What's the difference between a "word of wisdom" and a "revelation" (1 Cor. 12:8; 14:26)—I'm sure someone's figured it out but

One by One – Each One of You Has

don't you like surprises? I do, and such revelations and words of wisdom sound surprising to me—WE NEED THEM in the Body of Christ! We need them VERBALLY EXPRESSED! And, if you're deaf and unable to speak—find Aaron and have him do the honors!

VARIETY! "Are all apostles? Are all prophets? Are all teachers? Are all workers of miracles? Do all have gifts of healings? Do all speak with tongues? Do all interpret?" HOW DULL IT WOULD BE IF OUR "ALL" WAS ALL THE SAME THING!! (1 Cor. 12:29-30)

Imagine—the Body of Christ coming together where the same Spirit operating in various members of the Body will manifest the "*gifts of healing*," another will, by the same Spirit pull off some miracles (can't imagine that, but there it is)—someone else (notice, not the same person all the time) will be "*discerning of spirits*"—and then "*tongues and interpretation of tongues!*"—so much for cessation (1 Cor. 12:8-10).

Perennial "Control Freak" – Alpha Male (or Jezebel)

Figure 41 - "I'M SO IN CONTROL!"

Now the hard part for the "control freaks" out there:

"*But one and the same Spirit works all these things* (not the "control *meister*"), *distributing to EACH ONE INDIVIDUALLY AS HE WILLS*" (1 Cor. 12:11)—OUCH! That one hurt! Why? Because not only do we like to control the meeting (or assign some to do the same)—we'd like to think that "we're in control" distributing to people we think are deserving of whatever gifts or talents we think they should manifest as in: *"Brother so and so, you are gifted in music—why not give us a Psalm . . . Sister Debbie, isn't it time for you to discern the spirit of this situation with so-and-so?"* Why can't we let the SAME SPIRIT do the distribution, instead of Mr. Control Freak? That's because we can't trust the Spirit of God to do the manifestation—*"Individually as HE WILLS."* Forbid this "thing" gets out of control!

Yes, we want to see everyone functioning, sharing, prophesying—but there's a thin line between allowing the same Spirit distributing and manifesting vs. manipulating God's people to come out of their hiding places and join in on the feast . . . the Spirit of God must be in "operation" where the *"spirits of the prophets are subject to the prophets"*—meaning, everyone has a human spirit which is controlled by that individual not by some individual in the room controlling everyone's spirit! Let's be honest now: When was the last time you heard a pastor-teacher expounding on an Ekklesia-style gathering like this—good grief, might put the guy out of a job—but isn't that the ultimate goal wherein all the members of the same Body are prophesying and thereby expressing MEMBERS INDIVIDUALLY—*"distributing to each one individually as He wills"*?

Forgive me if I sound like I'm beating a dead horse—*"you can all prophesy one by one, that all may learn and all may be encouraged."* The initiative for such a display of an Ekklesia is NOT in the hands of the "elder" in the group, or "group leaders" or the "host" of the Ekklesia—it's the SAME SPIRIT Who's supposed to be in control. The saints may need some instruction from a Paul or whoever, but once they "get the knack of it"—they (the saints) should be up and running without anyone's interference. Now, THAT'S being a real pastor-teacher!

We've Got this "Thing" under Control . . .

But, isn't a "controlled environment" such as the traditional "Christian Service" where everyone files in, sits down, listens to some special worship-style music, some announcements, takes in a special prayer time, greets other folks in the pews nearby, and then listens to the same preacher week after week (with some variations when an outside speaker steps in—just keep it short, we've got lots of plans today); then there's something called a wrap-up or an offering and then we go home—YES! No casualties—everything is done "decently and in order" and nothing weird really goes down—it all happens just as it always happened—"safety, certainty" with a little bit of enjoyment (sort of) but you really can't wait to get a bite to eat and/or watch some football game . . . it's methodical, and no one's "out of order"—well, even a graveyard has a lot of "decently and in order" going on—really? Yep— "there's no there, there" because nothing's happening aside from the fact they're "dying to get in!"

I'm adding this rather peculiar title into the text because it is exceedingly essential if an Ekklesia is to succeed—technically speaking, that is. *"Let two or three prophets speak, and let the others judge. But if anything is revealed to another who sits by, let the first keep silent. For you can all prophesy one by one"* (1 Cor. 14:29-30). I call this "priming the pump"—once the water gets flowing, no need to keep priming the pump! Notice "two or three prophets" commence to speak—never any single individual—sorry, the guy "hogging the show" will have to share. Then as the "two or three" get things going in a gathering, that'll stir the troops—then LET THE PARTY BEGIN! Stop with manipulating, and monopolizing via prophesying, worshipping the way you want to worship, praying your way; frankly, doing anything your way. Look around: YOU'RE NOT THE ONLY GAME IN TOWN. If you really cared for the saints, you'd prime the pump—then sit back; you just might learn a thing or two and experience the rest of the Body of Christ! I know, I sound very cruel—but an Ekklesia isn't your private fiefdom—it's the Body of Christ!

Ending on a "Happy Note"

I'd like to end on a happy note, let me close by saying PRACTICING EKKLESIA is a whole lot more difficult today than it was back in Paul's day because the Greeks in Corinth had around 600 years to practice what a "civil ekklesia" looked like . . . the closest

So, You want to do Ekklesia?

thing we have today here in America is a "town-hall meeting" (and these can become quite spirited, even rowdy). The Greeks knew the rules of the game—but this *"I will build My Ekklesia"* was very different: THIS WAS THE LORD'S EKKLESIA He was building . . . the similarities stopped at the word EKKLESIA but it did have one thing in common—they all had to come together and all could participate . . . eventually, when a vote was taken, the majority decision was made for the benefit of the community (hopefully).

Well, our consensus (actually, unanimous) vote must conclude: JESUS IS LORD—we all agree, there is *"ONE BODY, ONE SPIRIT, ONE HOPE OF YOUR CALLING, ONE LORD, ONE FAITH, ONE BAPTISM, ONE GOD AND FATHER OF ALL, who is above all, and through all, and in you all. But to EACH ONE of us grace was given according to the measure of Christ's gift"* (Eph. 4:4-7) . . . therefore: *"Endeavoring to keep the unity of the Spirit in the bond of peace"* (Eph. 4:3-5) we press on as His EKKLESIA which shall prevail against the *"gates of Hades"* and shall shortly *"crush Satan under our feet!"* (Rom. 16:20)

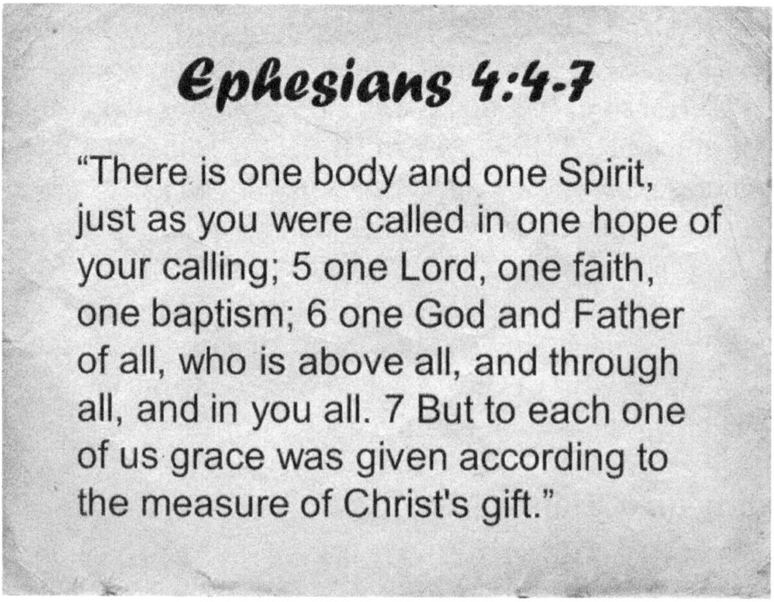

Ephesians 4:4-7

"There is one body and one Spirit, just as you were called in one hope of your calling; 5 one Lord, one faith, one baptism; 6 one God and Father of all, who is above all, and through all, and in you all. 7 But to each one of us grace was given according to the measure of Christ's gift."

Figure 42 - EPHESIANS 4:4-7

Chapter 7:
Balancing Act Between Clergy & Laity – Part 1

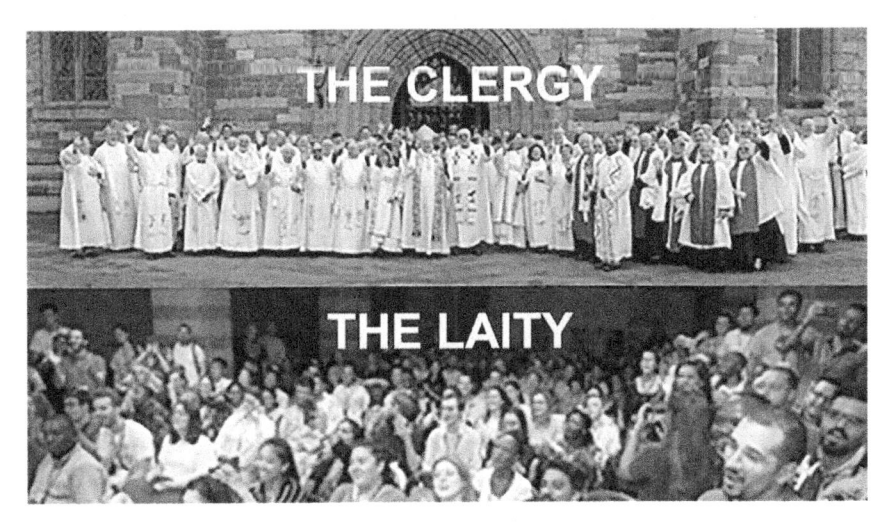

Figure 43 - THE CLERGY AND THE LAITY

There you go again, Krieger, trying to rearrange chairs on the top deck of the ***Titanic*** when we should be getting into the lifeboats and letting this "thing" sink! Yes, I guess I'm guilty of at least trying to move things around a bit because it's a little chaotic between clergy/laity—pulpit/pew—ministers/congregants—elders/members—I could go on; but I'm not trying to destroy the obvious. Let me explain . . .

To suggest that there is not this dichotomy within the Body of Christ (and, consequent "tension") one simply has either not read the Word of God—especially the New Testament—or (let me be a bit sinister here) has an agenda to have their own "tension system" of controlling the saints (not that the clergy doesn't), but to say "we're all the same" without gifted members of the One Body standing out vs. the "average Joe," well, the one saying we should all be "equal" is often guilty of that which they protest the most—viz., "some are more equal than others."

This (clergy vs laity) is a very "touchy" subject and grossly misunderstood—especially, among the growing number of Christians in America who are so DONE (aka, "the *Dones*") with

So, You want to do Ekklesia?

the traditional denominational or even non-denominational "Church-going" system. This perspective may outrage some "who are in control" but, believe me, there's plenty of blame to go around—i.e., the abuse wrought by ministries/ministers vs. congregant manipulations is endless. Need I say more than what is already known regarding "clergy abuse" either in moral matters or "financial issues" vs. congregants who "hire and fire"—at will—pastors.

Figure 44 - THE RISE OF THE DONES

Clergy Abuse/Exploitation

Now, bear with me, we've got to get the clutter taken out of the room before we can "rearrange" things. I know, somewhat presumptuous of me to suggest some of these "alternatives"—but someone's got to do it. Clergy exploitation (e.g., material, moral, psychological, spiritual) is known in the book of Revelation as Nicolaitanism:

> *But this thou hast, that thou hatest the deeds of the Nicolaitans, which I also hate.* — Revelation 2:6

Allow me to quote Renner on this:

> Jesus was proud of the church of Ephesus for their "hatred" of the deeds of the Nicolaitans, which He also "hated." The word "hate" is a strong word, so let's see exactly what it means. It comes from the Greek word *miseo*, which means to hate, to abhor, or to find utterly repulsive. It describes a person who has a deep-seated animosity, who is antagonistic to something he finds to be completely objectionable. He not only loathes that object but rejects it entirely. This is not just a case of dislike; it is a case of actual hatred.
>
> AND . . .
>
> The name "Nicolaitans" is derived from the Greek word *nikolaos*, a compound of the words *nikos* and *laos*. The word *nikos* is the Greek word that means *to conquer* or *to subdue*. The word *laos* is the Greek word for *the people*. It is also where we get the word *laity*. When these two words are compounded into one, they form the name *Nicolas*, which literally means *one who conquers and subdues the people*. It seems to suggest that the Nicolaitans were somehow conquering and subduing the people.

Renner goes into detail wherein Nicolaitans were those who followed the pattern of Nicholas, a proselyte from Antioch with a pagan background who converted to Judaism and then to Christianity and was somehow, as a result of his background, able to bring pagan practices into the congregation of the faithful (Acts 6:5; Rev. 2:14-15) *a la* Baalim who was hired by the Moabite king to prophesy against Israel, but could not (Numbers 22-24). These "guns for hire" are utilized to wreak havoc over God's people—aka, "clergy abuse." Today's Christianity is fraught, sadly so, by these "*Baalimites*" who are requisitioned to afflict the people of God (at their worst) or at their semi-best, simply control the laity . . . maneuvering them at their whims.

Congregant Malfeasance – The Laodiceans

However, within the seven distinctly different expressions of the EKKLESIA (aka, churches) in Asia as found in Revelation 2-3, I find the most egregious, even disgusting Lampstand, was the Church in Laodicea. Why? Because the very name conjures up a lukewarm condition which is *"neither cold nor hot"* so that the Lord would *"vomit you out of My mouth"* (Rev. 3:16)? How's that? Well, this rather prosperous outcropping of saints found itself in the midst of trade routes where lots of commercialism took place—this Ekklesia had "money issues" big time. And, money is power (in case you haven't yet figured that one out).

> *"Because you say, 'I am rich, have become wealthy, and have need of nothing'—and do not know that you are wretched, miserable, poor, blind, and naked"* (Rev. 3:17).

So, with "riches" comes control—normally, the clergy treats you differently if you have the big bucks. The Greek words which comprise "Laodicean" are two: λαος (*leos*) meaning "the people" and δικη (*dikay*) meaning "justice or fairness" wrought by the people; thus: "people justice." It has a "judicial context"—the best way to put it would be in a court of law where a "jury of your peers" render a decision, juxtaposed to the "court" (i.e., a judge only) rendering a decision; thus, "people justice" vs. "court justice." In other words: THE PEOPLE RULE vs. the JUDGE RULES. Put crudely: We, the people (aka, the congregants), will act as "judge and jury"—we control this "thing"—not some judge (aka, the clergy).

Figure 45 - LAODICEA - THE LUKEWARM CHURCH

Oddly enough, it was the very Council in Laodicea in 363-364 A.D. of some 30 bishops which solidified the separation between Jew and Christian and forbid worship on the Jewish/Sabbath as well as Hebraic Feast Days, among other things, but also, sought the following:

- ·Maintaining order among bishops, clerics and laypeople (canons 3–5, 11–13, 21–27, 40–44, 56–57)
- ·Enforcing modest behavior of clerics and laypeople (4, 27, 30, 36, 53–55)

My, my, how the clergy turned things around and sought not only to control the laity but themselves! But I think one can clearly see the extremes represented by the Lord's hatred regarding the Nicolaitan system and His disgust (vomiting) toward the Laodicean system—amazing how the Lord sees things vs. how we see them, isn't it?

The "Congregational System"

Today, the "congregational system" is celebrated where the Board of Deacons or Elders (depending on whether your Baptist [deacons] or Presbyterian [elders] tell the pastors "where to get off" (I know, sounds a bit negative) or on the positive side provides a wide-base of support to said pastor almost to the point of the ridiculous (e.g., "pastor appreciation days"—all sorts of "vacation perks"—inordinate expressions of adulation, etc.).

However, sometimes a member of the clergy will "gain the upper hand" and create a "leadership environment" where the congregants are, in the main, subservient to some type of administrative leader, patriarchal figure, nigh cult-like character or the assembled are mesmerized by some charismatic "Lollapalooza or Wallapalooza"-style leadership (viz. "an extraordinary or unusual thing, person, or event; an exceptional example or instance").

So, You want to do Ekklesia?

Figure 46 - WALLAPALOOZA

Balance Between "The Work" & the "Congregants"

Three things are at stake here:

(1) The congregants—the regulars—the "whole Ekklesia" when it comes together.

(2) Gifted members—Apostles, Prophets, Evangelists, Pastors-Teachers—sometimes affectionately known as "the clergy" . . . closely associated with them but a little different are the . . .

(3) Ministries—gifted members normally not connected, *per se*, with immediate "Church leadership" yet having ministries supporting what are known as "churches" (aka, "para-church ministries").

Can we find these three entities in the New Testament? Of course, in some fashion we can . . . known as (1) the "churches" (aka, the Ekklesia); (2) the gifted ones (viz., those who should be equipping the "saints for the ministry" as found in Eph. 4:11-12) or "workers" as per 2 Tim. 2:15 and illustrated by the workers from Antioch "when they were sent off" to Asia Minor in Acts 15:30-41 and (3) the elders/deacons of local congregations (e.g., Phil. 1:1; 1 Tim. 3:1-13—with all THREE designations found in Acts 15:23: *The apostles* (aka, gifted ones); *the elders; and the brethre*n (congregants).

Who's in Control – Why I Left a "Christian Cult"

Herein lies the rub. Somebody must be in control, right? In remembrance of a brother, who once considered himself (as well as others who so considered him) the **ORACLE OF GOD** (a bit of a stretch but, nevertheless, God's insurmountable mouthpiece on the earth today, would be more like it—yeah, I know, sounds nigh Papal, and it was/is).

Another brother and I after nearly eleven years within the "confines" of this man's "ministry" knew exactly what we stood for:

> "We are the OVERCOMERS who are 'standing on the local ground of unity'—for within any jurisdiction we may find ourselves—we are absolutely for the Body of Christ for we are the Body of Christ locally expressed; therefore, either we find others who are standing as we are (***EXCEEDINGLY RARE TO FIND***) or we "take the ground of unity" wherein all other believers who are in confusion (viz., Babylon) and, therefore, must meet with us to express the same 'ground of unity in that locality'—otherwise, if they don't align with us, they abide in division, sectarianism, and sundry factions (especially, the overt denominations)."

I generously labeled this, after I was "excused" from this concept/Church the "doctrine of the dirt."

Now, you may think this a somewhat odd "awareness" (shall we say) of "Body Life"—but the "doctrines of demons" are extremely clever and rabidly sectarian (although initially, they present themselves as most benign and gregarious—open to all, said the spider to the fly). Normally, such groups result in some form of "cultic expression"—although, they may be Christian, at least in name. Frankly, you can normally consider something ***cultic*** by dent of the fact these beloved members have an intense "superiority complex" and delight they have discovered truth and mysteries unknown by most Christians. Again, the closer one gets to the epicenter of their movement, the harder it is to digress from the dictum which normally are ensconced and/or broadcast by

So, You want to do Ekklesia?

their leader or "ministerial council"—any deviation is at best suspect and at worst pure rebellion and must be excised from the "group." This sometimes is referred to as "leaven"—in other words, once one is designated as "rebellious" by the "authorities" that person is stigmatized and shunned, lest anyone within the group "touch the unclean thing" and become contaminated [aka, leprous]—forbid!

Figure 47 - "I KNOW THE 'GROUND OF UNITY' IS OUT THERE SOMEWHERE"

They "become cultic" because, although they may give allowance in recognition that Christians can be found "all over the place"—there can be little doubt the REAL, GENUINE, COMMITTED ones are found within the wagons they have circled! Those "circled wagons" normally restrict or consign the "ministry" of that group to the singularity of that minister/ministerial council. To leave the group is more than dangerous and can result in some form of "dis-fellowship"—censor—shunning—and in extreme cases "curses be upon you" and even (as was the case with the inquisition) DEATH (normally, suicide)!

So, "Christian cults" can be very large or very small—do you follow? Oh, sure, since YOU are the problem, the group's members may from time to time see you at "neutral functions" (someone's going away party known by everyone—or a funeral, aka, Memorial Service or a wedding) but, in the main, stay out of your sight or give you a smile (if you're lucky) but, other than that, YOU'RE THE ENEMY!

Rejection? "Seems Antioch was Controlling Them"

Another brother and I, along with a few other young people, raised up a work (aka, "church") in, of all places, Berkeley, California back in the heyday of the Jesus Movement (early 1970s). We contended that we were standing on the "ground of unity" and all other believers in Berkeley, CA were just in some form of "degraded Christianity" (derogatorily known as "poor *Churchanity*").

But, as we continued to minister among the young people, hippies, university students in Berkeley, we realized many of the "other believers" who were doing similar works in leading young people to Jesus were still in the same "Household of Faith/God" as we—you see, that was "part of our doctrinal belief system" (in theory, at least)—notwithstanding, they still weren't on the "ground of the dirt" as we were!

So, there were Pentecostals doing a work there in the form of a place called Resurrection City, which was an outcropping of the Assemblies of God; then there was the rump-session of **Campus Crusade for Christ** known as the **Christian World Liberation Front** (by then) and then eventually as the Dwight House and, finally, as the "***Spiritual Counterfeits Project* or SCP**" (although the latter came "transforming itself" and it was hard to figure that one out).

We got into all sorts of trouble when one day a bunch of our "kids" gathered in Sproul Plaza near Ludwig's Fountain on the UC Berkeley Campus and "held hands" in prayer and worship with those, oh forbid, who were "not meeting on the ground of oneness" with us, of all people! Word of this and other "encounters of the worst kind" got back to "headquarters" and we were in hot water . . . not just for the fact that we had a "jug band" creating "jug people" (long story, there) but the fact that we were compromising (in the eyes of THE MINISTRY) with other believers who were "so different" from us! How DARE YOU meet with DEGRADED CHRISTIANITY—especially, with those NOT "meeting on the ground of unity" (sounds rather ostentatious of us, but we

So, You want to do Ekklesia?

were the "cat's meow" and all others were obliged to join our form of "oneness" and end their sectarianism post-haste)!

In order to "smooth things out"—I and this other brother who was as "radical" as I was—took off for Southern California to meet with the Oracle of God (although, at the time, he had not yet "ascended" to such heights—but was heading in that direction) . . . we sat in his living room to "discuss the matter". . . stupidly thinking there could be some kind of compromise or terminus to our dilemma of being "out of the flow" vs. "in the flow"—meaning, "How's about our 'ministry style' being a little different than that of 'central command' in that we were in a little different environment (to say the least) than "command central."

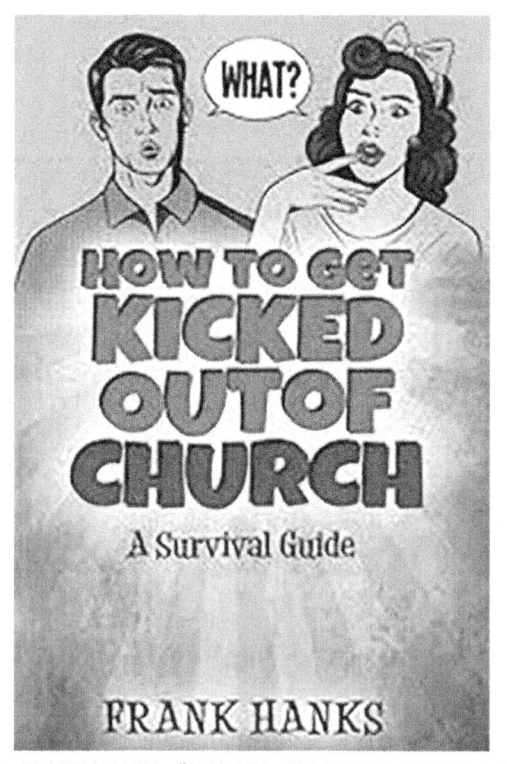

Figure 48 - FRANK HANKS - "HOW TO GET KICKED OUT OF A CHURCH"

He informed us of a quote taken from a text by Watchman Nee's *FURTHER TALKS ON THE CHURCH LIFE*. Nee's comments (at the end of this section) in the relationship among the **churches**, the **workers** and the **eldership** of those sundry churches in Asia Minor went something (not word for word) like this (from the lips of the Oracle):

"In Acts 13 we read:

'Now in the church (Ekklesia) *that was at Antioch there were certain prophets and teachers. Barnabas, Simeon who was called Niger, Lucius of Cyrene, Manaen who had been brought up with Herod the tetrarch, and Saul. As they ministered to the Lord and fasted, the Holy Spirit said, 'Now separate to Me Barnabas and Saul for the work to which I have CALLED THEM.' Then, having fasted and prayed, and laid hands on them, they sent them away . . . So, being sent out by the Holy Spirit, they went down to Seleucia, and from there they sailed to Cyprus,* etc. (Acts 13:1-4)."

The "Oracle of God" continued:

"*Now, Barnabas and Saul* (Paul) *went to Perga* (Acts 13:14); *Iconium* (Acts 14:1); *and Lystra* (Acts 14:8) . . . *and then they returned to Antioch* (Acts 14:21) . . . *and then they* (Barnabas and Paul) *appointed* (or "pointed out") *elders in every church* (Acts 14:23).

"According to this 'pattern' it APPEARS **ANTIOCH WAS CONTROLLING THEM**"—(so said the Oracle).

Then he said:

"What is the antecedent of 'them'?" —

In other words, what does **them** refer to?

Figure 49 - TOXIC CHURCH ENVIRONMENT

"Was Antioch (the Church in Antioch from whence the workers were sent out by the Holy Spirit) CONTROLLING the *workers* (Barnabas and Saul/Paul); the *churches* these 'apostolic workers' founded in Perga, Iconium, and Lystra; or the *elders* they pointed/appointed in every Ekklesia they established?"

The actual comments by Watchman Nee in his text, **FURTHER TALKS ON THE CHURCH LIFE**, "appear" to be as follows:

"From Antioch, some went forth to other places to do a work. When churches came into being, elders were appointed to be responsible for the oversight of the churches. **But it seems that Antioch was responsible for them, because the workers lived in Antioch**." (Chapter 6, Section 2 or 7 sections)

Please note, the word "controlling" replaced the word "responsible" by the Oracle ... how convenient was that? Also, the "them" was clarified to us as being the workers from Antioch, the churches those workers established, and the local leadership/eldership of those churches.

Wow, that was a mouthful—in point of fact, as we discovered— far too much for us to swallow and VERY ROMAN CATHOLIC-sounding for this direct descendant of Martin Luther. How's that ... listen up to the answer to the "antecedent" ... "*the workers, the churches, the elders*"?? Imagine, as well, an entire book dedicated to meticulously restructuring the Scriptures in formulating a system of control over all aspects of the work (ministry), the churches, and the leadership of those churches!

ALL THE ABOVE ... the Church in Antioch was CONTROLLING (and THAT was precisely the operative word used by the Oracle) the *workers, the churches* the workers founded, and *the elders* appointed by these workers—Antioch was controlling ALL OF THEM.

SHOCK AND AWE was our response. Gish, we thought, based on the Oracle's previous ministry that it was "Administration local, each answering to the Lord; communion universal, upheld in one accord"—not some central ministerial regional center controlling workers, churches, and elderships ... I mean, after all, weren't Barnabas and Paul "*sent out by the Holy Spirit*" (Acts 13:4) and "*separated out*" by the same Holy Spirit (Acts 13:2)—even though the brethren in Antioch "*fasted and prayed, and laid hands on them, they sent them away*" (Acts 13:3)—wasn't that naught but a CONFIRMATION and blessing, rather than some system of CONTROL of those workers, and eventually churches and elders?

We were at least signaling for a "congregational approach" to ministry, juxtaposed to an intense centrality of control that appeared like the Catholic, Mormon, Scientology, Jehovah Witness-style system of control. What was really going on in this brother's ministry was obvious: The "ministry" was in control—of the workers, the churches and the leadership of those churches—plain and simple. Ultimately, the ministry subsumed all—IT was like the BORG in that it "absorbed" everything into the collective! The "regional centers" (e.g., Antioch, Jerusalem, etc.) were replaced by one magnanimous center of the work/ministry HQed in the Los Angeles area—and YES, it sounds like Roman Catholicism or Mormonism out of Salt Lake, UT—I could go on but you get the drift.

So, You want to do Ekklesia?

We drove up along the coastal highway back to Berkeley, stopping off in Goleta, CA near UC Santa Barbara where another brother (we'll call him Eddy) had left some years back this movement . . . whatever happened to Eddy? What's it like when you find yourself outside of "God's final move on the earth today?" Can't imagine.

We sat there in this, what appeared to be a youth hostel, in a large living room. As we sat on one of the many couches in the room, we began to hear the sound of Eddy singing the Crusader hymn: **Fairest Lord Jesus** in melodious tones with gusto . . . coming ever closer to the disenfranchised. There he was, still with thunderous baritone voice standing arms outstretched before us. I whispered to my associate: "Does Eddy see us, recognize us . . . is he in his right mind?"

Shaken from the episode—especially when Eddy told us: "You can leave the 'group' but the 'group' never leaves you!" With that affirmation—we got in the car and drove off. My associate immediately froze up on the steering wheel and I proceeded, at his injunction, to pound his back and shoulders to release him from his bondage at the wheel. A cop saw what I was doing, stopped us, and wanted to know what on earth was going on? Of course, we told him the truth about leaving God's final move on the earth today and then our visit with Eddy—at which point he thought we were nuts and sent us on our way but warned us to quit with the shenanigans!

Figure 50 - "THE BORG"

This "Christian cult" we discovered touted our "spiritual unity" (i.e., the *"unity of the Spirit in the uniting bond of peace"*— Eph. 4:3) then criticized "spiritual unity" on the basis that our unity in Christ HAD TO BE EXPRESSED in any given locality— viz., "the doctrine of the dirt!" (IT HAD TO BE TANGIBLE, MATERIAL). I can sure see why (now) one of the critics of this "movement" once said to the Oracle when it came to this issue of the "dirt" (aka, the Church's standing in a locality): "Your Christ is too small."

Denominations were anathema—accursed—but, ALAS! That which we feared the most came upon us—we became one of the most sectarian organizations ever to countenance the flat earth (not to offend those who embrace a "global cosmology"). There can be no other "churches" but those founded upon certain jurisdictional land (and, by our group)—and, furthermore, all those in a given "region" must be one in coordination and practice (viz., the aforementioned Antioch Model—"*all the above*"). Specifically, that "regional coordination" demanded that the work, churches, and eldership among those churches were all "one with the ministry" (or else).

Suffice it to say, this Christian cult, like the others in the USA has experienced little or no growth for decades! Their elaborate orchestration of control may slake the thirst of the inquiring mind—but twisting the Scripture to fabricate such a system of control is as old as the devolution of the Early Church into its present Romish practice of the College of the Cardinals, with Pope and subservient laity.

"Work & Ministry" vs. "Ekklesia/Congregants?"

Unfortunately, most churches today act like ministries—yes, we're all members of the Lord's One Body—whether you're a pastor or a "pew sitter"—you're in the Ekklesia; you have FULL MEMBERSHIP (and, yes, it is a SPIRITUAL UNITY—notwithstanding those involved in the "ground of the dirt" doctrine of locality). That said, however, is the minister equipping the saints *"to do the work of the ministry"* and are the saints coming together, wherever (on a piece of dirt included), to literally "practice

So, You want to do Ekklesia?

Ekklesia?" No, I'm NOT badmouthing ministers, pastors, teachers, evangelists, or even prophets and apostles (those founding various Ekklesia/Churches).

FOR THE EQUIPPING OF THE SAINTS FOR THE WORK OF SERVICE, TO THE BUILDING UP OF THE BODY OF CHRIST; EPHESIANS 4:12

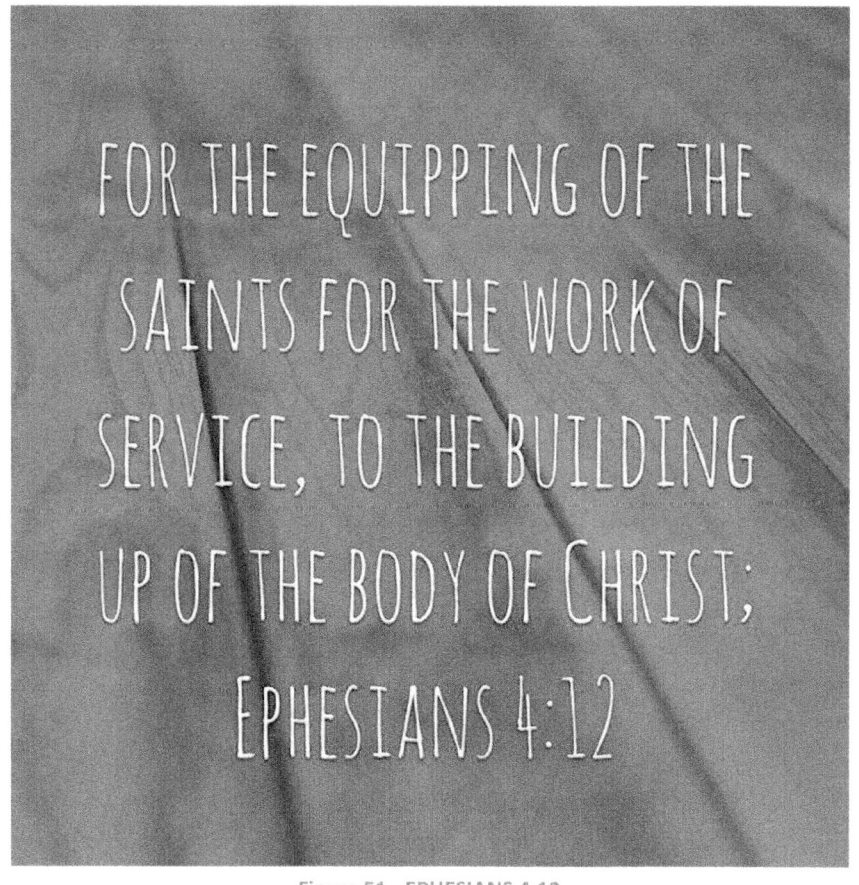

Figure 51 - EPHESIANS 4:12

What I am saying is this: If ministers really did the following:

"*And He Himself* (the Head of the Body, our Lord Jesus Christ) *gave some to be apostles, some prophets, some evangelists, and some pastors and teachers, for the EQUIPPING* [lit. "fitting or preparing fully" as in "perfecting"—Strong's G#2677—**katartismos**] *of the saints for the work of ministry, for the building up of the body of Christ, till we all come to the unity of the faith and of the knowledge of the Son of God, to a perfect man, to the measure of the stature of the* *fullness of Christ; that we should no longer be children, tossed to and fro and carried about with every wind of doctrine, by the trickery of men, in the cunning craftiness of deceitful plotting, but, HOLDING THE REALITY in love, may grow up in all things into Him who is the head—Christ"* (Eph. 4:11-15).

. . . however, instead of equipping God's people to *"do the work of the ministry"*—these ministers of God, far too often, gather the faithful around themselves for "fear they will lose them!" Dare they equip them to become "pastors and teachers" themselves? Dare they create "other ministries" (Seemingly, NOT in direct coordination with their original ministry!) based upon the principle that *"each of you has a gift"* and that gift should be exercised?

No, the pastor-teacher demands (or strongly suggests) we "use his notes" from the week's previous sermon and the "home group" should go over them as an "outline" to keep the congregants "on track" lest they be sidetracked (That's a ministry FOR the Ekklesia—but that's NOT the Ekklesia coming together to experience "Body Life."). *Ekklesias* are not "orchestrated" they are the antithesis of orchestration but still "decently and in order"—who knew?

Forbid that the pastor-teachers (who now, in the main, dominate the congregants—because, as well, the congregants want them to do so, lest they have to do the work of the ministry themselves!)—so, in essence you have a "collaborative conspiracy" of sorts—the clergy find themselves "running the show" and the congregants are more than willing to see this to be the case lest they become more involved in doing the "work of the ministry" themselves—BOTH ARE COMPLIANT—BOTH are caught in an ever-devolving spiral where the pastor-teachers are the targets of the congregants praise or wrath AND the congregants, because they lack "ministerial skills" are ill-equipped to strike out on their own. Indeed, if they (the congregants) were to shrink to their actual "spiritual size" most would be whisked out the front door of the "church" in baby carriages!

So, You want to do Ekklesia?

Part 2 of this three-part segment on the issues of clergy/laity, is even more "inflammatory"—especially, if you're a "gifted one" (which there are such in the Body of Christ) but who are NOT maximizing their gift for the true building up of the Body of Christ—viz., *"perfecting* (or "equipping") *the saints for the work of the ministry, to the building up of the Body Christ"* (Eph. 4:12) . . . which, according to 1 Corinthians 11-14 displays to the *"uninformed"* and the *"unbeliever"* that *"God is among you of a truth"* (1 Cor. 14:25) while the *"secrets of his heart will be revealed"*—it doesn't get any better than that because these uninformed and unbelievers will SO WORSHIP GOD by stating the obvious!

Isn't that what every gifted member of the Body of Christ should desire? We can only hope so . . .

Chapter 8:
Balancing Act Between Clergy & Laity – Part 2

Figure 52 - "I'M IN CHARGE OF THIS EKKLESIA - WHO'D LIKE TO SHARE?"

If "Each Has"—Then Why Do Some Dominate?

IN OUR PREVIOUS CHAPTERS WE SET OUT TO "PRACTICE EKKLESIA" IN ACCORDANCE WITH ONE OF THE RAREST OF GLIMPSES FOUND IN THE ANCIENT CITY of Corinth in today's Greece—1 Corinthians 11-14; wherein:

> "The whole Ekklesia comes together in one place . . . if all prophesy, and an unbeliever or an uninformed person comes in, he is convinced by all, he is convicted by all [NOT JUST BY THE PREACHER] and thus, the secrets of his heart are revealed; and so, falling down on his face, he will worship God and report that God is truly among you" (1 Cor. 14:23-25).

There's nothing—absolutely nothing here—that bespeaks of some charismatic preacher or faithful pastor doing his job—NO, NO, NO—it's the WHOLE CONGREGATION or Ekklesia doing the job of testifying, prophesying, convicting and convincing. The minister, pastor-teacher, preacher, evangelist, apostle, prophet may just have to (for a refreshing change) sit there and behold the work of equipping he has done! Such a gathering of the Ekklesia

So, You want to do Ekklesia?

is NOT under the control of a central/regional work, ministry, or preacher/pastor, teacher or evangelist!

PASTORAL ATTITUDE CHECK: THANK GOD, my congregants are taking up the burden and are ministering to one another as the Body of Messiah—FOR A CHANGE! Shouldn't this be the goal of anyone's ministry—DUPLICATING disciples who will in turn minister to the saints, teaching them to STAND ON THEIR OWN—to "meet and greet" other members of the One Body of Christ to avoid division in fellowship with other "factions" within the One Body—those "differing" from you? After all, we're not supposed to be COMPETING with other "churches"—or are we?

Someone coming in from the outside into a place of business, a home, a "cottage meeting" atmosphere with DIFFERENT TYPES OF CHRISTIANS (some Pentecostal, some Baptist, some Redeemer Church of God, some Anglican, some Seventh-Day Adventists, some Catholics, some DONES, and some believers who "haven't a clue"—can you imagine!?) and sharing Jesus with one another wherein *"each of you has a psalm, has a teaching, has a tongue, has a revelation, has an interpretation"* (1 Cor. 14:26) and the whole gathering is an environment where *"the spirits of the prophets are subject to the prophets"* and not to the "known spiritual authorities" in the room?

Tell me, in such a gathering as described in 1 Cor. 11-14 do you see someone "directing traffic"—telling "members individually" how to pray, how to sing, how to worship, when to pray, when to sing, when to worship? I don't think so. In point of glaring fact, trying to find ministers "doing their duties" in such an environment is antithetical to the very reading of the text. Good grief! How can anyone ever, aside from the "pastor-teacher" have a "teaching"—well, perhaps if they were given instructions by the INSTRUCTOR on what, when, why, how and where to teach . . . then it "might" be permissible (if kept to a minimum).

WHO KNEW SOMETHING LIKE THIS CAN BE DONE DECENTLY AND IN ORDER without an "overlord" hidden in the hollow orchestrating the whole thing or "central headquarters" lurking in the background "calling the shots?" No, the saints have been TRAINED by you, the pastor-teacher to GROW UP INTO

CHRIST IN ALL THINGS—to start functioning as the very Body of Christ you've equipped them to be! YOU SHOULD BE PROUD OF YOURSELF when your kids grow up and learn to stand on their own two feet!

Why, oh why, do you fear, as a pastor-teacher that your training of the congregants in this manner will "put you out of a job"—and, besides, isn't that why you were hired: To minister as a pastor-teacher? Or, try this out for size: Hasn't the HEAD OF THE BODY ordained you to EQUIP THE SAINTS TO DO THE WORK OF THE MINISTRY instead of you doing all the work?

Yet, one would think that the "clergy" or "ordained pastors/teachers" or, for that matter, prophets and evangelists, would delight to see their congregants exercising their GOD-ORDAINED "EACH ONE HAS" when the Ekklesia comes together. Tragically, most (thank God, not all) see such "Ekklesia-style gatherings" as either a nuisance or a threat to their "ministry." "If it *ain't* building my ministry, it *ain't gonna* happen!" Well, just what kind of a "ministry" allows saints week after week, year after year, awaiting for the next message from the pulpit when you haven't taught them to have a "teaching" themselves . . . you're seeking "revelation" from the Word when you should be equipping them to have their own "revelation" from the same: JUST LIKE YOU!

You tout your prophetic gift, but forbid you would ever consider a "mini-school of the prophets" wherein scores would be raised up by your insightful training—shouldn't that be the "equipping gift" of the prophet? And, spare me an environment where all can prophesy ONE BY ONE wherein all may be encouraged and all may be edified! Here you go: "*Or did the word of God come originally from you? Or was it you only that it reached?*" (1 Cor. 14:36). What does that mean? Frankly, you're not the only one in Corinth who received the revelation of the prophetic gift—others did too—and, it's about time you acknowledge that and to discover who they are!

You've become quite the evangelist—no doubt a real gift to the Body of Christ . . . yet, how many evangelists have you raised up, equipped, for the work of evangelism as in "*Do the work of an evangelist*" (2 Tim. 4:5)? No, it's not that Paul is suggesting, via Apostolic authority, Pastor Timothy should exclusively do the work of an evangelist but that he (Timothy) would practice the following: "*And the things that you have heard me say among many witnesses, entrust these to faithful men **who will be qualified to teach others as well***" (2 Tim. 2:2). That goes for every one of those so gifted—be they Apostles, Prophets, Evangelists, Pastor-Teachers . . . commit your gift to the faithful brethren who will "teach others as well"—that's doing the work of an evangelist . . . get the point?

Separate the "Gifted" when Needed in the Trenches?

Excuse me, another pet peeve. I can hardly deprecate the worth of Bible Schools and seminaries—I went to one and it was of inestimable value; however, why is it that we send off to such centers of learning potentially gifted brethren into environments which are, in the main, somewhat artificial and hardly attached to the so-called real world—the trenches? Shouldn't the "Household of Faith/God" be places where gifted members of the Body of Christ are being raised up in order for them to affect the ministry of their "disciples" who shall "*be able to teach others also?*" Have we forfeited the "*work of the ministry*" apart from the very Ekklesia that we are attempting to edify? Are we, instead, sending our most gifted (or they are sending themselves) off to these institutions, thereby "qualifying them," whereupon we inadvertently or purposefully perpetuate a system which caters to the raising up of gifted ones outside the immediate environs of the regular members of the Body of Christ?

Do you understand what I'm getting at here? In other words, are we strengthening a system which strengthens the concept of a "clergy-laity" system which accentuates the already wide gulf between the gifted members of the Body of Christ (aka, the "clergy") and the "regular members of the Body of Christ" (aka, the congregants)? Perhaps you wish to keep that gap which already exists— and you ask: Why does such a gap matter? It matters because within the context of 1 Corinthians 11-14 there is simply nothing which would enhance such a differentiation (i.e., gulf).

Prior to *"God has appointed these in the Ekklesia: first apostles, second prophets, third teachers, after that miracles, then gifts of healings, helps, administrations, varieties of tongues. Are all apostles? Are all prophets? Are all teachers? Are all workers of miracles? Do all have gifts of healings? Do all speak with tongues? Do all interpret?"* (1 Cor. 12:28-30) we have this verse:

"Now you are the body of Christ, and members individually" (1 Cor. 12:27).

The entire thrust for unity and diversity in One Body (1 Cor. 2:12-30) appears to take place within the normal setting of an Ekklesia with a quest for all of us to *"earnestly desire the greater gifts . . . and yet I show you a more excellent way"* (1 Cor. 12:31)— which is 1 Corinthians 13:1-13; the *"more excellent way"* is LOVE. Therefore, can we "safely say" the emphasis is NOT on the multiplicity of gifts within the Ekklesia but the exercise and embrace of divine love expressed to one another within the context of what appears to be a "normal Ekklesia setting"? I think so.

If we get caught up in training our elite outside the atmosphere of the Ekklesia/assembly, then aren't we separating out from the congregation those who should be doing the "practicum" within the context of the Ekklesia in the first place? I commend those "schools of Tyrannous" (Acts 19:9-10) which appear to have been Paul's most dynamic training center where this training *"continued for two years, so that all who dwelt in Asia heard the word of the Lord Jesus, both Jews and Greeks."* If you would, a rather "hands-on" style training with the Ekklesia receiving the immediate benefit of such a center of ministry. Obviously, what Paul was teaching received immediate application by those being trained.

It seems to me that "Christian Service" at Christian institutions of higher learning should consume a much greater portion, if you would, of the curriculum. Some of my most memorable times at the Bible School I attended were the weekly evenings

So, You want to do Ekklesia?

when nearly 50 of us hit the streets in downtown Portland, Oregon to share the gospel of Jesus Christ—we desperately needed much more instruction along those lines of sharing our faith, not just teaching on defending it. Likewise, such corporate exercise made us keenly aware of the Body of Christ and the realization that it was when we "fought the good fight" together that we discovered we were "*members one of another.*"

"House Churches" Don't Guarantee Ekklesia

Then there's always the "house church" where in miniature the "control mechanism" and habits of the "clergy-laity system" replicate. How's that? Well, for one, some in the clergy (and the laity) suggest you really can't have a "house church" without an ordained pastor present. No, really, that's ingrained both in "leadership" as well as in the run-of-the-mill saint (and in the culture of the clergy-laity "systems"); after all, how can things be "*done decently and in order*" without an ordained pastor taking charge! God forbid if the clergy hear you're pulling off a "house church" without a properly "ordained member of the clergy" actually present! Or, for fear of being "out of order" the laity would recoil at pulling off such a gathering without ecclesiastical approval? Come on now, folks, YOU can do better than that!

Figure 53 - "HOUSE CHURCHES" DON'T GUARANTEE EKKLESIA

In 1 Corinthians 11-14 it mentions NOTHING, absolutely nothing about any "leadership" qualification aside from those who are "genuine" or "approved" (1 Cor. 11:19) who only need to manifest themselves when "factions" (which are necessary in a gathering) become "factious" and "divisions" become divisive— that's when the "peace-makers" come forth!

Ekklesia isn't Therapy-Intimate Sessions

But we're so used to having things "organized"—we have to have our "time of worship" and then our time of sharing. Some think that the Ekklesia is a time when saints can vent—as in therapy or a time when we can have "intimate fellowship" and bear our hearts one to another (so let's keep it small, less intimidating for fear of the "crowds" of 30 or 40). Well, try to find "therapy sessions" or "intimacy" in 1 Corinthians 11-14—it isn't there—the entire focus is on saints edifying one another through a psalm, a revelation, a teaching, a prophecy, a tongue, an interpretation— THERE'S NO ORDER set; there's no one setting the pace; there's no mention of a pastor, evangelist, teacher, apostle, prophet. And, frankly, there's little mention of a "therapy session" nor of "let's get real" and bear our hearts (not that some of that won't happen, but that's NOT the norm of an Ekklesia gathering). Why? Because EACH ONE HAS, and that includes these so-called gifted members of the assembly. Hard to imagine: WE'RE ALL IN CHARGE . . . rather, praise God, the Holy Spirit is the ADMINISTRATOR of the gathering for:

> **"But the manifestation of the Spirit is given to each one for the profit of all:** *for to one is given the word of wisdom through the Spirit, to another the word of knowledge through the same Spirit, to another faith by the same Spirit, to another gifts of healings by the same Spirit, to another the working of miracles, to another prophecy, to another discerning of spirits, to another different kinds of tongues, to another the interpretation of tongues.* **But one and the same Spirit works all these things, distributing to each one individually as He wills.**" (1 Cor. 12:7-11)

So, You want to do Ekklesia?

Did you pick up on that? **THE SPIRIT WORKS ALL THESE THINGS DISTRIBUTING TO EACH ONE INDIVIDUALLY**! No, since you're the ordained pastor or "sanctified teacher"—YOU or your cohort must "lead" or "organize" the gathering—follow me, *"I'm the "ordained leader"—you guys are out of control, not under authority, if you think you can pull this off without proper leadership, FORGET IT!"*

Why don't you try something new that's more in line with Scripture? Why not train your congregants to DO THE WORK OF THE MINISTRY and gather saints in homes, businesses, wherever, to PRACTICE EACH ONE HAS without trying to "organize them" aside from training them to "***do Ekklesia***"—oh, no, how can they do that if there's not someone leading them in the practice?

Again, I'm not suggesting you "shut down" gifted ministers and ministries who should be "specializing" in ACTIVATING the members of the Body of Christ to replicate the gifts of the gifted ones—that's precisely what I am suggesting! Seriously, if you, as an "ordained teacher-pastor" have not raised up but one or two who are "a lot like you"—then you're probably not (maybe, barely) one yourself (i.e., a "pastor-teacher").

You'd be shocked and surprised if you train them how well they can actually do things "on their own"—yet, if you keep giving them fish, without training them to fish for themselves—well, you know the rest of that line—they keep coming back TO YOU for more of YOUR FISH (and, sadly, that may be precisely what you have in mind), but once you're no longer in the picture, they'll starve, panic or whatever—yet, if you've taught them to fish, they'll survive. YES, they need training—that should be the job of the gifted members of the Body—that's when you really need to be a TEACHER, a PASTOR, an EVANGELIST, a PROPHET, or even an APOSTLE; but the "traditional dichotomy" says the only ones who apparently HAVE (HAS) is not EACH ONE but the GIFTED ONE HAS and we (the LAITY) better get used to it! So sad, so very, very sad.

We'll be speaking about the origins of the "church service" in later chapters; however, "when the whole Ekklesia comes together" why is it, if everyone **has**, is there this propensity to structure what goes down in that gathering? First we'll do this; then will do that; and, finally, we'll end with this—so-and-so opens in prayer and the same person closes in prayer; meanwhile, if our gathering goes over one hour, it's time to close this "thing" down. Here's another "pet peeve" of mine: Try mixing it up— DON'T SIT IN THE SAME CHAIR, COUCH or on the floor in the same place . . . that's another "habit" which can lead to the "traditional service" model . . . it nigh becomes the "chief seats in the synagogue" mind-set!

Again, if it's a ministry, you could get away with that course of action (having things more organized)—but if you're trying to have "Ekklesia" (especially in a "home environment")—well, all bets are off—THERE IS NO ORDER OF SERVICE! Apparently, there's a meal—some type of "breaking of the bread and drinking of the cup" (we're not clear how that goes down either). You may think, especially pastors: **Krieger, you're simply describing a FREE-FOR-ALL.** No, I'm not, because I've got "*decently and in order*" on my side vs. same old, same old on yours. I should know, I did it for years, as "Pastor Krieger." And, one more peeve, what's with the "Lord's Table" being a "me focus" time (e.g., I'm such a sinner, wretch, crook—WE ALL KNOW THAT!) No, No, No! It's DO THIS IN REMEMBRANCE OF ME. If Jesus isn't lifted up in such a gathering of HIS FEAST, then however you wish to have it, it isn't happening—it's only when He's the center of our worship, praise, testimony that there's a real REMEMBRANCE OF ME!

But I digress—Titles (especially Clergy titles), by the way, are relatively meaningless IN THIS SENSE: It's NOT who you say you are or who others acclaim you to be—it's what you do that matters. You could be "untitled" or heavily titled, such as: The Very Right Reverend, the Honorable, Senior Pastor Emeritus, Dr. D. R. Putz, PhD, or just Sister So-and-So—it doesn't matter for "*the manifestation of **the Spirit is given to each one for the profit of all**"* (1 Cor. 12:7). If you say you are a teacher—then you should be equipping members of the One Body to be teachers as well.

So, You want to do Ekklesia?

Back at the House Church: But brother Parks "*gets-a-goin*'" and we can't shut him up—he literally monopolizes the meeting as if he's the only one who's got something to say (viz., prophesying as in testifying). Bro. Parks is utterly oblivious to anyone else in the room! Or, worse, what about the "dramatic Pentecostal-style sister" who goes off on a "Yea, verily, My people, unto thee I speak, if you will humble yourselves, etc.?" and offends just about everyone in the club room or the guy who can't wait to unleash his latest California Fire Storm prophecy?

There is a big difference between T-Ball and College-Age Baseball. Children need to grow up—but once they do, it doesn't take them long before they're playing a good game of sandlot baseball themselves without any coach at all telling them how the game is played or WHAT TO DO! Indeed, some companies have discovered that management is far more creative, dynamic, and successful when done with "teams" where INPUT accomplishes far more on an "even playing field." Yes, such "management teams" need practice and training on how this is done—but once trained, they're off and running with "fine tuning" here and there to keep things on track. Again, we're NOT deviating from the plain Word of Scripture given in a rare glimpse of how Ekklesia is actually manifested "*when the whole Ekklesia comes together.*"

"*Your expectations are either supercilious or unrealistic . . . you can't expect God's people to 'hit the tarmac' running—not after nearly 2,000 years of 'doing it the wrong way!' Don't we have to ease our way into this kind of gathering?*" ANSWER: Yes, and no.

Some instruction is helpful but I would suggest the least amount is better because once you "overdo it" you simply create another "method" and worse structure than you had before—the very "nature" of such an expression of Ekklesia militates against organization, structure, federation, methodology, and traditional leadership!

The way it reads, again, in 1 Corinthians 11-14 sounds like folks are all allowed (not that they will) share EQUALLY and in ORDER and normally, so it appears, in twos and threes . . . there's no place for a "one-man show or band"—it's corporate, it's exceedingly "user-friendly" where everyone feels the urge to contribute, participate, cooperate, as in: EACH ONE HAS.

JUST WHAT I THOUGHT: MAJOR FOOD FIGHTS WILL BREAK OUT IF WE DON'T CONTROL THESE CHILDREN - I MEAN "CONGREGANTS"

Figure 54 - SOMEONE HAS TO CONTROL CHILDISH FOOD FIGHTS

By dent of the number of folks present if someone is prophesying, don't be surprised if they're INTERRUPTED by someone:

"Let two or three prophets speak, and let the others judge. But if anything is revealed to another who sits by, let the first keep silent. For you can all prophesy one by one, that all may learn and all may be encouraged" (1 Cor. 14:29-30).

"For in fact the Body is not one member but many" (1 Cor. 12:14). You know something's off when the pastor opens the building, arranges the chairs, turns on the A/C or Heat, greets everyone at the door, leads the worship and most certainly gives the sermon, and wraps it all up somehow by shaking everyone's hand as they're leaving the building before locking the place up (again). You'd never guess that to be the case since this Pastor espouses the notion *"for in fact the Body is not one member but many!"*

So, You want to do Ekklesia?

The rest of THAT BODY is in charge of "showing up"—getting their fish from the pulpit—then going home with a little praise, worship and friendly exchange . . . the exhausted pastor rejoices that another service is over! Not good!

Let's look at this sequence of passages and the order of "preference" or emphasis:

"And if they were all one member, where would the body be? But now indeed there are many members, yet one body. But God composed the body, having given greater honor to that part which lacks it, that there should be no schism in the body, but that the members should have the same care for one another. And if one member suffers, all the members suffer with it; or if one member is honored, all the members rejoice with it. Now you are the body of Christ, and members individually. And God has appointed these in the church: first apostles, second prophets, third teachers, after that miracles, then gifts of healings, helps, administrations, varieties of tongues. Are all apostles? Are all prophets? Are all teachers? Are all workers of miracles? Do all have gifts of healings? Do all speak with tongues? Do all interpret? But earnestly desire the best gifts. And yet I show you a more excellent way" (1 Cor. 12:9-31, excerpts).

First of all, please notice the stress upon the more "insignificant members" of the One Body—God gave greater honor to the part that lacked it! Also, if one suffers, everyone suffers and if one is honored, everyone is honored and rejoices. The emphasis is upon the "little guy"—the sister who drones on with her, what appears to be, a somewhat trite testimony (BUT IT IS HER PORTION—stop with the criticism; she's just as important as anyone else in that gathering). Remember, if we were all one member, WHERE WOULD THE BODY BE?

Listen up, we are the Body of Christ and MEMBERS INDIVIDUALLY or IN PARTICULAR. What sets us apart is not how different we are, but how essential we are one to another. THEN, it shifts to *"God has appointed these in the church: first apostles, second prophets, third teachers, after that miracles, then gifts of healings, helps, administrations, varieties of tongues. Are all apostles? Are all prophets? Are all teachers? Are all workers of miracles? Do all have gifts of healings? Do all speak with tongues? Do all interpret? But earnestly desire the best gifts. And yet I show you a more excellent way."* What's going on here?

Well, Paul's not saying that apostles, prophets, teachers, workers of miracles, gifts of healing, speaking in tongues, interpretation of tongues are of no account—THEY ARE—but duly noted, little **sister Insignificance** is, in an Ekklesia gathering, critical due to the fact that all members have NOT the same function. They are MEMBERS INDIVIDUALLY. But, please notice, the "entitled ones" are secondary when it comes to the experience of the One Body, with the BEST WAY to practice "Body Life" (aka, Ekklesia) is the greatest gift: LOVE! And, it's this kind of love—smack, dab in the midst of 1 Corinthians 11-14 which we so desperately need if we are going to defer to one another and honor one another in participating as His Ekklesia where EACH ONE OF YOU HAS!

Somehow we've taken 1 Corinthians 13 OUT OF CONTEXT and reserved it for weddings and whatnot! We've made it a "stand alone." When we're talking about "biblical things in general" we always, so it seems, come back to 1 Corinthians 13 and state with all confidence: THE GREATEST OF THESE IS LOVE—not this or that, but LOVE! Well, yes, but please note where it's found—again, smack dab in the middle of 1 Corinthians 11-14 where having an actual Ekklesia-style gathering takes place.

Yes, the greatest of "these" is LOVE—but IT'S FOUND IN AN EKKLESIA SETTING. If we don't have this kind of LOVE domiciled in the Ekklesia gathering—then we're missing the whole point of 1 Corinthians 13! This is beyond tolerance, diversity, etc. How are we going to accept the biblical fact that EACH ONE HAS if we are void of the GREATEST OF THESE IS LOVE? Nope! You and I will never experience real Ekklesia without the Greatest of These!

So, You want to do Ekklesia?

Too Big OK – But Keep Ekklesia Intimate

Figure 55 - 12,000,000 MEETING AT NIGERIA'S REDEEMER CHURCH OF GOD

Let's be realistic—once the "whole Ekklesia" shows up in one place, how are you going to "practice an Ekklesia-style gathering" if there's more than 30 or 40 people in the location where this is taking place? I've seen some gatherings with a hundred or so and it was still possible if everyone, in the main, kept things "brief" so everyone could participate who wanted to (for you can *all prophesy one by one that all may be encouraged*)—but it's pretty rare once you get a little crowd going—the "problem" is this: Such an assembled group, all prophesying (aka, participating) becomes so attractive, everyone and their brother or sister wants to come to such a gathering.

Or, you can show up at the HQ of the Redeemer Church of God in Lagos, Nigeria with 12,000,000 in attendance—trust me, it's awesome, and folks are "really into it" but such a massive gathering does not an actual Ekklesia-style gathering make! Folks there are all members of the Ekklesia—no doubt—and the ministry is terrific . . . but does it resemble 1 Corinthians 11-14 in that sense? Be honest, it doesn't; but that's not to say members of Redeemer Church of God do not meet from "house to house" enjoying the Lord as His Ekklesia with all sorts of "other Christians" in attendance—that's Ekklesia!

Well, when it gets that crowded, split up and have another Ekklesia-style gathering elsewhere or at a different time. Once again, the tendency is to "federate" such gatherings so that "someone" keeps a lid on "fires" that keep breaking out all over the place—forbid that revival might look like this! The urge to CONTROL such outbreaks is insatiable—I know, I must be dreaming—forbid the Holy Spirit has this whole Ekklesia under this overarching decree: *"I will build my Ekklesia and the gates of Hades shall not prevail against it."*

Obviously, if you're going to have a meal, a brunch, or a food-fest/BBQ at such a gathering, the best place is probably in someone's home—and you are allowed to rotate homes, you know—just let folks know where to show up and when (that's as far as "organization" needs to go). Sure, if you are bringing certain dishes it would be nice if there were variety—but don't count on it! Better to keep "organization" to a "bare-bones minimum."

Consistency? The only consistency we need is EACH ONE HAS and we ALL ought to be prophesying ONE BY ONE—that's it, plain and simple! Bring some UNINFORMED and UNBELIEVERS to your gatherings—mix it up—having the same people showing up every time creates a "mutual admiration society" of sorts and, frankly, is indicative of a "fishing hole" that's be thoroughly fished—move on to a new fishing hole.

But what about being "built up" as a holy temple unto the Lord? Doesn't that take time, energy, and space? They tried that in Jerusalem until the Holy Spirit allowed persecution to scatter the saints hither, thither, and yon! We get too comfortable—once we've figured this "thing" out, once we've lost the sense of excitement and surprise, once we bog down into a certain routine—IT'S OVER! But isn't an Ekklesia like a marriage? Then the kids come along and the "romance" is a bit humdrum, right? Well, whose fault is that? PUT SOME ROMANCE INTO YOUR MARRIAGE; some excitement—do some things together that put the spark back into the marriage—if you don't, well, get some help, and fast! I know, "Easy for you to say!" But, really, an Ekklesia-style gathering is a lot like a new romance—if you don't keep the spark going, it'll play itself out and some form of division will be the by-product. Having children should NOT dampen the marriage but enrich it! That's why we're called the HOUSEHOLD OF GOD, HOUSEHOLD OF FAITH!

So, You want to do Ekklesia?

Oh, you can hold your "communion service" or "bread breaking" or "Lord's Table" (whatever you wish to call it)—but don't get too organized about it—one week you do it one way, another week you do it another way. And, really, do you have to meet on a certain day to enjoy Ekklesia? Try meeting Thursday morning at 7 A.M. like this place I used to meet with in Loomis, CA called the "Upper Room"—eventually, we gathered upwards of several hundred each Thursday morning—sometimes we had food, other times we didn't . . . we had all sorts of worship, bands, groups of singers, whatever and everyone felt free to participate. Probably the biggest blessing was we didn't know what we had, nor what we were doing! Folks from some 26 different "churches" (or more) that we knew of, participated—yes, and there were pastors there—most remained "anonymous" and just enjoyed the gathering (imagine that). There was some organization—but the "leadership" was so low key, anyone coming in from the outside had no idea who was at the helm!

Brethren—may the Lord open our eyes—the FINAL HARVEST of the Earth will be harvested by the Son of Man (Rev. 14) but it will go something like this:

> *"Then He said to His disciples, 'The harvest truly is plentiful, but the laborers are few. Therefore pray the Lord of the harvest to send out laborers into His harvest'"* (Matthew 9:37-38).

LORD OF THE HARVEST—SEND FORTH **LABORERS** INTO YOUR HARVEST FIELD! That's what will earmark this as the final revival—we're all in this together and He, the Spirit of God, is the LORD OF THE HARVEST . . . but look around, there are other LABORERS working on this harvest too!

Chapter 9:
Balancing Act Between Clergy & Laity – Part 3

Figure 56 - BEWARE OF WOLVES IN SHEEP'S CLOTHING

What About the Flock-less Shepherds Taking Over?

THERE'S NOTHING LIKE ATTEMPTING TO HOLD AN EKKLESIA-STYLE GATHERING AND HAVING A STRONG-WILLED "TEACHER-TYPE" OR PROPHETIC ministry-type show up and do a "take-over." What's a "take-over"? Well, it looks like something found in Judges 17:1-18:31 when Micah decided he'd have his own little sanctuary (aka, "Shrine of Micah") apart from the Tabernacle in Shiloh with his own hired Levite Priest. The Levite came up from Bethlehem and was looking for, you might say, a "pulpit."

Prior to this, this fellow Micah, who hailed from the mountains of Ephraim, and his mother (who was apparently involved in some form of witchcraft, putting curses on 1100 hundred shekels of silver—bizarre, but in the story) . . . which, by the way, the number set of "11" is most definitely a very negative set indeed (11

So, You want to do Ekklesia?

sons of Canaan; 11 with Haman and his 10 sons vs. the Jews of Persia; the younger horn of Daniel making the 11th horn; Judas' betrayal and subsequent suicide, making the number of disciples "11" – I could go on . . . but "11" is most definitely connected in Scripture to the Antichrist) . . . in any event, Micah stole the 1,100 shekels of silver. His mom was so impressed with Micah's confession that he'd stolen it from his mother that she gave Micah back 200 silver shekels, because (so she says) she fully had *"wholly dedicated the silver from my hand to the LORD for my son, to make a carved image and a molded image"* (slight "mixture" going on here). Yes, I know, a rather convoluted series of phony righteous acts taking place. I mean, really, taking a bunch of silver and making idols, images, and whatnot from this silver.

So, this Micah gave these 200 hundred shekels of silver to the silversmith and out popped *"a carved image and a molded image"* which Micah placed in his house—but Micah also had this little shrine in which, although he was right next door to the Tabernacle in the Wilderness (now in Shiloh, Ephraim), he decided the Shiloh Tent wasn't all that attractive with its badger skin, so he *"made an ephod and household* (or "angelic"—Heb. *Teraphim) idols"*; then, ordained his son to be the priest (Side Note: What's up with preachers anointing their sons to take over pastorates of the same "church"—just sayin'?)

Well, Micah knew that his own son was no Levite like the Levites next door at Shiloh, so up comes this young Levite from, of all places, Bethlehem, wholly qualified!

Eventually, as the story reads from Judges, this Micah found this wandering Levite priest (looking for a "pulpit") to administer his little sanctuary (aka, Shrine of Micah). Then, shortly after Micah set up his little Shrine with Levite in hand, along came the rebellious members of the tribe of Dan up from the plains unsatisfied as they were with their inheritance; I mean, having to fight incessantly with the Philistines for "property rights" really bugged these Danites—they wanted an "easy hit" like the "softies" up by the gateway to Phoenicia . . . not promised to the Tribe of Dan, but why not? So, let's go for it. But, they needed the "blessing" in their illegal pursuits; but they knew they weren't going to get it from the

Balancing Act Between the Clergy and the Laity – Part 3

Levites at the Tabernacle at Shiloh but, well now, there's this Levite guy at the Shrine of Micah . . . not quite the same but the guy's still a Levite, so, that should qualify.

They knew they wouldn't get a "blessing" from that old badger-skinned Tabernacle in Shiloh, but "fortunately for them" they discovered the exciting Shrine of Micah nearby. So, they decided to give this ambitious Levite priest a "better deal" (unbeknownst to "Shriner Micah") —having him be the high priest of an entire tribe vs. a one-horse operation known as the Shrine of Micah with its little idols and paraphernalia! The opportunity for such a grandiose position went to the Levite's head and off he went lifted upon a palanquin upwards to the northern acquisition taken over by Dan wherein all sorts of apostasy took place and where Dan became the "toilet bowl" of Israel as far as corruption goes, pouring in from Baal's base in Phoenicia!

Levite Priest atop Palanquin under escort from the Tribe of Dan heading north from the "Shrine of Micah"

Figure 57 - THE LEVITE PRIEST AND THE "SHRINE OF MICAH"

There's always—well, most of the time—going to be OPPORTUNISTS (like this young, qualified Levitical priest who appears destined to exploit "things" in an Ekklesia environment). When that inevitability takes place, the locals must rise up and "*mark them that cause divisions among you*" . . . as Romans 16:17-18 states:

So, You want to do Ekklesia?

> *"Now I urge you, brethren, note those who cause divisions and offenses, contrary to the doctrine which you learned, and avoid them. For those who are such do not serve our Lord Jesus Christ, but their own belly, and by smooth words and flattering speech deceive the hearts of the simple."*

Paul & Barnabas NOT Controlled by Antioch

This is not a sidebar—this is most essential in our understanding of the relationship between "the work" and the "Ekklesia" (aka, the so-called Church—but by this we mean the "people" not the "church buildings").

So, let's examine, more closely, the New Testament pattern and/or association between the "work" (ministry) and the Ekklesia (aka, "the churches").

Cutting to the chase: churches don't control the workers. If that were the case, when Paul and Barnabas had their contentious falling out over John-Mark . . . Paul taking Silas and going off in one direction (modern-day Turkey), and Barnabas taking John-Mark and heading off, apparently to Cyprus . . . then why isn't there some record where they "brought the issue of their dispute to the Church?" (In their case to the Church in Antioch.)

> *"Now Barnabas was determined to take with them John called Mark. But Paul insisted that they should not take with them the one who had departed from them in Pamphylia, and had not gone with them to the work. Then the CONTENTION became so sharp that they parted from one another. And so Barnabas took Mark and sailed to Cyprus; but Paul chose Silas and departed, being commended by the brethren to the grace of God"* (Acts 15:37-40).

No, they didn't bring it to the assembly, congregation, congregants or "Central Command" as per Matthew 18:15-17 because it had nothing to do with sin, *per se*. *"Per se"* because it was simply a matter of a brother (John-Mark) NOT being "profitable" for the work (i.e., "the ministry"). Hey, the guy took off to Pamphylia and forsook "the work"—according to Paul, this John, called Mark, was not all that committed for whatever reason.

Paul and Barnabas became quite contentious over John-Mark's "profitability" for the "work of the ministry." Eventually, which proves Paul and Barnabas apparently had some "fellowship" as time wore on, because later Paul brought John-Mark back into his own ministry (2 Tim. 4:11).

Besides, the churches do not control the workers, PERIOD! The workers of that given work have got to resolve the matters of "contention" between and/or among themselves. We may think it expedient for there to be "much more coordination" between the "work" and the "churches"—true, there should be—but such collaboration should never result in either the "clergy" or the "laity" trying to control one another! To suggest that since the workers (in this case Barnabas and Paul) were commissioned by the Holy Spirit and "sent forth" by the brethren from the Church in Antioch (as a confirmation of the Holy Spirit's choice in the first place)—somehow this can be interpreted "that Antioch was controlling them" (i.e., the workers, and eventually the churches and the elders established by these workers)—is the height of eisogesis; consider:

> **EISOGESIS:** The art of making a text say what YOU want it to say. Usually the *eisogete* already has certain beliefs and is simply looking through the Bible to find passages that will support that belief. The eisogete will ignore any passages that would dispute his belief and is simply looking to *proof-text* what he or she already desires to advocate. If there are any passages that seem to dispute his preconceived ideology, he simply seeks to reinterpret them or apply a different hermeneutic to it (dispensational, cessationist, allegorical, etc.) (See: Christian Forums)

The HEAD of the Body gave some to be . . . (Acts 15:36-41). Once you open the door to "centrality of control" (in this case, the Church in Antioch) in the name of so-called unity, better co-ordination, greater impact, regional collaboration—you're up and running as a cult-like entity. Your "work" or "ministry" may be small or large, but the goal is to RELEASE MINISTRIES on their own, not to build a homogeneous work/ministry over which to gloat. Let Paul be our example and imitate him—he wound up with NOTHING BUT CHRIST HIMSELF. The "divine destiny" of what happened to Jesus was a complete forsaking. Think about it.

No, the workers don't control the churches; just as the churches (Ekklesia) do not control the workers. Paul admonished and encouraged the Ekklesia—but did NOT control them—he certainly sought to exercise "spiritual encouragement" with them, but by saying to the Ekklesia in Corinth: *"I am of Paul, or 'I am of Apollos,' or 'I am of Cephas,' or 'I am of Christ'"*—it seems rather obvious that all sorts of "apostolic" input had gone into the Corinthian Ekklesia—the Corinthian believers apparently had a multiplicity of *influences* in their midst. The problem was they went off into factions based upon the "apostle they liked the best" with those of Christ standing off by themselves. They had become factious, divisive.

What About Local *Eldership*?

So, what about the ELDERS and/or the "leading ones" in their midst. Well, we have this rather peculiar text:

> *"For first of all, when you come together as an Ekklesia, I hear that there are divisions* (lit "factions") *among you, and in part I believe it. For there* **must** *also be factions among you* (NOTE: It is **NECESSARY** there be **FACTIONS** in an Ekklesia), *that those who are approved* (lit. "genuine") *may be recognized* (lit. "manifest, evident") *among you"* (1 Cor. 11:18-19).

Elders aren't "voted in"—they need factions in order to **manifest their genuineness** (the stress is not laid on the "position" of so-called elders but upon their "actions"—not "who they are" but "what they're doing" . . . it's functional, not positional)—i.e., *genuine* in that they are mature enough to "keep the peace" among the factions so the folks do not become FACTIOUS. Yes, *"I hear there are divisions among you"*—AND I PARTLY

BELIEVE IT—of course, Paul believed it. But he also believed that those who had some maturity in Christ would manifest in such a situation as to bring in the peace of Christ into their midst and not allow a factious spirit to divide the Ekklesia!

Some translations mistake the word *"factions"* or *"divisions"* as SCHISMS and HERESIES. No, we're talking here of plain old-fashion factions and divisions—having absolutely NOTHING to do with schisms and heresies. Folks are simply embracing sundry doctrines and super apostolic stars like Paul, Cephas (Peter) and Apollos to the point where factions have arisen among the brethren (as in *"I am of Paul, I am of Apollos"* etc.) and as a result, there are these divisions. Factions can result from all sorts of issues—be they personalities, styles of ministry, doctrinal emphases, methods, etc. I discovered there's a whole denomination in Nigeria called: THE CHURCH WITHOUT SHOES . . . for the "ground we walk upon is holy ground" (Who knew?).

Again, we're not saying that folks will not be overly influenced by various apostles or ministers—it's when it becomes factious and divisive that we have problems. Again, there MUST be these factions—but someone(s) has/have got to be the reconcilers; the genuine or approved ones who keep the congregants from falling into factious, divisive traps of their own making!

Aren't these "genuine" brethren the real "elders" of the Ekklesia? According to Paul, I think so. Ministries and dynamic ministers have some amazing influence upon the Ekklesia—and should have such impact . . . but why is it, far too often, these gifted brethren come into an Ekklesia-environment and "continue their old habits?"

Let me explain. Let's say a brother gifted as a pastor-teacher steps down from his ministerial role as a "pastor-teacher" to attend a general gathering of the assembly where a great deal of diversity among brethren takes place. As discussed, folks from "different persuasions" are gathered with the express intent to be under the direct headship of Christ (just like the ministers should be—"***HE*** GAVE SOME TO BE"). But this time it's a purposeful, intentional, gathering of the "general assembly" where EACH ONE HAS, not just the gifted pastor-teacher, evangelist, prophet,

So, You want to do Ekklesia?

or even an apostle (whether you believe or don't believe in cessation).

Two things here:

(1) The pastor-teacher does NOT give up his gift—it will probably manifest itself in some form of caring and teaching at and during such an Ekklesia-style gathering; however,

(2) The pastor-teacher should NOT dominate the meeting with his gift fully exercised; after all, this isn't "his meeting."

What do I mean by that? Well, in the common vernacular: TONE IT DOWN, brother—there's room in here for everyone—this is NOT your "ministerial pulpit"—this is the general assembly where EACH ONE HAS and you can all prophesy ONE BY ONE. That's all—use some common sense and get excited that your sheep who are in the gathering are exercising their God-given right to participate, contribute at such an Ekklesia-style gathering.

Likewise, it might—I didn't say *always*—be good if you have a gifted prophetic ministry, to "**keep your gift to yourself**" to allow others to participate . . . sometimes it's healthy for you/we gifted brethren in the Ekklesia to keep silent (for a change) and be a good listener. The problem—and it IS problematic—strong-willed prophets, pastor-teacher types, find it virtually impossible to "stay out of the fray" and just, at best, privately minister on a one-to-one basis rather than a "group-basis"—but the "force in them is strong" . . . much like the wandering Levite from Bethlehem who accepted the "exciting pulpit" at the Shrine of Micah but even that did not satisfy—he sought to be the high priest of the Tribe of Dan—and you know the rest of the story.

Well, "I'm hosting this Ekklesia"—so, I've got to take control of this "thing." Recently, I've had the very good pleasure of visiting a number of Ekklesia. All I was given was an address where it was to be held. I entered—the door opened to some kid who just happened to be there to open the door for me—he was very matter of fact and said: "You're in the right place; come on in"—that was all he said; except he told me to take my shoes off because everyone else had done so as not to dirty the carpet of the host. The whole gathering was wonderful—the food and the fellowship—I had no idea whose house we were meeting in and never did figure out who was hosting the gathering—now, THAT'S A REAL HOST for you! Just because you're the host doesn't mean you have to dominate things—remember, this is an Ekklesia . . . better to be the "unseen host at every meal" rather than the flamboyant host who decides to host an Ekklesia, giving the host a preeminent position—it's better to serve than be served and far better to serve without anyone knowing you are serving—that way, the Lord could possibly get more glory? Think about it. Imagine a host who makes everything happen without being noticed much—or at all! Hard to fathom—but such anomalies do exist within the Body of Christ. There's nothing worse than an overbearing host—someone who makes everyone know "they are in charge" and, furthermore, as a result of their "newly-found status as host" they can manipulate the entire gathering. My suggestion: Find another host!

The BBQ that got Busted!

I hope this gives us a little insight into the difference between a "work" or "ministry" (leadership) and an "ekklesia" (the brethren/congregants) coming together. I remember a brother telling me a rather dynamic gathering of brethren from the "same church" came together in a home for a BBQ. I may not have the entire story straight, but in any event, it went something like this:

They (members of the same church) decided to have additional BBQs until it became a weekly affair—like on a Saturday evening. Folks brought their playful kids, food, and they all gathered together for some time of singing, sharing and worship—praying for one another—it was sweet. When it got too cold—they all went inside the home and continued their fellowship—kids were encouraged to stay with the adults or go downstairs to play—you'd be surprised how many kids didn't think the adults were boring!

More and more kept coming until there were over 50 in the gathering. They loved it—friends brought friends, and other

So, You want to do Ekklesia?

friends from other churches started coming as well; along with the "uninformed" and "unbelievers." Some of the pastors from other "churches" heard about the meeting and decided it was "getting out of hand"—the little group needed to "come under authority" of the local eldership of the church that allowed this to happen in the first place . . . so one of the pastor-elders of that anchor "Church" (encouraged by local pastors who viewed this gathering as a "siphoning off mechanism" of their own members destined, in their own eyes, to leave their congregations and unite with the "BBQ Church"). So, the BBQ's elders (not participating in the BBQ, by the way) dropped in and started giving out "ministerial sheets" for the group to follow (stage one in the "disillusionment process"). So, they hurriedly went through the little "poop sheets" and then went back to having "fun in Christ!" Foiled again!

Figure 58 - THE BBQ THAT GOT BUSTED

Some had to answer questions from this BBQ's local pastors; as in: *Why are you inviting others from other churches—we're not proselytizing other churches—why not just bring "unsaved people" to your parties or whatever you call them?* Eventually, the little group grew to around 70 or so.

One day, they all wanted to go up to some campground in the mountains and have more fellowship (they had no intention of "forming a new church")—bringing additional friends, saved and unsaved, but who didn't go to their "church"—besides, it would be a whole lot of "Jesus fun" to sit around a campfire having s'mores while sharing Jesus with one another—a really "friendly environment" for would-be "uninformed" and "unbelievers"—they weren't trying to "evangelize"—just love on people . . . such a sinister motive!

Their "organized church" decided to hold a similar excursion on the same day the BBQ folks (just happenstance, of course). The "mother church" planned to stage theirs (Stage 2 of the disillusionment well on its way.) at exactly the same time as the BBQ bunch. The BBQB (the BBQ Bunch) were totally oblivious as to their "sinister activities"—they were just having fun!

That did it, the leaders of the "rebellion" were called before the church pastors-elders and the gathering was quashed once and for all! Again, who knew?

Instead of celebrating how the saints were spreading the gospel in this manner—the local eldership was threatened by its success! They were fearful of losing control—what a shame, what insecurity, what CONTROL! Of course, the Senior Pastor, informed the mother church's eldership that he'd seen this before and rightly knew the end result would end with scores of members wanting to "start their own church"—so, better to nip this one in the bud lest membership lag in his own church and finances suffer (God forbid!). Isn't that why some form sundry "eldership/deacon" boards either controlled by the Pastorate or these boards controlling the Pastorate; and, all in the name of "being responsible for the flock?" This should NOT be what's happening.

No, the workers do not control the Ekklesia—we are NOT suggesting "starting other churches" or creating divisions in the Body of Christ. To the contrary, we're asking gifted brethren to train, equip their flocks to grow up into Christ in all things and learn to function as the Ekklesia when they "spontaneously" gather together whenever and wherever!

Think of it? If Christians are trained by their leadership to "mingle with other Christians" as a PRACTICE—meeting and greeting one another . . . having other members of the Body of Christ over to such BBQs (if you would) without trying to RECRUIT them to their own churches—but to practice the "*unity of the Spirit in the uniting bond of Peace"*—THAT is precisely what we're talking about. We hold to a "common faith"—ONE LORD, ONE BAPTISM, ONE SPIRIT, ONE HOPE OF OUR CALLING... get the point? If so, why can't we encourage the brethren to *"greet the ekklesia that is in their house"* (the house of Priscilla and Aquila) or how's about Gaius who is hosting the *"whole Ekklesia"* passing on greetings to all the saints in Rome (what a heart this brother had) (Rom. 16:5, 23)?

How could you greet the Ekklesia in the home of Priscilla and Aquila (P-A) if you don't visit with the Ekklesia meeting in their house in the first place? Get off your duff and get over to P-A's—it's time to get out of your own "comfort zone" and just show up over at P-A's place . . . bring some food while you're at it! It would be nice to inform them of your intentions—but sometimes, it's just such a welcoming place, that showing up is all you need to concern yourself; P-A are used to handling such spontaneity; fire up the grill—and if we're short on food, we can always get some more.

I'll never forget it, my wife and three kids moved back to Sacramento from Denver, Colorado back in the mid-'80s. We rented this neat house near a local well-known park. There was a conference going on in one of the local churches and a lot of folks knew me from that group. Somehow, someone (I strongly suspect who it was.) invited everyone to my home for pizza and goodies—a kind of housewarming—except, I was being toasted! Deb, my wife, looked out the window to a large crowd of folks coming across the park—you see, she thought just a couple of couples who we personally invited were coming for an intimate dinner. One of our original invited guests casually informed Deb the crowd she was viewing was all coming to OUR PLACE! We freaked! I spent most of my time going back and forth to the corner store buying pizza, drinks, goodies. We must have had over a hundred people there. While passing through the living room I saw this older homeless-styled lady sitting in my rocker, and commenting to me: "Great party; how'd you find out about it?" She informed me she'd heard about the "free dinner" down at the local Union Gospel Rescue Mission (about 4 miles from my place). That's called being a host and having no idea you are—neither does anyone else!

What About Wolves & "Flockless Shepherds"?

Figure 59 - WE'RE JUST WAITING FOR THE FLOCKLESS SHEPHERD!

Of course, at this point in time, someone will inevitably remind us of Paul's exhortations given to the elders from the Church in Ephesus found in Acts 20:17-38 where Paul warns the elders *"that after my departure savage wolves will come in among you, not sparing the flock . . . also from among yourselves men will rise up, speaking misleading* (i.e., perverse) *things, to draw away the disciples after themselves"*—so, folks, look out for the wolves and the "flockless shepherds" who wish to ravage the flock and *"draw away the disciples after themselves."*

This provides, doesn't it, ample justification to keep "tight controls" over the flock lest wolves and flockless shepherds sneak in unawares? So it would appear; however, I wager that if the sheep are trained to be alert, and the elders commend them to instructions to be on the lookout—they, the congregants, would be much better equipped to handle such hostile action by such wolves and flockless shepherds.

Notwithstanding the great need to instruct congregants to both discern and "search the Scriptures" themselves like good Bereans who were Jewish believers, given the title as *"more noble than those in Thessaloniki"* because they diligently delved into the Scriptures—even when Paul had spoken to them of the revelations received of him . . . but did those revelations match with Scripture?

The vulnerability of saints can be measured by their lack of instruction from gifted brethren who ought to be preparing them to "discern" and "search the Scriptures" for themselves—not forever grace the pews being fed pablum from the pulpit when these gifted ones should be feeding them the "meat of the Word" and the ability to *"commit these things to faithful men who shall be able to teach others also"* (2 Tim. 2:2).

Listen up brethren:

"Preach the word! Be ready in season and out of season. Convince, rebuke, exhort, with all longsuffering and teaching. For the time will come when they will not endure sound doctrine, but according to their own desires, because they have itching ears, they will heap up for themselves teachers; and they will turn their ears away from the truth, and be turned aside to fables" (2 Tim. 4:2-4).

This ought to be our cry: **FULFILL YOUR MINISTRY** (2 Tim. 4:5) . . . and this is our plight:

"Although by this time you ought to be teachers, you need someone to reteach you the basic principles of God's word. You need milk, not solid food! For everyone who lives on milk is still an infant, inexperienced in the message of righteousness . . ." (Heb. 5:12-13).

And, who's fault is that . . . who's to blame when the saints ought to have been well trained in God's Word and the fundamentals of the Faith; yet, they continue year after year within the confines of the INFANTILE CHURCH because her leadership is remiss in going beyond the "basics"—so the flock abides "***inexperienced in the message of righteousness***"—sooner or later that infant must be POTTY-TRAINED?

Is it love spelled *LUV* that commits a teaching-pastor to leave his congregants as infants because children are so endearing? I don't think so. Is there some strange fear which keeps the babes in swaddling clothes—when they ought to grow up into Christ in ALL things?

Sure, there's plenty of blame to go around—we ought to be raising up teachers, but we've managed to secure overcrowded classrooms. Indeed, we'll always have a "teaching job" but there's a massive SHORTAGE OF TEACHERS . . . instead of "teaching ourselves out of a job" we manage to assure our own "job security"—OUTRAGEOUS!

Then, there's the compliant congregation who *"have itching ears . . . heaping up for themselves teachers"* who are predisposed to great stories (aka "fables"), while turning aside from the truth—because why hear the truth when you can be entertained? *"We'll settle for entertainment"* and *"blame the pastor when nothing ever happens around here! At least we have 'smoke and mirrors'!"*

I once was involved in an organization which figured out how to raise large sums of money but subjected the faithful to endless "trainings" and "materials" (the trainee would have to pay for these "trainings"—it was an obligation and privilege to do so; and if you wanted to "go up the ranks" you'd better get aboard these voluntary trainings)—it seemed these "trainings" were interminable! Forbid, the saints would grow up so that they themselves could be teaching others . . . yes, some squeaked by and basically regurgitated the "messages" from "Central Command" and, if one deviated from the "Oracle's message"—well, let's say, that "minister's lifespan" in the movement would be short-lived.

If he or she found themselves some distance from the "headquarters of the movement"—then, they would have to move back to the "starting blocks" and begin the race all over again—aka, RE-TRAINING would be in order. At the end of the day, the saints were kept in an infantile state, utterly dependent upon the ministry, ergo never to survive on their own. Tragically, all their "experience of God" was the movement itself—once they "left the ministry" most (not all) felt they had left God. Their God was the

So, You want to do Ekklesia?

ministry, the "church" became "God-like"—their identification was NOT found in the "fellowship of the saints" but all brethren were linked to the Oracle—or, upon later reflection, a Council of Brethren was formed wherein they were the inheritors of the "revealed truth" so that with the passing of THE LEADER, everyone who wished to stay in the movement, now had to buckle under to the "princes" who became the new overlords of the movement.

How tragic, so many who found themselves outside the movement—kicked out, drummed out, or disenchanted by the movement—not only left the movement, but left God, denied their faith, such as it was, became agnostic, even atheist . . . truly, damaged goods! Their "God" was actually the movement, that church, that group, that "thing"—and when they found themselves outside of it, they cast their lot with the world, going from one sinking ship to another; not good, so sad.

I've been known to tell folks: "Listen, if you haven't gone through a 'Christian Cult' or two, witnessed an old-fashioned Southern Baptist Church split; seen your home church ravaged by some progressive movement designed to debilitate the locals—then, you're probably not worth your salt!" Listen, many (especially, those panting hard after the Lord) have been "through it"—you have a choice: Be bitter about it all and QUIT THE RACE or regroup to fight another day (I know, it's not easy.).

Betrayal, dis-fellowship, brainwashing by well-meaning brain washers—yes, a whole cacophony of insults foisted upon the human psyche and spirit—have left scores of DONES in their wake. But God knows what we've all been through and still loves you and cares for His Own—remember, a "Church" or "Group" or "Doctrine" or "Charismatic Leader" did NOT save you, a Person did, and His Name is Jesus Christ our Lord and Savior! Let's give us all a little credit . . . we know that the "blame game" satisfies no one; sure, you found yourself "outside the fold" with your cozy safety net smashed to smithereens; but you know full-well, you still need God's people—you still need their fellowship. I'm not saying you need time to regroup from whatever fiasco you've gone through—but sooner or later you need His people and they need you! It may take some time; but getting back into the race is the lot of those who wish to press on into Him in all things. Fellowship with those who have "survived" oppressive "Christian cults" and who have left their bitterness behind, are probably your "best bet" for early recovery—no one said the Christian life would be a bed of roses.

Alas! You were only in "fellowship" if you were absorbing the ministry of the Oracle (known as a "Pyramid Model")—any criticism of the Oracle spelled certain "spiritual isolation" and immediate reprimand. *Cultic?* And, if you messed with people still inside the movement—you could be sued by the movement's leadership or even cursed! Listen, when you're "in it" you have little or no awareness how bound you are! All this can be justified by any given "movement" which is man centered.

Notwithstanding, real training should provide God's people the capability to discern on their own—to search the Scriptures on their own. But holding the saints in such a "suspended state of infantile animation"—justified by the ruse that "flockless shepherds" could be at fault, so we must keep guard over the sheep—belies the fact that the Oracle-Teacher has his own insecurities or has an agenda filled with self-aggrandizement (aka, filthy lucre) to enrich himself or his family—SHAME, SHAME, SHAME!

Let Paul be our Example

It never ceases to amaze me how Paul wound up in his ministry in a rented house in Rome under "house arrest" awaiting trial under Emperor Nero—eventually he was beheaded as a Roman citizen all by his lonesome (68 AD)—BUT GOD STOOD WITH ME (2 Tim. 4:17) (Incidentally, Nero committed suicide the same year/time that Paul was beheaded.). Seemingly, Paul shook and turned the Roman World upside down—but when he finished his journey, he had nothing left but the riches of His Savior—he had gathered no one around him—so, do we consider his "ministry" a failure? If that's failure, then bring it on! Paul's ministry did NOT control the churches, nor would he let churches control his ministry. I hope we're getting the picture here. You say: That was then, this is now! No, few desire to "finish the race" and finish strong—ministry can be a lonely road:

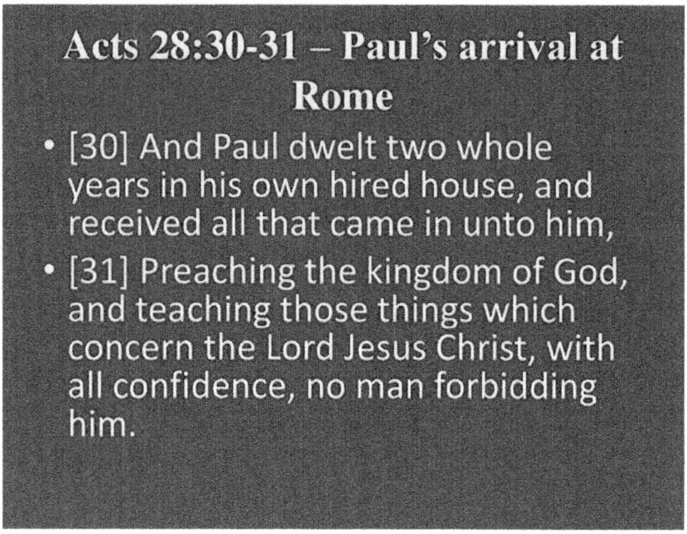

So, You want to do Ekklesia?

> **Acts 28:30-31 – Paul's arrival at Rome**
> - [30] And Paul dwelt two whole years in his own hired house, and received all that came in unto him,
> - [31] Preaching the kingdom of God, and teaching those things which concern the Lord Jesus Christ, with all confidence, no man forbidding him.

Figure 60 - ACTS 28:30-31

"For Demas has forsaken me, having loved this present world, and has departed for Thessalonica—Crescens for Galatia, Titus for Dalmatia. Only Luke is with me . . . Alexander the coppersmith did me much harm. May the Lord repay him according to his works . . . But shun profane and empty chatter, for they will lead to more ungodliness. And their message will spread like cancer. Hymenaeus and Philetus are of this sort, who have strayed concerning the truth, saying that the resurrection is already past; and they overthrow the faith of some" (2 Tim. 4:10-11, 14; 2:16-18).

These names all sound like co-workers with Paul—some good, some bad, and some indifferent. Ministry has its twists and turns, God knows. Yes, my heart goes out to those who "*work righteousness*" for the Kingdom's sake—their task is assuredly, at times, insurmountable . . . **BUT THE LORD STOOD WITH ME**! (2 Tim. 4:17)

I wouldn't be so cavalier about these issues. We're out of balance in most of Christendom. There is MUCH we can learn from these examples of ministry and Ekklesia. There is a balance—the one does not obfuscate the other. Both are needed for equipping the saints to do the work of the ministry so that when "*the whole*

Ekklesia comes together" His people will know and practice the *"unity of the Spirit in the bond of Peace."* God bless...

So, You want to do Ekklesia?

Chapter 10:
Ekklesia Replicates "Lord's Appointed Times" – Part 1

Figure 61 - KING SOLOMON - THE "FORMER HOUSE" - G. BONITO

An Introduction to the Topic at Hand:

YOU MIGHT BE WONDERING HOW THE NEW TESTAMENT EKKLESIA IS RELATED TO THE MAJOR "FEAST DAYS" OF THE LORD—"THE LORD'S APPOINTED Times" (Lev. 23). Especially, since Paul's reflections on Christians and their relations to the following:

> *"So let no one judge you in food or in drink, or regarding a festival* (aka "feast day") *or a new moon or sabbaths, which are a shadow of things to come, but the substance* (lit "the body" or "reality") *is of Christ"* (Col. 2:16-17).

This is even more affirmed when, again, Paul makes it abundantly clear in Romans 14:

> *"Who are you to judge another's servant? To his own master he stands or falls. Indeed, he will be made to stand, for God*

is able to make him stand. One person esteems one day above another; another esteems every day alike. LET EACH BE FULLY CONVINCED IN HIS OWN MIND. He who observes the day, observes it to the Lord; and he who does not observe the day, to the Lord he does not observe it. He who eats, eats to the Lord, for he gives God thanks; and he who does not eat, to the Lord he does not eat, and gives God thanks" (Romans 14:4-6).

When I originally wrote this two-part series for Commonwealth Theology's blog (which tends to be a bit more "heady" in its presentation), I pondered on the resurgent rise in Christian interest in celebrating the "Lord's Appointed Times" now taking place within large swaths of the Body of Christ. Critics are perplexed—why celebrate such "feast days" when we have the "reality in Christ" in any event; and, by the way, isn't this nothing more than keeping Jewish laws and regulations; after all, don't we have the New Testament? Why fool around with "signs and symbols" when today's "Temple" is the very Body of Christ? Some will go so far as to suggest: "We really don't need much of the Old Testament because it was written for the Jews; besides, the only way it can be understood is by reading the New Testament." The put down of the Old Testament gets more severe in certain circles where of late we've heard: "We really don't need the Old Testament with the Old Covenant and its 'rules and regulations'—so, why keep any of these feast days or, for that matter, the Sabbath day when every day should be celebrated—we can worship on any day of the week!"

I'm not here in this little introduction to convince anyone to celebrate these feast days or be regulated by the new moons or keep the Sabbath from sundown on any given Friday until sundown on Saturday. I have my own preferences—and that's what I'm talking about: *LET EACH BE FULLY CONVINCED IN HIS OWN MIND.* There are a whole lot of "doubtful things" out there in the Bible (Rom. 14:1) but there's a whole lot of DISPUTES over these doubtful things which separate believers into various "camps." Who ever heard of giving your brother or sister the "benefit of the doubt" on these "doubtful things?" No, if you're not worshiping on the Sabbath Day, you're under the Mark of the Beast! Sunday worship is BEAST WORSHIP! That little "gracious outburst" is spoken of by whole denominations—in case you didn't know.

Now, my preference, if I could be blunt, is to keep the Sabbath and to be gracious with anyone else who doesn't—so there. Mark of the Beast? Nonsense! Did the Emperor Constantine at the Council of Nicaea in 325 AD and then the Council of Laodicea in 363-364 AD eliminate and even forbid Christians to worship on Saturday AND forbid them to "hang out" with Jews, let alone celebrate any of their "feast days" when Christians had their own "Holy Days" like Christmas, Easter and whatnot? They sure did; and in doing so, virtually put Jews in a "theological ghetto"—a complete social, cultural, and tragic separation lasting until the present day (with some breaks in the barriers so erected now and again).

What Paul is calling for in Romans 14 is for believers to "*receive one who is weak in the faith*"—however one considers such a one as weak. It's a plea on his part for "brotherly tolerance"—the Ekklesia is a place where such "diversity of practice" should be the norm. Some who worship on the Sabbath as Saturday and some who do not—both can meet any time together on either day and gather as brethren. This is the bottom line:

> "*. . . and not holding fast to the Head, from whom all the body, nourished and knit together by joints and ligaments, grows with the increase that is from God . . . do you subject yourselves to regulations—'Do not touch, do not taste, do not handle,' which all concern things which perish with the using—according to the commandments and doctrines of men? These things indeed have an appearance of wisdom in self-imposed religion, false humility, and neglect of the body, but are of no value against the indulgence of the flesh . . . since you have put off the old man with his deeds, and have put on the NEW MAN who is renewed in knowledge according to the image of Him who created him, where there is neither Greek*

nor Jew, circumcised nor uncircumcised, barbarian, Scythian, slave nor free, but Christ is all and in all" (Col. 2:19-23; 3:9-11).

We'll never have Ekklesia—real fellowship in Christ—if we're "all the same" (e.g., we only meet with those who don't eat pork). Do you truly think that a bunch of Barbarians (and there are some amongst us) enjoy being around a group of sophisticated Greeks who deem intense study of the Word of God a much sought after goal of the believer, when Barbarians (no offense here) can't wait for the real action with wild worship and dancing before the Lord as a "divine art form" of the most profound exercise? Ultimately, there can be NO discrimination in the Body of Christ—and, by the way, Sunday mornings, especially in the West, are still the most racially-divided places you'll find around these parts. You bet we've got to do better than this—that's why the Ekklesia should be one of the most diverse habitats whenever it comes together—and, if it isn't, then we should pray it happens the sooner the better; while finding opportunity to experience such diversity as exemplary of being "in Christ!"

Now, how does all this introduction fit into our enjoyment of Christ in "The Lord's Appointed Times?" Much, in every way—first notice, the description abides: These are still "The Lord's Appointed Times"—His Feast Days—this is still His Calendar—and for good reason. For one, if these feast days are "a thing of the past," then why, pray tell, are we and the nations going to celebrate them as follows:

"And it shall come to pass that everyone who is left of all the nations which came against Jerusalem shall go up from year to year to worship the King, the LORD of hosts, and to keep the Feast of Tabernacles" (Zechariah 14:16)?

And, if they were so unimportant, why was it that Jesus frequented the Passover, the Feast of Tabernacles and even the Feast of Dedication throughout John's gospel and the other gospels? Well, you say, Jesus was Jewish, and just "fit right on into the culture of His day." That somewhat superficiality is meaningless, for *"ALL SCRIPTURE is given by inspiration of God and is profitable for doctrine, for reproof, for correction, for instruction in righteousness"* (2 Tim. 3:16). Brethren, allow me, we believers have been ripped off by placing these feast days either in theological obscurity or as part and parcel of our nigh 2,000 years in "forbidding all things Jewish" to enter into our "Christian house!" It is time we began to examine more closely what this Hebrew Sacred Calendar is all about and why we should hold it in esteem, far more than we ever have, because it truly reveals the Lord's eternal plan and purpose for the ages . . ..

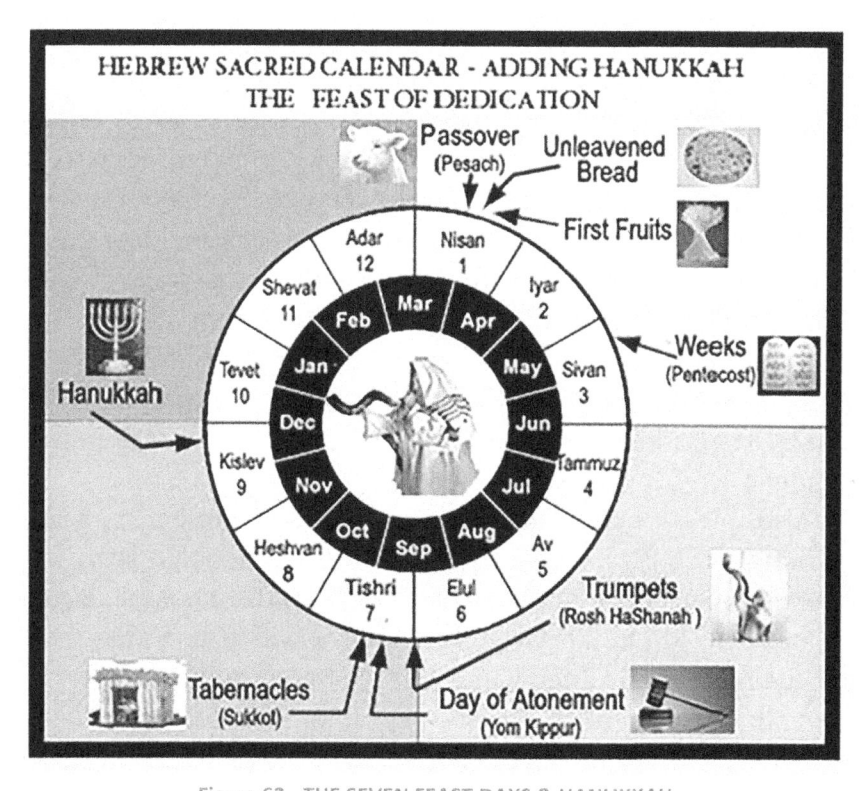

Figure 62 - THE SEVEN FEAST DAYS & HANUKKAH

Again this brevity was (in the main) released on Commonwealth Theology, Tishri 1—the Beginning of the Jewish Civil New Year (please view the Hebrew Sacred Calendar) will have passed (this was released around the end of September, 2019). It is celebrated on the Hebrew/Gregorian (somewhat of an admixture)

So, You want to do Ekklesia?

calendar date, this year, beginning on Sunday evening (6 P.M.) on September 29, 2019 and extending until Tuesday's commencement at 6 P.M. on October 1, 2019 (a 24-hour time frame on the Hebrew Sacred Calendar)... thus begins the CIVIL NEW YEAR on the Jewish Calendar... but we haven't quite made it to HAPPY HANUKKAH... Say, WHAT? Yes, these two feast days are "divinely connected"—we're going to find out how that "comes down" when Jesus in John's Gospel attended both feast days between John 7 and John 10, most amazing.

We'll get to the 24/25th Day of the Ninth Month (the month of Kislev) in a moment (viz., the Feast of Dedication—alluded to in Haggai 2:10-23 in "adumbrative" language)—but since the Civil New Year begins so soon (1 Tishri on the Hebrew Calendar) it is good that we examine the "prophetical issues" arising from the Fall Feast days—tracing the dates from 1 Tishri (Feast of Trumpets) to 10 Tishri (Day of Atonement/Yom Kippur) through to 15 Tishri (Feast of Tabernacles)—known as the High Holy Days on the Jewish Calendar with the Feast of Tabernacles ending on 21 Tishri [7 days]... but we still haven't made it unto 24/25 Kislev some **70 days beyond 15 Tishri** (i.e., 15 days left in the 7th month of Tishri + 30 days in the 8th month of Cheshvan + 25 days into the 9th month of Kislev for a total of 15 + 30 + 25 = 70 days). (See End Note #1 in this chapter and all endnotes in this chapter.)

Also, please note, the "day one" was the "evening and the morning" (Gen. 1:5) wherein the "day one" begins at sundown and extends to the next sundown; so, if the 24th of Kislev begins around 6:00 PM in the "evening"—then, it will extend unto 6:00 PM the next "day" which will in turn commence the new day of the 25th of Kislev at that time—so, often, we'll see a "day" expressed, on behalf of the Gregorian calendar as 24/25 because whatever day we are considering on the Gregorian Calendar and comparing it with the "Jewish" or "Hebrew Festival Calendar" it must be "spliced" into a "two-day" happening. Therefore, when we read in Haggai the Ninth Month and the Twenty-fourth Day of the month, we actually have the 24/25th day of the Ninth Month.

Therefore, in that 70 days is betwixt the terminus of the High Holy Days (15 Tishri) unto 24/25 Kislev—there is more than an obvious connection; therefore, 1 Tishri was a logical starting point in unraveling this "prophetic potential."

The 70th Week of Daniel and the multitude of "70s" throughout Scripture should signal to us that "something's going on here" of immense significance. Thus, we begin, "at the beginning" of 1 Tishri but start the "countdown" to 24/25 Kislev at 15 Tishri (The commencements of the Feast of Tabernacles or Nations) which is the final "Divinely Ordained Seven Feast Days" with the Feast of Tabernacles being the final and seventh such Feast Day on the Hebrew Sacred Calendar . . . but this "70" bears our attention in that "something else is going on here" as well.

The Hebrew Festival Calendar (aka, the "Hebrew Sacred Calendar") has of late experienced a revival of interest among Christians—Christians who have recognized their association as Ephraim (those "lost among the nations" or Gentiles) with Judah (viz., the Jewish people).

That's a rather loaded introduction which is as mystifying as the secondary title (which I did not use): THE HEBREW SACRED CALENDAR & THE ANTICHRIST. Naturally, arising in the hearts and minds of well-meaning believers in Yeshua, are these "festival days"—such as the spring feast days which start after the commencement of the "Religious Year" on 1 Nisan (in the spring) (NOTE: We shall dispense in attempting to synchronize the present Gregorian Calendar days with those of the Jewish Calendar days and simply use the "Prophetic Calendar" and the 30-day "prophetic month" or 360-days in a "Prophetic Year"—each of the 12 months being 30 days or 12 X 30 days = 360 days). And, yes, we are keenly aware that it was at the time of King Hezekiah of Judah's "life extension" of some 15 years around 711 B.C. in which the luni-solar calendar was extended from 360 days to 365.2425 days (with a leap year of 366 days every 4 years).

The "Civil Year" on the Hebrew Calendar commences on 1 Tishrei (during the fall); whereas, 1 Nisan is in the spring of the year. Nisan is the commencement of the "Religious Year" on the Hebrew Calendar—thus, there are "two New Years" on the

So, You want to do Ekklesia?

Hebrew Calendar—all divinely designed around harvests, early and latter. The first Passover in Egypt—Exodus 12—made Nisan, instead of the Seventh Month, the First Month; and, Tishri became the Seventh Month instead of the First Month. In Noah's day the month of Tishri was the First Month and Nisan was the Seventh Month; therefore, when one examines the record they will find very significant time frames wherein, for example, when Noah's Ark landed on the Mountains of Ararat it states: *"Then the ark rested in the seventh month, the seventeenth day of the month, on the mountains of Ararat"* (Gen. 8:4); therefore, this was the month of Nisan. On 17 Nisan Jesus was resurrected from the dead (Saturday/Sunday evening)—thus, when Peter proclaims *"that ark* [Noah's Ark] *is Christ"* (1 Peter 3:18-22) we see that His resurrection from the "death waters" was foreseen when Noah's Ark touched the dry land which had been raised from the judgment of the waters which covered the earth.

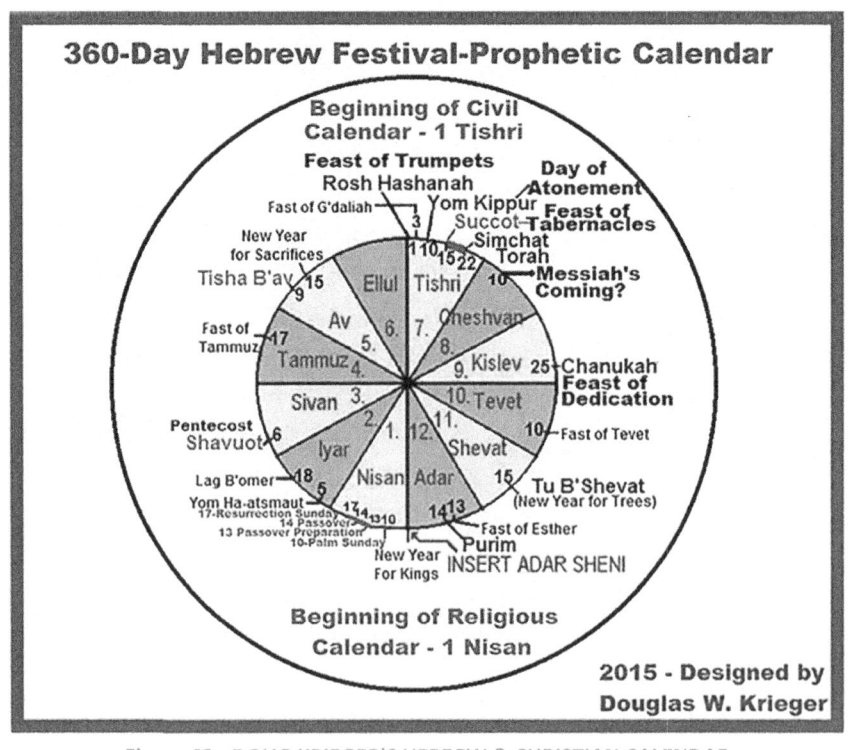

Figure 63 - DOUG KRIEGER'S HEBREW & CHRISTIAN CALENDAR

Ekklesia Replicates "Lord's Appointed Times" – Part 1

Seven Sacred Feast Days of the Hebrew Calendar

There are seven feast days (lit. "appointed times') accorded divine and perpetual celebration. They are considered as an "everlasting ordinance"—to wit:

"So this day [viz., Passover] *shall be to you a memorial; and you shall keep it as a feast to the LORD throughout your generations. You shall keep it as **a feast by an everlasting ordinance**"* (Ex. 12:14-15).

Please note: The Hebrew calendar day commences at 6 P.M. on any given ***day*** so that a date of 13 Nisan "flows into" 14 Nisan on the same Gregorian day; therefore, a Hebrew day is sometimes seen as 13/14 on the Gregorian calendar day but on the Hebrew calendar it is simply 14 (Ref. "The EVENING and the MORNING were the first ***day***"—Gen. 1:5).

The Seven (7) Divinely Ordained Feast Days are:

1. Passover (Pasach or Pesach)—13/14 Nisan—Exodus 12:1-14; Lev. 23:4-5; Numbers 9:1-14; 28:16; Deut. 16:1-7
2. Unleavened Bread—14/15 Nisan—Exodus 12:15-20; 13:3-10; Numbers 28:17-25; Deut. 16:3-4, 8; Lev. 4:6-8 – (Literally 7 days or 14/15 through 20/21 Nisan)
3. Firstfruits—16/17 Nisan—Leviticus 23:9-14; Num. 28:26
4. Feast of Weeks (Shavuot or Pentecost)—6 Sivan—Exodus 23:16; 34:22; Lev. 23:15-21; Num. 28:26-31; Deut. 16:9-12
5. Feast or Trumpets (Rosh Hashanah or Yom Teruah—Beginning of the Hebrew "Civil Year")—1 Tishri—Leviticus 23:23-25
6. Day of Atonement (Yom Kippur)—10 Tishri—Leviticus 16; 23:26-32; Num. 29:7-11
7. Feast of Tabernacles (Sukkot or Weeks or Booths or Nations)—15 Tishri—Exodus 23:16; 34:22; Lev. 23:33-36, 39-43; Num. 29:12-38; Deut. 16:13-15 and Zechariah 14:16-21

So, You want to do Ekklesia?

Each of these "Feast Days" have their reflection/fulfillment in our Lord Jesus Christ; to wit:

1. Passover: John 1:29; 1 Cor. 5:7
2. Unleavened Bread: Rom. 6:4; 1 Cor. 5:8
3. Firstfruits: 1 Cor. 15:20-23; 1 Cor. 12:27
4. Pentecost: Acts 2:1-4; 1 Cor. 12:12-13
5. Feast of Trumpets: Matthew 24:31; 1 Thess. 4:16; 1 Cor. 15:52; Rev. 8-9; 11:15-18
6. Day of Atonement: Matthew 24:21; 23:39; Heb. 9:11-12; Rev. 6:12-17; 11:15-18
7. Feast of Tabernacles: Matthew 24:30; 16:27; 24:44; 24:27; 25:23; John 7:2-39

The general understanding of these Feast Days in their "prophetic context" affirms that the first four Feast Days were fulfilled in Christ at His First Coming—viz., Passover, Unleavened Bread, Firstfruits, and Pentecost (spring feast days); whereas, the final three Feast Days will be fulfilled at His Coming again in Glory—viz., Feast of Trumpets, Day of Atonement, and Feast of Tabernacles (the fall feast days).

Yes, Christians have, in the main, and as a result of Emperor Constantine (Nicaea Council of 325 A.D.) and the Council of Laodicea (363-364 A.D.) completely abandoned the Hebrew Sacred Calendar, along with any association between Christians and Jews—literally placing a "theological ghetto" around "all things Jewish." The Sabbath was changed from Saturday to Sunday—with all worship among Christians to be on "the first day of the week" commemorating the resurrection of Christ.

Now, I am keenly aware that Christians have utterly abandoned these feast days and have declared them (as a result of these unbeknownst tragic rejections by civil and clerical leaders) inconsequential (to say the least) and have justified their abandonment using such passages as:

> "So let no one judge you in food or in drink, or regarding a feast (as in "festival day") or a new moon or sabbaths, which are a shadow of things to come, but the substance is of Christ . . . one person esteems one day above another; another esteems every day alike . . . let each be fully convinced in his own mind . . . He who observes the day, observes it to the Lord; and he who does not observe the day, to the Lord he does not observe it. He who eats, eats to the Lord, for he gives God thanks; and he who does not eat, to the Lord he does not eat, and gives God thanks" (Col. 2:16-17; Romans 14:5-6).

The problem here is that those brethren who are "fully persuaded in their own mind" to celebrate these feast days MAY (Note: I didn't say "they do.") have a tendency to look down their noses at those believers in Yeshua who do not; yet, those who do not MAY (Note: I didn't say "they do") look down their noses at those who do celebrate these feast days as UNTO THE LORD. Both could readily be doing so—either way—as UNTO THE LORD . . . why can't we come to terms with that? It's called extending grace to all believer!

Furthermore, the pendulum has swung so far in the opposite direction over the course of nearly 1,700 years (viz., "away from celebrating these feast days") that for believers to commence to acknowledge these "feast days" as having any significance is a most refreshing sign, as far as this writer is concerned, in the bringing together of Ephraim and Judah at the end of the age! (Please review my article @ COMMONWEALTH THEOLOGY or http://commonwealththeology.com/)

Now, getting back to 10 Tishri—the Day of Atonement...

There are some, I being one of them, who see in the futurity of the Day of Atonement, the *"Wrath of God and the Lamb"* (a time of world judgment) is wrought by the "Worthy Lamb" Who is "worthy to open the Seven-Sealed Book" to claim His legal inheritance (i.e., the Earth).

In His First Coming He atoned for the sins of the world and is, therefore, worthy to Judge "*all they that dwell on the earth.*" In other words: The Lamb of God Who "*takes away the sin of the world*" is likewise, the coming "*Wrath of the Lamb*"—thus, the Day of Atonement is yet future.

The Feast of Dedication . . . Connecting the Dots

There are "other feast days" and/or "days of significance" of alleged "lesser importance" such as the Feast of Dedication (again, 70 days beyond the Seventh of these feast days—Feast of Tabernacles, and final, divinely orchestrated seven feast days on the Hebrew Calendar), Purim, Tisha B'av or 9th of Av (destructions of the First and Herodian Temple—aka, the Second Temple), etc. We could, and multitudes of writers have, written about the significance of these feast days as they pertain to the Messiah.

What garners this writer's immediate interest in this brevity is the Feast of Dedication—I know, why bring up all the other feast days and then jump to a feast day which is NOT accorded as one of the major seven feast days? Well, that's because it has such profound prophetic importance and is, in the main, casually given short shrift because it allegedly is considered either "prophetically obsolete" (i.e., having already been fulfilled) . . . or pertains "only to the Jews" (the Christians having absolutely nothing of interest in the topic of the Feast of Dedication). It is, however, intrinsically tied to the three final fall feast days due to a number of peculiar calendric associations; the least of which is, of course, the "**70 days**" from 15 Tishri (commencement of the Feast of Tabernacles) to 25 Kislev (commencement of the Feast of Dedication).

King Solomon's Temple Dedication & Haggai's 9/24

In 2 Chronicles 5:2 it clearly states that "*. . . all the men of Israel assembled with the king* (Solomon) *at the feast, which was in the **seventh** month.*" It is clear from the context that this was most likely the Feast of Tabernacles (15 Tishri—Lev. 23:34; 1 Kings 8:2—the "seventh month" called *Ethanim* or *Tishri*) in that 2 Chronicles 7:8-10 states:

*"And on the **eighth day** they held a sacred assembly, for they observed the DEDICATION of the altar seven days, and the feast seven days. On the **twenty-third day of the seventh month*** [which was the "eighth day" from 15 Tishri unto 23 Tishri some 487 years beyond 1445 B.C. Passover or in the year 965 B.C. less 7 years of building the temple or from foundation dedication to completion of the Temple = 958 B.C.— Refs. 1 Kings 6:1 and 1 Kings 6:37-38] *he sent the people away to their tents, joyful and glad of heart for the good that the LORD had done for David, for Solomon, and for His people Israel* (cir. 957 B.C.)" **(See: End Note #2)**

Figure 64 - KING SOLOMON'S TEMPLE DEDICATION

We carefully note that Solomon's Feast of Tabernacles commenced on 15 Tishri and extended for 7 days (or 15 + 7 [inclusive] = 21 Tishri) in that:

"At that time Solomon kept the feast seven days (15 Tishri to 21 Tishri–inclusive) . . . *and on the **eighth day*** (22 Tishri) *they held a sacred assembly, for they observed the*

dedication of the altar seven days, and the feast seven days . . . On the twenty-third day of the seventh month (23 Tishri) *he sent the people away to their tents, joyful and glad of heart for the good that the LORD had done for David, for Solomon, and for His people Israel"* (2 Chron. 7:9-10)

This sheds much greater light upon the connectivity between Haggai's 9/24s and the Feast of Dedication in that Tishri 21 (the terminus of the 7-day Feast of Tabernacles—for it was designed to be a 7-day Feast Celebration and an additional Eighth Day to be that of a Holy Convocation (Lev. 23:34-36). Why? Because it was on Tishri 21 that we hear:

"In the seventh month (Tishri), *on the twenty-first of the month* (Tishri 21—the final seventh day of the Feast of Tabernacles), *the word of the LORD came by Haggai the prophet"* (concerning the 9/24s which was 9/24-25 the very future Feast of Dedication) (Haggai 2:1).

In other words, **the final seventh day of the Feast of Tabernacles readily foresaw the coming of the Feast of Dedication**? I think so—for it was all about the Temple and its miraculous restoration upon Judah's return but had, likewise, in view that LATTER TEMPLE—THE GREATER HOUSE (Haggai 2:6-9)—From Tishri 15 unto Kislev 24/25—some **70 days**! The introduction to the 9/24s is given in Haggai 2:6-9! The 7-day Feast of Tabernacles must be viewed as a "block"—in other words "singular" so that 15-21 Tishrei is seen as a "collective" number set or as ONE SET.

Thus, 15 Tishri holds a most powerful connection to the dedication of the Solomonic Temple. Now, one would conjecture that the dedication of the Second Temple would reflect 15 Tishri's Feast of Tabernacles akin to that of Solomon's dedication of the First Temple; however, the actual dedication of the Second Temple took place on the *"third day of the month of Adar* [early spring]. . . *then the children of Israel, the priests and the Levites and the rest of the descendants of the captivity* [Babylonian

Captivity] , *celebrated the DEDICATION of this temple of God with joy*" (Ezra 6:15).

Thus, a somewhat arbitrary date is selected (3 Adar) which bears little (at this time) significance—for, we affirm, that the significance of the Second Temple's FOUNDATION laid on the 24/25th Day of the ninth month (24/25 Kislev) bears far more significance (as recorded in Haggai 2:10, 18, 20—some 3 times). .. but first ...

Feast of Dedication 24/25 Kislev—2,300 Days of Dan. 8

The great dispensational prophetic commentator, Dr. John Walvoord, suggests in his commentary of Daniel (***Daniel – The Key to Prophetic Revelation***) that the 2,300-day prophecy as recorded in Daniel 8:13-14 has already been fulfilled as "days" (not as years as the Seventh-Day Adventists, Mormons, and Jehovah Witnesses suggest)—already fulfilled in 165 B.C.

Dr. John Walvoord's accounting of these 2,300 days found in Daniel 8:14 divorces the "Abomination of Desolation" found in these verses from the prototype of the future Antichrist pre-figured in Antiochus IV Epiphanes (AE). In other words, the 2,300 days is a "fulfilled prophecy" (P. 190, Daniel, the Key to Prophetic Revelation, Walvoord, 1971); whereas, this author affirms that the 2,300-day vision of the "evenings-mornings" is yet future, beyond today's date of 2019 (See: 2300-Days, Conservapedia @ https://www.conservapedia.com/2300_Day_Prophecy_of_Daniel_8.).

AE, in his attempt to Hellenize the Jews, stirred up the Maccabees, leading to the uprising known as the Maccabean Revolt. The revolt led to the "cleansing of the Temple" desecrated by AE and ultimately the celebration of their victory over AE with the re-dedication of the Temple; hence, the Feast of Dedication or "Happy Hanukkah" or the "*Festival of Lights*" (with the miracle of the sacred oil lasting eight days instead of but one day on the Menorah) and the specificity of the 24/25 Kislev date as the commencement date of the actual Feast of Dedication which is a 8-day celebration with the eighth day falling on the 10th Month or on 2/3 Tevet. (NOTE: AE's attempts at Hellenizing the Jews commenced in earnest in 171 B.C. with the desecration of the Temple taking place on December 25, 167 B.C. with the death of AE occurring in 164 B.C.—Walvoord's Daniel Commentary, p. 190).

Figure 65 - JUDAH - THE MACCABEE

Walvoord states:

Taking all the evidence into consideration, the best conclusion is that the twenty-three hundred days of Daniel are fulfilled in the period from 171 B.C. and culminated in the death of Antiochus [IV] Epiphanes in 164 B.C. The period when the sacrifices ceased was the latter part of this longer period. Although the evidence available today does not offer fulfillment to the precise day, the twenty-three hundred days, **obviously a round number**, *is relatively accurate in defining the period when the Jewish religion began to erode under the persecution of Antiochus, and the period as a whole concluded with his death . . . As far as* Daniel 8:1-14 *is concerned, there is no adequate reason for considering it in any* *other light than that of fulfilled prophecy from the standpoint of the twentieth century. It is adequately explained in the history of the Medo-Persian and Greek empires, and specifically, in the activities of Antiochus Epiphanes.*

(Walvoord, p. 190: **Commentary on Daniel**, *Moody Press, 1971)*

The ambiguity of Walvoord's calendric math disturbs this author. God Almighty is far more precise on His calculations. Since Walvoord accords the futurity of the Seventieth Week of Daniel's major prophecy found in Daniel 9:24-27, and its Abomination of Desolation, then how can he take Daniel 8:13 when it speaks clearly concerning? . . . .

"How long will the vision be, concerning the DAILY SACRIFICES and THE TRANSGRESSION OF DESOLATION?"

These two items are juxtaposed the one to another—viz., SACRIFICE and DESOLATION. When Daniel wished to comprehend/understand the vision of the 2,300 days, we read:

"Then it happened, when I, Daniel, had seen the vision and was seeking the meaning, that suddenly there stood before me one having the appearance of a man . . . so he came near where I stood, and when he came I was afraid and fell on my face; but he said to me, 'Understand, son of man, that the VISION REFERS TO THE TIME OF THE END.'" (Daniel 8:15, 17)

Apparently, Walvoord's "time of the end" terminated somewhere around 164 B.C.? Whereas, the fulfillment of the 2,300 days is given in this context:

"And the vision of the evenings and mornings [Note: Clearly a 24-hour time frame as per Genesis 1:5.] *which was told is*

true; therefore seal up the vision, **FOR IT REFERS TO MANY DAYS IN THE FUTURE**" (Daniel 8:26).

The juxtaposition of the "Sacrifice" and the "Desolations" are again recited and/or alluded to in Daniel 9:27; 11:31; 12:11—all within a "prophetical context" with the final allusion being found in Daniel 12; to wit:

"And at that time . . . until the time of the end . . . the end of these things . . . the time of the end . . . go your way till the end" (Excerpts from Daniel 12).

Furthermore, the prophetic time frame as to when the "*time of the end*" takes place is within the context found in Daniel 12:7:

"Then I heard the man clothed in linen, who was above the waters of the river, when he held up his right hand and his left hand to heaven, and swore by Him who lives forever, that it shall be for **a time, times, and half a time**; *and when the power of the holy people has been completely shattered, all these things shall be finished."*

This same phraseology is used in the book of Revelation regarding the vision of the Woman who flies and flees into the wilderness:

"But the woman was given two wings of a great eagle, that she might fly into the wilderness to her place, where she is nourished for a **time and times and half a time** *from the presence of the serpent"* (Rev. 12:14 – See Daniel 7:25; 12:7).

Inadvertently, at best, Walvoord would have us interpret the 1,290-days of desolation (Dan. 12:11) as being fulfilled in history past at the time of Antiochus IV Epiphanes, the Seleucid-Syrian-Grecian King (aka, the "Madman" or *Epimanes*)?

Not so! Since there are 1,290 "Days of Desolation"—counted from the "middle of the future 70th Week of Daniel" when a yet future "Abomination of Desolation" shall occur whereupon the

Ekklesia Replicates "Lord's Appointed Times" – Part 1

"Sacrifice" shall cease; we must, therefore, calculate the "unknown" in this manner:

X = Days of Sacrifice

1,290 days = Days of Desolation ([Daniel 12:11](#))

2,300 days = Total Days of Sacrifice and Desolation/Transgression ([Daniel 8:14](#)); thus:

X + 1,290 Days of Desolation = 2,300 Days of Sacrifice and Desolation

SOLVE FOR "X" –

X + 1,290 Days = 2,300 Days

X = 2,300 Days less 1,290 days

X = 1,010 Days

Proof:

1,010 Days + 1,290 Days = 2,300 Days

Therefore, the Sacrifice must commence 250 days into the 70th Week of Daniel because the Abomination of Desolation will occur "in the middle of the Week" (i.e., after 1,260 days or 3 1/2 years/prophetic months) – again:

X + 1010 Days = 1,260 Days (1/2 of the 70th Week)

X = 1,260 Days less 1,010 days

X = 250 Days

Proof:

So, You want to do Ekklesia?

250 days + 1,010 days = 1,260 Days (first half of the 2520-day Week or 7 prophetic years @ 360 days X 7 years = 2520 days

Obviously, the 1,290-days of desolations (Dan. 12:11) is 30 days beyond the total 70th Week of 2,520 days (1,260 days [3 ½ years] + 1,260 days [3 ½ years] = 2,520 days or one heptad or "70" or 7 prophetic years or 7 X 360 days (prophetic year) = 2,520 days + 30 days beyond the "Week" = 2,550 days). [Side Note: These 2,520 days are a fractal or resemblance of the Hebrew Sacred Cubit's measurement of 25.20 inches—See: Signs in the Heavens and on the Earth, Man's Days are Numbered and he is Measured, by Doug Krieger]

As the "dust clears" what I assert is simply this:

The entire 70th Week of Daniel is yet future—even Walvoord concludes this and so do most dispensational writers; however, the majority of them do not conclude the "whereabouts" of the 2,300 "evenings and mornings" (Daniel 8:26)—therein lies the rub. It is NOT in the ancient past (cir. 164 B.C. with Antiochus IV Epiphanes—exclusively) nor is it calculated in years (the 2,300 years [into the future] allegedly ending in 1844 A.D. as the SDA's affirm—which date was transferred from the Second Coming of Christ to the commencement of the "Investigative Judgment" orchestrated by Ellen G. White).

Thus, the futurity of the Abomination of Desolation which commences the 1,290 days of desolation (Dan. 12:11) is yet to be—precipitated by the Abomination of Desolation "*in the middle of the week*" (Dan. 9:27); which, in time past, was what inaugurated the Feast of Dedication itself!

Indeed, the initial Feast of Dedication celebrated the cleansing of the Temple under the Maccabee brothers—it did, in fact, take place on the 24/25th Day of the Ninth Month or on 24/25 Kislev—THAT is why we salute with HAPPY HANUKKAH—this glorious Festival of Lights in celebration, not only of the Second Temple's Re-dedication on this very date in 165 B.C. by Judas Maccabeus, but recalls that the foundation of the Second Temple was originally laid on that very day (thrice mentioned in Haggai 2:10, 17 and 20) in 536 B.C. with the Temple Dedication likewise on 24/25 Kislev in the year 515 B.C.—a span of some 350 years between 515 B.C. and 165 B.C.

It's as if the remarks in Haggai regarding Kislev 24/25's laying of the foundation for the House of the Lord in 535 B.C. FORESAW the very Feast of Dedication in 165 B.C.—some 370 years later.

Our attention, therefore, is riveted on the origins of the Feast of Dedication; its 9/24 (165 B.C.) association with the original laying of the Foundation of the Second Temple in Haggai's time (535 B.C.) and of the futurity of the Abomination of Desolation—there is an obvious association with all of these time frames bearing profound prophetic significance!

Haggai's 24/25 Kislev – "Glory of the Latter House"

First off, there can be little doubt that Kislev's 24/25 dates are directly associated with the defeat of the archetype of the Antichrist (both then and yet future—2 Thess. 2:3-12; Matthew 24:15; Mark 13:14; Revelation 9:11; 12:7-17; 13:1-18; 17:8-11).

Secondly, the "devotional" aspects of the 9/24 (Kislev 24/25—Hanukkah or Feast of Dedication) as seen three times in Haggai are given in two brief chapters wherein Haggai chides the returnees from the Babylonian Captivity, for they took care of themselves (their own houses) but did nothing to rebuild the House of the Lord; therefore this decree upon them was made by Haggai:

> *"You have sown much, and bring in little; you eat, but do not have enough; you drink, but you are not filled with drink; you clothe yourselves, but no one is warm; and he who earns wages, earns wages to put into a bag with holes ... Thus says the LORD of hosts: 'Consider your ways! Go up to the mountains and bring wood and build the temple, that I may take pleasure in it and be glorified,' says the LORD"* (Haggai 1:6-8).

Much more is said concerning Judah's indifference to the Lord's Temple ... but suffice it to say, all this corporate rebuke

So, You want to do Ekklesia?

was tempered when *"the LORD stirred up the spirit of Zerubbabel ... and the spirit of Joshua ... and the spirit of all the remnant of the people; and they came and worked on the House of the LORD of hosts, their God"* (Haggai 1:14).

We will continue our theme regarding these specific "Feast Days" in Part 2 of the next chapter and how these "days" impact the Ekklesia.

****

END NOTE #1: (Note: For those interested in Biblical *Numerics* this will be most fascinating; however, for those who feel such numeric meandering is a non-essential of the faith, feel free to leave the building—but please do so with a pleasant grin on your face; thank you.)

I felt that the sufficiency of the "70" days between Tishri 15 and Kislev 25—that is, between the High Holy Days of the fall season (harvest) and that of the Temple's Dedication (Feast of Dedication/Festival of Lights)—was able to highlight there readily could be a linkage between the two (i.e., the High Holy Days and the Feast of Dedication). There are "70" days, which "70" is a cardinal number set within Scripture (e.g., the 70 Heptad/Weeks of Daniel's prominent prophecy (Daniel 9:24-27) and the association between the Year of Jubilee's short cycle of 49 years (7 * 7 = 49 years Leviticus 25:8) or Jesus' injunction to forgive 7 * 70 = 490 – Matt. 18:21-22; and, then, there is the 70 years Babylonian Captivity (Jer. 29:10) and sending out the 70 via 2 by 2 (Luke 10:1), etc.

That said, the 3 sets of 9/24 are fascinating in that there are 8 months of 30 days or 240 days and then 24 days of the Ninth Month. Once we've determined this, it is simple to calculate that there were 3 sets of these time frames so that 240 days X 3 = 720 days and 24 days X 3 = 72 days; thus, we have two sets of "72" or 72 X 2 = 144. The "144" is a prominent number in the New Jerusalem's Wall being 144 cubits and of each of the faces of the six-

Ekklesia Replicates "Lord's Appointed Times" – Part 1

faced measurements of the "cubical" New Jerusalem in that 12,000 furlongs X 12,000 furlongs = 144,000,000 sq. furlongs or 6 sets of "144" no matter what angle one views the New Jerusalem the appearance of "144" is displayed (Ref. Rev. 21:16-17). Furthermore, in the Revelation there are two sets of 144,000 (Rev. 7; Rev. 14)

Again, if we wish to extrapolate these 72-day number sets we find that 72 days X 24 hours in a day = 1,728 hours which is 12 * 12 * 12 which, as well, can be found in the measurement (cubical) of the New Jerusalem in that 12,000 cubits X 12,000 cubits X 12,000 cubits (for its length, height, and width are the same according to Rev. 21:16) = 1,728,000,000,000 cubic furlongs or "1728."

Furthermore, we can determine that the 24th Day of the Ninth Month can be seen as 9/24 wherein if 9 and 24 are added we have: 9 + 24 = 33. The number set "33" has by this author and many others, considered to be the Savior's age at 33 years when He was "cut off" most likely in the year 33 A.D. Also, King David reigned from the City of David (Jerusalem) for 33 years (2 Sam. 5:4-5).

If we take the 3 sets of "33" we have 3 * 33 = 99. Here we are reminded of the 99 sheep and the one who was lost whereupon the Shepherd of the sheep sought the lost sheep (Matt. 18:12; Luke 15:4).

There is another most remarkable calculation which can be derived from the 9/24 in that 8 months X 30 prophetic days in a month = 240 + 24 days of the Ninth month itself or:

240 + 24 = 264 days

3 sets of 264 = 3 * 264 = 792 days

So, You want to do Ekklesia?

The "792" number set equates as a mathematical "fractal" or "resemblance" of the edge of the New Jerusalem and of the circumference of Solomon's "mystical sea of cast bronze"—as follows:

Revelation 21:16 = 12,000 furlongs X 660 ft. (one furlong = 660 ft.) = 7,920,000 linear feet or "792" which is a precise reflection of the New Jerusalem—again, validating the connection of the 9/24 Feast of Tabernacles to that of the ultimate New Jerusalem. Solomon's Laver is given as 10 cubits in diameter (1 Kings 7:23), with the circumference configured at 3.142857 (Pi); therefore, if the Hebrew Sacred Cubit is 25.20 inches (the 2520 being the number of degrees in the rotation of the earth each day or 3600 * 7 days = 25200); therefore 10 cubits X 25.20 in. = 252 inches X 3.142857 (Pi) = 792 inches (Circumference) in that the circumference of a circle is determined by D * Pi or Diameter X 3.142857 (simple Pi).

Finally, in my text on *Signs in the Heavens and on the Earth, Man's Days are Numbered and he is Measured*, the number set of "6336" is prolific in measurements throughout antiquity. When we take the 24 hours of every day and use it as a factor with the 264 days of the time frame given in the three sets of 9/24 we discover the following:

24 hours X 264 days (8 months = 240 days + 24 days of the 9th Month = 264 days) = 6,336 hours or "6336"—this numeric expression can be seen as "6...33...6" and is symbolic, I would say, of "man's" number being "6" (for on the sixth day was he, male and female created); and, of course, the "33" is the Savior's number set as previously discussed; therefore, this could readily be seen as the Savior being "cut off" between two thieves on the cross.

Likewise, it fascinates in that this "6336" if used as factors appears as follows:

Ekklesia Replicates "Lord's Appointed Times" – Part 1

6 * 3 * 3 * 6 = 324 (one set) – this "324" is the very WALL of the New Jerusalem in that 144 Cubits (Rev. 21:17) X 2.1 ft. (the length of the Hebrew Sacred Cubit of 25.20 inches ÷ 12 inches = 2.1 ft.) = 302.4 ft. wherein if the zero is removed we see the "324" appears once again.

There are a multiplicity of mathematical expressions which can be viewed from the three sets of 9/24 found in Haggai 2.

END NOTE #2: Please Note: 1 Kings 6:38 states, as well, that the Solomonic Temple took 7 years in building it [from the 4th year of Solomon's reign until the 11th year of Solomon's reign– from the month of Ziv [Ayar/Lyar around April/June] the foundation was laid unto the month of Bul/Heshvan or Cheshvan [October or November] it was finished; therefore, we must subtract from the foundation's inaugural date of 965 B.C. some 7 years+ or cir. 957 B.C. as the actual Temple Dedication date on the Gregorian Calendar . . . the establishment of the 1445 B.C. for the Passover/Law + 480 years unto the laying of the foundation of Solomon's Temple unto 965 B.C. MAY be contested; however, numerous scholars contend the 1444/1445 B.C. date to be the Passover/Exodus with the Jewish Calendar contrived in cir. 133/160 A.D. [the Seder Olam Rabbah being some 243 years deficient– i.e., it is currently not the year 5780 as of Sept. 29/30 in the Gregorian year of 2019 AD].

(RE: The absence of the 243 years—see: *Daniel Reveals the Bloodline of the Antichrist*, Jr. R. Church, 1st Edition, 2010, Prophecy Publications, Oklahoma City, OK, pp. "The Jewish Calendar's Missing Years," Appendix 1, pp. 237-254—mainly, accounting for all the Persian Kings [8 of them] is sorely absent from the Jewish Calendar.)

One would add to 5780 A.M. (in 2019 A.D.) + 243 years = **6023 years** (since Adam's creation) meaning that if man were given 6,000 years, then the Jewish Calendar is some 23 years beyond 6,000 years which comports to Bishop James Ussher's calendar

So, You want to do Ekklesia?

of 4004 B.C. to the present of 2019 A.D. in which the total is: 4004 + 2019 = **6023 years** or, again, some 23 years beyond the 6,000 years—meaning the creation of Adam had to have been somewhere cir. 3975 B.C., not 4004 B.C. Could it be that if Adam's creation date was in 3975 B.C. + 2019 AD = 5,994 years; meaning, we could be within six years of the end of "man's days."

In my study of the calculations of the generations of the Patriarchs, I can account for 21 of them from Adam to Isaac, Son of Promise, and some 2,100 years from Adam's Creation until the reception of the Promise made to Isaac in Genesis 26:1-6 at the age of 52, having twins (Esau and Jacob) when Isaac was 60 years of (Gen. 25:26)—there were 430 years from the Promise made to Isaac until the Passover (Ex. 12:40-41; Gal. 3:15-18). Thus, 2,100 years + 430 years = 2,530 years from Adam to the first Passover. Therefore, if the first Passover was in the year 1445 BC, we would add 2,530 years to this date or 1445 BC + 2,530 years = 3975 BC (the year of Adam's Creation). Thus, again: 3975 BC + 2019 AD = 5,994 Years—in sum, we appear to be "running out of time!"

Chapter 11:
Ekklesia Replicates "Lord's Appointed Times" – Part 2

Figure 66 - KING SOLOMON DEDICATES THE FIRST TEMPLE

9/24 Amplified in Latter House Dedication

AND, ALTHOUGH THE SECOND TEMPLE WAS ALTOGETHER INFERIOR TO SOLOMON'S MAJESTIC FIRST TEMPLE, THE LORD SO ENCOURAGED HIS "TWO Sons of Oil" (Zerubbabel the Governor and Joshua the High Priest—Haggai 2:4) that He declared this far-reaching prophecy regarding the ultimate manifestation of the Holy District and New Jerusalem's Temple/House as seen in Ezekiel 40-48 and Revelation 21; to wit:

> *"For thus says the LORD of hosts; 'Once more (it is a little while) I will shake heaven and earth, the sea and dry land; and I will shake all nations, and they shall come to the **DESIRE OF ALL NATIONS**, and I will fill this*

temple (house) with glory,' says the LORD of hosts. The silver is Mine, and the gold is Mine,' says the LORD of hosts. **The glory of this latter temple (house) shall be greater than the former**,' says the LORD of hosts. 'And in this place I will give PEACE; says the LORD of hosts'" (Haggai 2:6-9).

Figure 67 - GLORY OF THIS LATTER HOUSE - GREATER THAN THE FORMER

This is a marvelous prophecy—it does NOT refer to the Second Temple, nor the glory of Solomon's Temple nor of Herod's "redo" of the Second Temple—but of the ultimate manifestation of the Oneness of His people who shall constitute the very Temple of the Lord—this is the PEACE, the Good News of the Gospel of Peace which would ultimately resound in the bringing together of the TWO (both Jew/Judah and Ephraim/Gentile) to be ONE NEW MAN—SO MAKING PEACE through the "blood of His cross"— THE DESIRE OF ALL NATIONS, our Lord Jesus Christ, HAS COME . . . for we read:

*"For **He Himself is our peace**, who has made both one, and has broken down the middle wall of separation . . . that He might reconcile them both to God in one body through the cross . . . and He came and preached peace to you who were afar off and to those who were near. Now, therefore, you are no longer strangers and foreigners, but fellow citizens with the saints and members of the HOUSEHOLD OF GOD, having been built on the foundation of the apostles and prophets, Jesus Christ Himself being the chief cornerstone, in whom the whole building, being fitted together, grows into a HOLY TEMPLE in the Lord, in whom you also are being built together for a DWELLING PLACE OF GOD IN THE SPIRIT"* (Eph. 2:14-22, excerpts).

And again . . .

"Yet once, it is a little while, and I will shake the heavens, and the earth . . . I will shake all nations . . . and I will fill this house with glory" (Haggai 2:6-7).

And the prophecy is repeated in Hebrews 12:26-29:

"Yet once more I shake not the earth only, but also heaven. *And this word, Yet once more, signifies the removing of those things that are shaken, as of things that are made, that those things which cannot be shaken may remain. Wherefore we receiving a Kingdom which cannot be moved, let us have grace, whereby we may serve God acceptably with reverence and godly fear: for our God is a consuming fire."*

No, this is NOT far-fetched—this is God's ULTIMATE INTENTION and PURPOSE! This is the *"Glory of the Latter House shall be greater than the former!"*

"Behold the TABERNACLE OF GOD is with men, and He will dwell with them, and they shall be His people. God Himself

will be with them and be their God . . . But I saw NO TEMPLE IN IT [i.e., the Holy City, New Jerusalem], *for the Lord God Almighty and the Lamb are its temple"* (Rev. 21:3, 22).

This is the eternal relationship wrought between YHWH and His people for eternity! This has always been His Eternal Purpose:

"I will set My tabernacle among you . . . I will walk among you and be your God, and you shall be My people" (Lev. 26:11-12);

"But this is the covenant that I will make with the house of Israel after those days, says the LORD: I will put My law in their minds, and write it on their hearts; and I will be their God, and they shall be My people" (Jer. 31:33);

"'Thus they shall know that I, the LORD their God, am with them, and they, the house of Israel, are My people,' says the Lord God. 'You are My flock, the flock of My pasture; you are men, and I am your God,' says the Lord God" (Ezk. 34:30-31);

"My tabernacle also shall be with them; indeed, I will be their God, and they shall be My people. The nations also will know that I, the LORD, sanctify Israel, when My sanctuary is in their midst forevermore" (Ezk. 37:27-28)

It is after the Lord's final statement: *"'And in this place I will give peace,' says the LORD of hosts"* (Hag. 2:9) that the three 9/24s are mentioned in Haggai 2—connecting the Feast of a future Feast of Dedication with the Temple and its association with the Antichrist archetype, Antiochus IV Epiphanes (which automatically connects to the final Antichrist who *"shall sit in the Temple declaring himself as God in the Temple of God"* as found in 2 Thess. 2), before the final Feast of Dedication is celebrated, I believe, prior to the Millennium and the manifestation of the Holy District with Holy City found in Ezekiel 40-48 whereby the fulfillment of this prophecy found in Daniel 9:24 shall come to fruition: *"To seal up vision and prophecy, and to ANOINT THE MOST HOLY PLACE"* (which is His Temple and Messiah in absolute union).

Jesus at Feast of Dedication vs. Antichrist

In John's gospel (John 10:22-42) Jesus declares: *"I and My Father are one"* (vs. 30). By this He declared His divinity. He was NOT saying, as some ignorantly extrapolate "I and My Father are in agreement!" The Father and the Son agree but more so: The Father and the Son are ONE! Jesus came to the Temple and declared this:

> *"Now it was the **Feast of Dedication** in Jerusalem, and it was winter (24/25 Kislev—the ninth month is always around the Gregorian Christmas time). And Jesus walked in the TEMPLE, in Solomon's porch . . . then the Jews surrounded Him and said to Him, 'How long do You keep us in doubt* (lit *"suspense")? If You are the Christ, tell us plainly.'"* (John 10:22-24).

The Jewish leadership (religious) obviously knew the implications of the Lord's statement: *"I and My Father are one."* For we read:

> *"The Jews answered Him, saying, 'For a good work we do not stone You, but for blasphemy, and because You, being a Man, MAKE YOURSELF GOD.'"* (John 10:33).

Please notice—not "equal with God" but "make yourself God!" Dancing around reinterpretations of the text is naught but eisogesis to the extreme—how else can one interpret Jesus' final statement recorded by John in Solomon's Porch, in the temple: ". . . *believe that the Father is in Me, and I in Him"* (John 10:38). It was shortly thereafter that Jesus raised Lazarus from the dead—

So, You want to do Ekklesia?

that WORK was incomparable to all His other works during His earthly ministry . . . and many believed in Him (John 11).

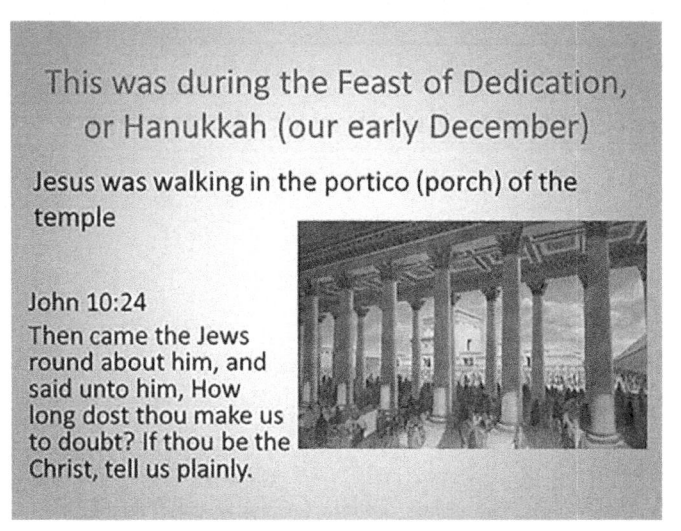

> This was during the Feast of Dedication, or Hanukkah (our early December)
>
> Jesus was walking in the portico (porch) of the temple
>
> John 10:24
> Then came the Jews round about him, and said unto him, How long dost thou make us to doubt? If thou be the Christ, tell us plainly.

Figure 68 - JOHN 10:24

What we have here is **JESUS DECLARING HIMSELF AS GOD IN THE TEMPLE OF GOD!** That is precisely what Satan incarnate into the spirit of the Antichrist shall do. Thus, the Man of Sin will be revealed as the Son of Perdition, the Lawless One who with at his coming shall perform:

> "... according to the working of Satan, with all power, signs, and lying wonders, and with all unrighteous deception among those who perish, because they did not receive the love of the truth, that they might be saved" (Ref. 2 Thess. 2:3-10) . . . and as "Satan entered into Judas, surnamed Iscariot, who was numbered among the twelve" (Luke 22:3) . . .

. . . to commit his dastardly deed of betrayal, even so shall Satan enter into the body/temple of the Antichrist and commit not only the desecration of a rebuilt Temple in Jerusalem but the desecration of the human spirit—from thenceforth this final Antichrist shall be entitled THE BEAST, for a beast cannot fellowship with the Living God—for a beast is NOT made in the image of God . . . animals have no spirit.

And where shall this Abomination of Desolation transpire?

". . . the Son of Perdition, who opposes and exalts himself above all that is called God or that is worshiped, so that he sits as God in the temple of God, showing himself that he is God" (2 Thess. 2:3-4).

This understanding of Jesus' divinity took place at the Feast of Dedication—Kislev 24/25.

Feast of Tabernacles Tied to Feast of Dedication

Yes, both the Feast of Tabernacles—the dedication of the Solomonic Temple in the year 958/957 BC (some 7 years in its building and being completed in the eleventh year of King Solomon's reign—2 Chron. 3:2; 1 Kings 6:1, 37-38--i.e., between 965 B.C. [480 years after the first Passover in Egypt in 1445 BC unto 965 BC in the fourth year of King Solomon's reign] and 958 BC (7 years in building from 965 BC unto 958 BC) and the ultimate Feast of Tabernacles celebrated at the dedication of the Solomonic Temple in 958/7 BC . . . AND . . . the Feast of Dedication celebrated in 165 BC on 24/25 Kislev (the 24/25th Day of the Ninth Month) and connected by the Prophet Haggai . . . thus, we must see the New Testament's "spiritual implications" recording of Jesus at the Feast of Tabernacles!

In John 7:2-39 the Triune God—Father, Son and Spirit are revealed. The ultimate revelation centers on these passages:

*"Now about the **middle of the feast** Jesus went up into the temple and taught . . . On the last day, that great day of the feast* [the Feast of Tabernacles' Seventh Day of the Feast], *Jesus stood and cried out, saying, 'If anyone thirsts, let him come to Me and drink. He who believes in Me, as the Scripture has said, out of his innermost being will flow rivers of living water.' But this He spoke concerning the Spirit, whom those believing in Him would receive for the Holy Spirit was not yet given, because Jesus was not yet glorified"* (John 7:14, 37-39).

So, You want to do Ekklesia?

I bring to our attention Jesus' arrival at the Feast of Tabernacles *"about the **MIDDLE OF THE FEAST**."* Why? Because this was a seven-day feast and He did not show up until "the middle of the week" (7 days or at the mid-point at 3 1/2 days). Is this somehow a reflection of both the final week of Daniel's 70th Week and, as well, of our Lord's 3 1/2 years of earthly ministry?

Is this a possible reflection of the very Passion Week in which from Nisan 10–His Triumphal Entry into Jerusalem on Palm Sunday unto His crucifixion on Nisan 13, Passover Preparation Day–Wednesday (morning) or 3 1/2 days of the Week–i.e. Sunday (morning only); Monday Evening/Morning; Tuesday Evening/Morning; Wednesday Evening/Morning unto Nisan 13/14–and from thence, Thursday Passover Evening/Morning; Friday Evening/Morning; Saturday Evening/Morning; Sunday (evening only) unto Nisan 17–thus, 3 1/2 days for a complete 7 days total or one week?

I believe so–for when Jesus came mid-way during the 7-day Feast of Tabernacles He was declaring his opposition to Satan's inhabiting the spirit of the Antichrist (as well) by declaring that at the end of the 3 1/2 days left in the Feast of Tabernacles (i.e., at the end of 7-days) He would shortly be glorified and from thence, all who would believe into Him would receive the Holy Spirit and all the Promise of fellowship within the Triune God!

Whereas Satan would "enter into the body/temple of the Antichrist" akin to that of entering into Judas Iscariot (Luke 22:3)– deadening the spirit of man–this same Jesus, when glorified, would declare: *"If anyone thirsts, let him come to Me and drink . . . out of his innermost being* (the spirit of man) *will flow rivers of living water . . . He spoke concerning the Spirit"* (John 7:37-39).

DEATH vs. LIFE and life more abundantly! That is precisely why Jesus participated first in John 7 at the Feast of Tabernacles as the Life-giving Spirit and secondly, at the Feast of Dedication to declare His Divinity in the Temple of God which Temple today we are! Thus, the Life-Giving Spirit of Christ resides in His Holy Temple–His Life infuses the Temple of the Lord, the Latter House with GLORY–for He is glorified in His saints! Even His ultimate glory: "*On the day He comes to be glorified in His saints*" (2 Thess. 1:10; Eph. 3:21–"*Unto Him be glory in the Ekklesia*").

Thus, will the future Antichrist present himself "in the middle of the week" of Daniel's yet future Seventieth Week in the Temple of God, declaring that he is God at some future Feast of Tabernacles, Nations, Weeks? This desecration of the spirit of Antichrist wherein his entitlement is transformed to that of "the Beast" (in the middle of the week) is most striking in contrast to the Life-Giving Spirit of Christ! (Ref. Revelation 13)

Thus, Christ's visitation at the Feast of Tabernacles in the middle of the week (John 7:14) is a super-abundant contrast between the Abomination of Desolation "in the middle of the week" (the manifestation of the Beast) versus the 3 ½ days unto the terminus of the 7-day Feast of Tabernacles (the 3 ½ days akin to the 3 ½ years of Jesus' earthly ministry) resulting in the regeneration of the human spirit from whence as the Holy Spirit of Promise (John 7:39) outflowing from the human spirit "rivers of living water" (John 7:38) were promised.

What is Haggai Really Saying?

Now, with the aforementioned remarks as a backdrop, the THREE uses of the **Twenty-fourth Day of the Ninth Month** (date of the Feast of Dedication) made by Haggai in Haggai chapter 2 take on profound consequence:

> "*10 On the **twenty-fourth day of the ninth month**, in the second year of Darius, the word of the Lord came by Haggai the prophet, 11 "Thus says the Lord of hosts: Ask the priests about the law: 12 'If someone carries holy meat in the fold of his garment and touches with his fold bread or stew or wine or oil or any kind of food, does it become holy?'" The priests answered and said, "No." 13 Then Haggai said, "If someone who is unclean by contact with a dead body touches any of these, does it become unclean?" The priests answered and said, "It does become unclean." 14 Then Haggai answered and said, "So is it with this people, and with this*

nation before me, declares the Lord, and so with every work of their hands. And what they offer there is unclean." (Haggai 2:10-14)

At issue here is the defilement of the people of Judah who have returned—they were condemned by Haggai for their mixture. The "holy" and the "profane" were NOT separated—neither were they. Because they were contaminated by these mixtures "*every work of their hands; and what they offer there is unclean*" (Hag. 2:14).

It is a sad commentary upon God's people who "offer unto the Lord" that which has become unclean. Yes, it starts out as "holy meat" and kept from anything dead—but then the Lord's servants contaminate the holy with the profane and vainly attempt to offer it unto the Lord . . . but now it is UNCLEAN!

Yes, you have received the "holy meat" as from the Lord but then you place it in the "*fold of your garment*" and then the "*edge*" of that garment "*touches bread or stew, wine or oil, or any food*" and you think that by so touching you can make these items "holy"? Answers the priest: NO!

No, because the SELF has gotten into the mix and destroyed the purity of the message. The message is pure, but the vessel conveying it is impure—and everything that "selfish garment" touches will be considered unholy for it was NOT holy to begin with! We think that since we bear "holy meat" that everything we touch will somehow bear witness to the original "holy meat"—but such "transference" is contrary to the work of the Holy Spirit. We cannot distribute holiness akin to a commodity. Sanctification is the work of the Holy Spirit—it is not gained by osmosis or "being around" someone . . . it is sanctified by the Holy Spirit of God and cannot be contaminated by the flesh, nor by the *soulish* man.

Be aware, God Almighty has been known to speak through Balaam's ass! His preference is to speak through you and me—but is the vessel out of whom He pours His Living Water prepared for the Master? Sure, we can offer all we want—"*and what they offer there is unclean.*"

*15 Now then, consider from this day onward. Before stone was placed upon stone in the temple of the Lord, 16 how did you fare? When one came to a heap of twenty measures, there were but ten. When one came to the wine vat to draw fifty measures, there were but twenty. 17 I struck you and all the products of your toil with blight and with mildew and with hail, yet you did not turn to me, declares the Lord. 18 Consider from this day onward, **from the twenty-fourth day of the ninth month**. Since the day that the foundation of the Lord's temple was laid, consider: 19 Is the seed yet in the barn? Indeed, the vine, the fig tree, the pomegranate, and the olive tree have yielded nothing. But from this day on I will bless you."* (Haggai 2:15-19)

Now, the "TEMPLE OF THE LORD" (vs. 15) comes into view. We are to consider the "diminishing results" of our own futility because we have not taken to heart the Temple of the Lord . . . and we must consider this in light of *"The glory of this latter temple shall be greater than the former"* . . . for *"In this place I will give peace"* (Hag. 2:9).

Again, NOT to extrapolate this to the ONENESS (peace) of God's people—the ultimate TEMPLE, the foundation, place of ONENESS with the Almighty—well, in a word, one is simply spiritually MYOPIC!

FOCUS:

"The latter house shall be greater than the former" (Hag. 2:9) . . . For *"From the day that the foundation of the LORD'S temple was laid—consider it"* (Hag. 2:18).

Indeed:

"For no other foundation can anyone lay than that which is laid, which is Jesus Christ" (1 Cor. 3:11) . . . *"Having been built on the foundation of the apostles and prophets, Jesus Christ Himself being the chief cornerstone, in whom the whole*

building, being fitted together, grows into a HOLY TEMPLE IN THE LORD, in whom you also are being built together for a dwelling place of God in the Spirit" (Eph. 2:20-22).

It is only then that our barns shall be filled; only then will there be an abundant yield of fruit ... ***BUT FROM THIS DAY (9/24) I WILL BLESS YOU.***

Really, do you actually think without the laying of the foundation there can be any blessing? Is it possible, without standing together upon such a foundation being laid in Zion—signaling our ONENESS IN MESSIAH, in His One Body (the "latter house") that there can be any blessing? It is only when we take this definitive stand with His People—FOR THE LORD—that we hear: *"from this day I will bless you."* What day? *"Consider now from this day forward, FROM THE TWENTY-FOURTH DAY OF THE NINTH MONTH . . . from the DAY that the foundation of the LORD'S temple was laid—CONSIDER IT!"*

How many of us have labored "outside of this reality"—outside the Temple—we have built upon false foundations, sadly so, "wood, hay, and stubble" and not "gold, silver, precious stones"— why? Because even that which we have built upon and the materials we have utilized have been incapable of building the House of the Lord IN SPIRIT—these temporal items will be BURNED on that day.

Is the Seed still in the Barn?

Before we move to the final 9/24 (the third in the set of 9/24s), we must:

> *"'Consider now from this day forward, from the **twenty-fourth day of the ninth month,** from the day that the foundation of the LORD's temple was laid–CONSIDER IT: **IS THE SEED STILL IN THE BARN?** As yet the vine, the fig tree, the pomegranate, and the olive tree have not yielded fruit. But from this day I will bless you.'"* (Haggai 2:18-19)

It is abundantly clear that since the prophetic vision given through the prophet Haggai pinpoints *"the glory of this latter house* (lit. Temple) *shall be greater than the former . . . and in this place I will give peace"* (Hag. 2:9) it, therefore, bespeaks beyond the laying of the foundation of the Second Temple–it projects into the future reality: *"Unto Him be glory in the Ekklesia by Christ Jesus to all generations, forever and ever, Amen"* (Eph. 3:21) . . . with BOTH foundations linked!

In Ephesians 3:1-20 the great Mystery concerning the Messiah (the Christ) and His Ekklesia (aka, "the Church") is amplified:

"That the Nations (aka, the Gentiles) *should be fellow heirs, of the same body, and partakers of His promise in Christ through the gospel . . . that I should preach among the Gentiles the unsearchable riches of Christ, and to make all see what is the DISPENSATION OF THE MYSTERY, which from the beginning of the ages has been hidden in God who created all things through Jesus Christ; to the intent that now the manifold wisdom of God might be made known by the EKKLESIA to the principalities and powers in the heavenly places, according to the ETERNAL PURPOSE which He accomplished in Christ Jesus our Lord"* (Eph. 3:1-12, excerpts).

This is the LATTER HOUSE–GREATER THAN THE FORMER . . . This is the bringing together of Judah and Ephraim/the Nations. Therefore: IS THE SEED STILL IN THE BARN?

No, EACH ONE HAS been given a portion of the "riches of the land"–There are vine seeds, fig tree seeds, pomegranate seeds, and olive tree "seeds"–they cannot yield their fruit aside from being on this **foundation**! Brethren don't leave your seeds in the barn–bring them forth–plant vineyards, orchards–your seeds need to yield fruit that remains! This is the LATTER-GREATER HOUSE!

So, You want to do Ekklesia?

> **20** *And again the word of the Lord came to Haggai on* **the twenty-fourth day of the month***, saying,*
>
> **21** *"Speak to Zerubbabel, governor of Judah, saying: 'I will shake heaven and earth'*
>
> **22** *'I will overthrow the throne of kingdoms;*
> *I will destroy the strength of the Gentile kingdoms.*
> *I will overthrow the chariots*
> *And those who ride in them;*
> *The horses and their riders shall come down,*
> *Everyone by the sword of his brother.*
>
> **23** *'In that day,' says the Lord of hosts, 'I will take you, Zerubbabel My servant, the son of Shealtiel,' says the Lord, 'and will make you like a signet ring; for I have chosen you,' says the Lord of hosts."* (Haggai 2:20-23)

Yes, now the fruit of blessing pours forth from the Almighty—we (Zerubbabel, the governor of Judah) is/are expressing the KINGDOM. This IS Kingdom Living at its utmost! All authority is given to them who will take such a stand with the LORD OF HOSTS. He repeats Haggai 2:6:

> *"Once more (it is a little while) I will shake heaven and earth, the sea and dry land; and I will shake all nations, and they shall come to the DESIRE OF ALL NATIONS (Messiah) and I will fill this TEMPLE WITH GLORY."*

Do we see it? *"I will overthrow the throne of kingdoms; I will destroy the strength of the Gentile kingdoms . . . I will make you like a SIGNET RING; for I have chosen you"* (Hag. 2:22-23).

Why would the Almighty commit such divine authority to Zerubbabel (representing the Kingship)? Why would He give such as to overthrow kingdoms—destroy the strength of the Gentile kingdoms? Why would he place the SIGNET RING upon Zerubbabel? Because He chose him? More so, I believe, because

Zerubbabel is upon the right foundation—the TEMPLE OF THE LORD!

The SIGNET, normally placed in a ring, is used as a STAMP OF OWNERSHIP and is used instead of or with a signature to give authentication to an official document. Zerubbabel is given authority to place the SIGNET RING of the Almighty upon that which he would declare as His/his own! This is MY SIGNATURE . . . My ownership . . . My Kingdom!

The SIGNET upon the head of Joshua, the High Priest, bears the very NAME OF YHWH!

That same SIGNET, as we later view, is placed in the frontal of the three braided crowns placed, not upon Zerubbabel's head, but upon the head of Joshua, the High Priest—the other, of the "two sons of oil" (Zerubbabel, the Governor . . . and Joshua, the High Priest).

> *"Take the silver and the gold, make an elaborate crown* (lit. *"crowns"), and set it on the head of Joshua the son of Jehozadak, the high priest . . . 'Behold, the Man whose name is the BRANCH! From His place He shall branch out, and He SHALL BUILD THE TEMPLE OF THE LORD, Yes, He shall build the temple of the LORD. He* (Joshua, the High Priest) *shall bear the glory, and shall sit and rule on His throne; so He shall be a priest on His throne, and the counsel of peace shall be between both offices* (Kingship and Priesthood) *. . . Now the ELABORATE CROWN shall be for a memorial in the temple of the LORD . . . even those from afar shall come and build the temple of the LORD"* (Zechariah 6:11-14).

The SIGNET is so profound and its association with BOTH the Kingship and Priesthood (Zerubbabel and Joshua) breathtaking, because it so overtly declares the personage of the Messiah of whom we read in the Revelation:

> *And his eyes are a flame of fire, and upon his head are many diadems; and he hath a name written which no one knoweth but he himself.* (ASV – Rev. 19:11)

So, You want to do Ekklesia?

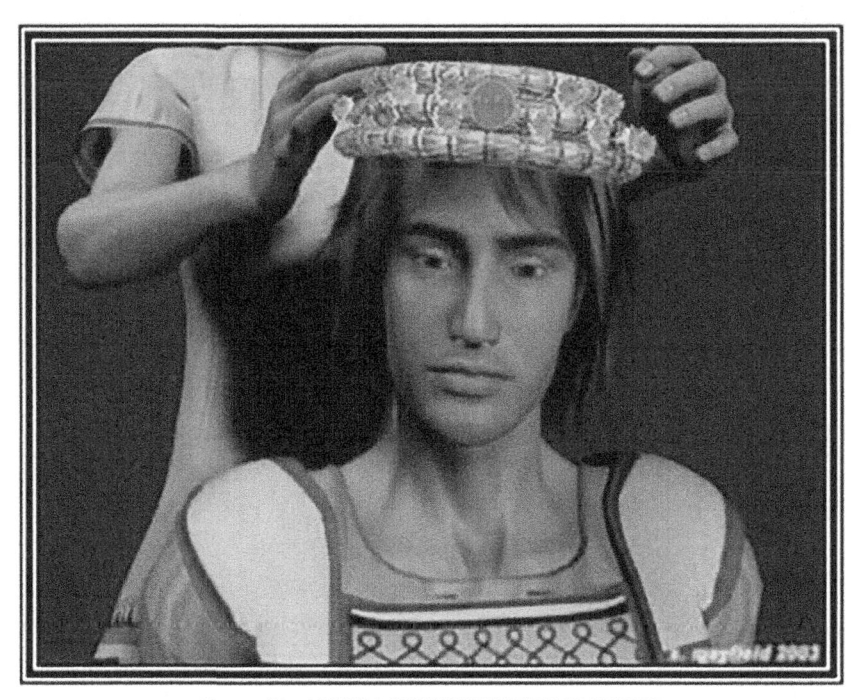

Figure 69 - JOSHUA THE HIGH PRIEST CROWNED

The King of kings, and Lord of lords, yea, **THE DESIRE OF ALL NATIONS**, unto Him shall all the nations of the earth come! He is our KING-PRIEST—our Melchizedek:

> *This Melchizedek was **king of Salem** and **priest of God Most High**. He met Abraham returning from the defeat of the kings and blessed him, 2 and Abraham gave him a tenth of everything. First, the name Melchizedek means "**king of righteousness**"; then also, "**king of Salem**" means "**king of peace.**" 3 Without father or mother, without genealogy, without beginning of days or end of life, **resembling the Son of God**, he remains **a priest forever**.* (Hebrews 7:1-3 NIV)

But He bears the TRIPLE CROWN—for not only is He our King-Priest (our Melchizedek; and, as well, Zerubbabel/Joshua), He stands in the midst of His People—in the midst of the Seven

Golden Lampstands (Revelation 1), as the BOWL in the midst of the Two Sons of Oil (Zechariah 4), pouring His anointing oil into their offices—for He is our PROPHET—He is our PROPHET, PRIEST AND KING—THE TRIPLE CROWN!

These be the meaning of the three sets of 9/24s found in Haggai surrounding the Feast of Dedication of the Temple, the Foundation, the Priest-King and the Triple Crown with Signet thereon—TO GOD BE THE GLORY . . . may our spirits be stirred up by the Holy Spirit to FOCUS, CONSIDER IT—all of IT!

Alas! This IS a fight to the finish line—but He:

"Will shake all nations, and they shall come to the DESIRE OF ALL NATIONS . . . and I will fill this temple with glory,' says the LORD of hosts" (Hag. 2:7). Yes, *"The Man, whose name is BRANCH, He shall bear the GLORY . . . From His place He shall branch out, and He shall build the temple of the LORD"* (Zech. 6:12-13).

Laboring on the "Good Land" = Surplus of Christ

It is of "Calendric Interest" to this author regarding the following on the Hebrew Sacred Calendar:

Nisan 10 - Joshua 4:19:

*"Now the people came up from the Jordan on the **tenth day of the first month** [now the Month of Nisan]"*

Nisan 10 - Ezekiel 40:1-2:

*"In the twenty-fifth year of our captivity, at **the beginning of the year** [the month of Nisan—beginning of the religious year—for Ezekiel was a priest himself], on the tenth day of the month, in the fourteenth year after the city was captured* [586 B.C. less 14 years = 572 B.C. or 608 B.C. to 538 B.C. = 70 years of captivity, so 608 B.C. to 572 B.C. = 36 years or 34 years unto 538 B.C.] , *on the very same day the hand of the LORD, was upon me; and He took me there,*

So, You want to do Ekklesia?

> *in the visions of God He took me into the land of Israel and set me on a very high mountain; on it toward the south was something like the structure of a city."*

Nisan 10—Zechariah 9:9-10; Matthew 21-22; Mark 11-12; Luke 19-20; John 12 (Reading from Zechariah 9:9-10 concerning Messiah's First and Second Comings and from John 12 only):

"'Rejoice greatly, O daughter of Zion! Shout, O daughter of Jerusalem! Behold, your King is coming to you; He is just and having salvation, lowly and riding on a donkey, a colt, the foal of a donkey.

"I will cut off the chariot from Ephraim and the horse from Jerusalem; the battle bow shall be cut off. He shall speak peace to the nations; His dominion shall be from sea to sea, and from the River to the ends of the earth.'"

"Then, six days before the Passover [Note: Passover evening at 6:00 P.M. on Wednesday/Thursday or on 14 Nisan], *Jesus came to Bethany, where Lazarus was who had been dead, whom He had raised from the dead* [NOTE: We must count back from Wednesday 13 Nisan; Tuesday, 12 Nisan; Monday, 11 Nisan; **Sunday, 10 Nisan**; Saturday, 9 Nisan; Friday, 8 Nisan—this would been 6 days before the Passover on 14 Nisan or Nisan 8, 9, 10, 11, 12, 13 and then 14 Nisan being the Passover—Jesus came to Bethany, where Lazarus was, to celebrate the Passover on Friday day (morning portion) and by that evening of 9 Nisan it was Saturday, the Sabbath)—NOTE: Any portion of the "morning/day" constitutes a 12-hour time frame—this is precisely why Jesus drew our attention to this 12 hours by stating in John 11:9: *"Jesus answered, 'Are there not twelve hours in the day?"*

The children of Israel crossed the Jordan River on 10 Nisan; Ezekiel saw the vision of the Holy City/Holy District (Ezk. 40-48) on 10 Nisan; and the Triumphal Entry of Jesus into Jerusalem (aka Palm Sunday) took place on 10 Nisan. How are these three events not connected?

Ekklesia Replicates "Lord's Appointed Times" – Part 2

The Land of Canaan is referred to as the "Good Land" (Ex. 3:8; Num. 14:7-9; Deut. 8:7) as found in the Hebrew Scriptures; however, in the Christian Scriptures we find that the **"Good Land"** (aka, "Entering into **His REST**"—Hebrews 3:11, 18; 4:1, 3, 5, 8-11) is an abundantly clear picture of Christ Himself upon we, as believers in Yeshua (Jesus), are called to labor—to secure the produce of the land:

> *"Therefore, since a promise remains of **entering His rest**, let us fear lest any of you seem to have come short of it. For indeed the gospel was preached to us as well as to them; but the word which they heard did not profit them, not being mixed with faith in those who heard it. **For we who have believed do enter that rest**, as He has said: 'So I swore in My wrath, They shall not enter My rest,' although the works were finished from the foundation of the world . . . **there remains therefore a rest for the people of God.** For he who **has entered His rest** has himself also ceased from his works as God did from His . . . Let us therefore be diligent to **enter that rest**, lest anyone fall according to the same example of disobedience"* (Hebrews 4:1-11, Excerpts).

Once believers have entered into the "Good Land"—into "His rest"—then the "manna and the quail" will cease:

> *"And they ate of the produce of the land on the day after the Passover, unleavened bread and parched grain, on the very same day. Then the manna ceased on the day after they had eaten the produce of the land; and the children of Israel no longer had manna, but they ate the food of the land of Canaan that year"* (Joshua 5:11-12).

It is altogether obvious, in order for the Good Land (Christ, our Rest) to continue to produce sustenance—the land must be "worked" and/or labored upon . . . no labor, no sustenance! THIS is what the Feasts of the Lord—the "Lord's Appointed Times" were all about—a CELEBRATION of harvests—OUR EXPERIENCE OF

CHRIST AS OUR REST—wrought by earnest labor upon the Good Land where Christ is one's Passover—derived from the Land; Christ is our Feast of Unleavened Bread, without sin or any such mixture; we bring to the Feast of First Fruits of His resurrection Life in our lives to the Feast; we celebrate the Feast of Weeks/Pentecost as a great harvest festival in the late spring; and finally, the three final feast days of the Feast of Trumpets, Day of Atonement and Feast of Tabernacles in the fall season. These are the "Lord's Appointed Times"—they are intrinsically connected to our "Ekklesia experience" as brethren bring the harvest of their experience with Christ, for EACH ONE HAS!

He Shall Bear the Glory

Allow me to expand upon the Man, Whose Name is BRANCH:

"I am the True Vine, and My Father is the vine-dresser. Every branch in Me that does not bear fruit He takes away; and every branch that bears fruit He prunes, that it may bear more fruit . . . abide in Me, and I in you. As the branch cannot bear fruit of itself, unless it abides in the vine, neither can you, unless you abide in Me. I am the vine, you are the branches. He who abides in Me, and I in him, bears much fruit; for without Me you can do nothing . . . By this My Father is glorified, that you bear much fruit; so you will be My disciples" ([John 15:1-8](), Excerpts).

This IS the where the Man, Whose Name is BRANCH—Who bears the Glory—then the Father is glorified when we, His disciples, abide in Him Whose Name is BRANCH and bear MUCH FRUIT. Therefore, how much more is this confession of Who He is and how He will defeat His enemy?

"'You are the Christ (Messiah), the Son of the living God' . . . **'And I also say to you that you are Peter, and on this rock I will build My Ekklesia, and the gates of Hades shall not prevail against it'"** ([Matt. 16:16, 18]())

Ekklesia Replicates "Lord's Appointed Times" – Part 2

Allow me to conclude by saying: Joshua entered the Good Land—but to secure the Good Land, the Rest, there was the "taking of the Good Land"—the battle for the Land! If we are going to labor upon the land, to gain experiences of the Lord to bring to the Feast, today's corporate feast—the Ekklesia of the Lord—then we must come to grips with "fighting the good fight" of faith. Likewise, we must come to terms with fighting such a "fight" as His Corporate Body (Eph. 6). You don't "take the land" by yourself—but with others in the Body of Christ! That's what we see in Joshua on 10 Nisan—they crossed on over the Jordan together with the Ark of the Covenant in the midst of the Jordan River.

Then, Ezekiel saw the Holy District/Holy City on 10 Nisan—THAT is what God's ultimate plan and purpose for the ages is all about. Today, we are the "Temple of the Lord" with the "ultimate manifestation" of God's eternal plan and purpose witnessed in the New Jerusalem (from heaven) and the Holy District (from the earth)—the New Jerusalem is this glorious "heaven and earth" manifestation of multi-dimensional glory!

Finally, His Triumphal Entry into Jerusalem on 10 Nisan bears His Witness: THE TESTIMONY OF JESUS, which is the very spirit of prophecy. We find that Zechariah 9:9-10 is recorded in all the gospels—it speaks of the First AND Second Comings of the Messiah. Verse 10 of Zechariah 9 speaks of His First coming and Zechariah 9:10 speaks of His Second Coming where the King's *"dominion shall be from sea to sea and from the River to the ends of the earth."* The Lamb of God was slain for us and our salvation in Zechariah 9:9 and is the Worthy Lamb yet to come to manifest His Dominion in Zechariah 9:10.

HAPPY NEW YEAR
&
HAPPY HANUKKAH

So, You want to do Ekklesia?

Chapter 12:
This is Not an Ekklesia – Part 1

Figure 70 - "MOM, DON'T TELL ME HOW TO DRIVE--I'M IN CONTROL!"

Backseat Drivers?

I'VE REPEATEDLY BEEN ASKED: WHAT DOES AN EKKLESIA (OR "ECCLESIA") LOOK LIKE? MAY I BE A BIT MORE AMBIGUOUS? SHOULDN'T AN EKKLESIA look a lot like my ministry? ANSWER: No. What about looking like brother so-and-so's ministry: ANSWER: No. Frankly, it shouldn't look like any person's ministry—It's not of Paul, of Peter, of Apollos, and not even "of Christ" (for the "spiritually discerning" types). But aren't these gifted ones rather obvious figures whose ministries have had amazing impact upon the overall Body of Christ, and shouldn't we honor them? Of course, to deny they exist is foolhardy—but once we come into an Ekklesia experience these beloved brethren must take a back seat.

Now, get this—they're still in the car—but they're not driving the Ekklesia. "No backseat driving allowed!" The Ecclesia's Driver is the Holy Spirit—no one-man's ministry drives it. I

So, You want to do Ekklesia?

know this analogy will infuriate some as too evasive: Yes, it should look like Christ; however, its essence looks a whole lot more like "spiritual democracy in action."

Sometimes—and I think this is one of those times—it's better to explain the negative, as in: Ekklesia isn't happening if the following elements are festering within those assembled. As we expose the negative, we might illuminate the positive!

Figure 71 - KEEP CALM AND SUBMIT TO MY AUTHORITY

Submit or Else ... or Else What?

"It's starring you right in the face!" "But I can't see it because I have a predisposition to follow the leader ... no matter where it leads (at times) because this ONE seems to know where they're going; and, since I don't, I may as well keep following someone who is so assertive ... well, I could go on, but this guy's utterly convinced me he's on the right train and if I don't get on board, I'll miss it!"

If you find yourself impressed by so-and-so's ministry and tend to follow that person around because you've gotten and keep on getting (as far as you are concerned) help from following that sterling apostle, oracle, prophet, evangelist, pastor, teacher, etc.—fine, all well and good, but be careful, be VERY careful, having UNQUESTIONED trust in the leadership expressed in any group is not only unwise, it can be flat-out dangerous.

The Scriptures suggest that we should be *"submitting to one another in the fear of God"* (Eph. 5:21). But, please note: It's to ONE ANOTHER. One-way submission may impress some but doesn't impress all—especially, some who are "more equal than others." What do I mean by that comment? Have you ever met a "wonderful leader" in a ministry or who shows up in an attempt to have Ekklesia practiced, who talks a good game about "submitting to one another in love" but rarely do you see him actually submitting to anyone . . . take note, some who acclaim the practice usually have difficulty in doing the same. In other words, they "talk a good game" but when the chips are down, you'll rarely see them defer to someone else's opinion—especially, on the big decisions.

It's like a family. Oh, sure, they humbly submit to the big decisions as in "Who's going to win the World Cup" but the little decisions like what house we're going to buy—then the real person shows up, digs in, and adamantly refuses to yield an inch!

In other words, "submitting one to another" is NOT a one-way street. You may be impressed that Brother Bob is such an *illuminator* of the Word of God that he is altogether worthy to follow and emulate—BE CAREFUL, your unquestioned following of that "leader-type" or of that "group think" (aka, known as "clump mentality") can be nothing more than what I call the "lemming longing" wherein everyone follows—right over the cliff!

It's a very thin line—trusting someone who is trustworthy (i.e., worthy to emulate) and then following him over the cliff. Usually, such a person comes in the person of an apostle, a prophet, an evangelist, and, most likely, a dynamic pastor-teacher type. Normally, it is considered a commendable trait to "receive the equipping" from such an individual; yet, doing so in an "unquestioned"

So, You want to do Ekklesia?

fashion provides fertile ground for the following—please note immediately following the "gifted" are issues less commendable:

Figure 72 - "SHUT UP AND DO AS YOU'VE BEEN TOLD!"

And he gave some, apostles; and some, prophets; and some, evangelists; and some, pastors and teachers; For the perfecting of the saints, for the work of the ministry, for the edifying [i.e., "equipping"] of the body of Christ: Till we all come in the unity of the faith, and of the knowledge of the Son of God, unto a perfect man, unto the measure of the stature of the fullness of Christ: That we henceforth be no more children, tossed to and fro, and carried about with every wind of doctrine, by the sleight of men, and cunning craftiness, whereby they lie in wait to deceive; (Ephesians 4:11-14).

Have you ever noticed how being tossed to and fro while being carried about with every wind of doctrine, along with the "*sleight of men*" with their "*cunning craftiness*" and deceitful ambushes immediately follows gifted brethren who should be equipping the saints to do the work of the ministry? Yep—THIN LINE, indeed!

This is Not an Ekklesia – Part 1

Seemingly, Prophet Jones, has a most unusual link up with the Almighty—whereas you don't? Isn't it grand that you can sort of kick back and let the biggie prophet in the group care for your spiritual well-being? What's so gratifying is to pursue further fetes of submission on your part whereby the perks given back by said noble leader in the form of greater responsibilities in the group; along with accolades heaped upon you whereby your level of submission accelerates. Wow—receiving the approbation of the "leading one" in the group (if that's what's manifesting) may put you on a "spiritual high" . . . all the while *"they lie in wait to deceive"* the unsuspecting! Beware of them bearing gifts—remember, **HE** GAVE SOME and *"But one and the same Spirit works all these things, distributing TO EACH ONE INDIVIDUALLY **as He wills**"* (1 Cor. 12:11).

An overweening sense of Brother Jones' propriety is probably a major red flag—the higher he's uplifted; the greater will be the fall. Wait 'til you find out he's only human! In sum: Keep your eyes on the prize—and guess Who the Prize is? In an Ekklesia experience the GIVER OF GIFTS and Rewards (even) is THE SAME SPIRIT, not brother so-and-so. He may equip but the Spirit gives the gifts!

We're it – the Overcomers – the Elite!

The Ekklesia the Lord's building is designed to withstand the *"Gates of Hades"*—consequently, if it doesn't achieve this, then something's amiss. The Ekklesia is not a social organization, a Masonic Lodge or Lion's Club. But we are a rather unique bunch—that's why He tagged us THE CALLED-OUT ONES—even, *"Many are called, few are chosen"* (Matt. 22:14).

> *"But you are **a chosen generation, a royal priesthood**, a holy nation, His own special people, that you may proclaim the praises of Him who called you"* (1 Peter 2:9).

Don't let it go to your head . . . say what? That's right. You can claim to be God's tiny, little elite corps of the "chosen few"—the

So, You want to do Ekklesia?

"remnant"—but, again, BE CAREFUL, lest you get the "***Babylon Complex***" wherein all others are in Babylon (especially the APOSTATES) but we, the few, the noble, the extremely humble, are standing for the "one true faith once delivered" while we bemoan everyone else who isn't!

Figure 73 - THE ELITE FORCES

How we get such a *high-falutin', rootin' tootin'* impression of ourselves MAY have to do with our "fearless leader" or the fact that we've become so insulated as a "click" (not an Ekklesia—which is "open-ended"). Here's a safeguard that's worthy of our consideration:

*"We do **not** have the audacity to put ourselves in the same class or compare ourselves with some who [supply testimonials to] commend themselves. When they measure themselves by themselves and compare themselves with themselves, they lack wisdom and behave like fools"* (2 Cor. 10:12- Amp. Ver.).

Think of it—we set our "elitist" standards and then measure ourselves by the standards we set for ourselves against the alleged standards of others who have no idea what we're talking about. In a word, Paul says we're nothing more than FOOLS!

The temptation to set up "religious standards" is the bane of cults which compose certain formula deemed as "spiritual standards" in which, if the compliant follower will achieve, then they will be given greater responsibilities and be acclaimed a more excellent inductee into the group's "inner circle"—having absolutely nothing to do with "*unto a perfect man—unto the measure of the stature of the fullness of Christ*" (Eph. 4:13).

It's US vs. THEM

We're under attack! An Ekklesia "environment" is—don't get me wrong here—assailing the "*Gates of Hades*"—which means: WE'RE ON THE OFFENSE. That's completely different than being on the defense. What am I getting at here? Simply put: The Ekklesia is not a place where we undergo securing a "persecution complex."

This is what I mean by "circling the wagons"—yes, we know the "world's out there" and that entanglement with it is antithetical to the Lord's calling for His Ekklesia. In other words, don't let the religious or worldly world squeeze you into its own mold. Notwithstanding our valiant cause in crushing Satan's head, we, nevertheless, tend toward a mentality when others criticize what we're doing in doctrine or practice, it must mean we're "under persecution" thereby validating our doctrine and practice is spot on!

A persecution complex leads to greater isolation which in turn reinforces circling the wagons ever tighter. How's that? Once the "attack" begins—especially from other Christians (all, of course, well-meaning) we tend toward ever greater security from the group's leadership.

In order to secure our people from the arrows of the enemy we resort to ever-greater scheduling of the saints with more "training"—more meetings—all justified or cloaked in the righteous garments of "enduring to the end" until the foe is defeated. We didn't plan on this kind of isolation from other believers but once we

So, You want to do Ekklesia?

became aware our critics were launching forays at our "doctrinal" positions and/or "practices"—that did it! We cut off fellowship with them posthaste (wasn't much to cut off; most contact was already gone) and simply figured out how to "talk among ourselves"—good grief, we begin to act like one another, dress like one another; it begins to look like we've gone tribal . . . drawn ever closer to the leader(s) of the group who has our best interests, no doubt!

Figure 74 - CIRCLE THE WAGONS

"Jezebel spirit": CONTROL, Control . . .

If it isn't controlling the actions and thought patterns of the group through indoctrination; then how about a few stories on what happens to members who dare leave the "ministry's" fearless leader—you know, the one whose life of dedication demands our own dedication to the same? Grief, I might be "cast out into outer darkness"—never "overcome"—all in the context if I ever leave the enchanting ministry of The Oracle of God—you know, the "prophet of the age."

Losing one's salvation is always another favorite theme of those who'd dare control the hapless adherent.

Where and how to live. From the sublime to the ridiculous— the infamous "schedule" of events during the week to occupy one's time cranks up in the wee hours of the morning for "corporate prayer"—then noon-time "fellowship" at the job site—then an evening meal together, along with "praise and worship"—forget so-called "free time" or any time alone with the Lord (let alone with your spouse if you have one)—it's o.k. to talk about that, but in practice, you're probably too exhausted; worn out by what's become a "fire hose ministry, Inc." Most activities are rather sublime, even absurd but it's when someone who has "left the group" and is killed in a plane crash (usually within proximity of having left the group) that the "curse" forecasted by the leader becomes a fulfilled prophecy!

Likewise, your "Ekklesia experience" is now fraught with scores of opportunities to express your "service to the Lord" by volunteering your labor (free of charge) on behalf of the leader and his astounding ministry. Shame, shame, and a whole lot more shame, be upon those "Leaders" who heap riches upon themselves at the expense of the saints. Isn't it plain as day when the "fearless leader" flits around in a private jet and lives a life of extravagance? Frankly, how dumb can we be to support such selfish aggrandizement? Answer: Really dumb!

In her chapter on "Notes On How To Rule From An Ivory Palace" from her text, *Jezebel vs. Elijah . . . the great end time clash*, Dr. Bree M. Keyton elucidates upon the controlling spirit of Jezebel:

> "Jezebel knew how to 'stir up' her victims. She manipulated her husband, everyone and everything around her.
>
> *"But there was none like unto Ahab, which did SELL himself to work wickedness in the sight of the LORD, whom Jezebel his wife STIRRED up"* (1 Kings 21:26).
>
> "The word 'stirred' (*cuwth*) means seduce, stimulate, inspire, soothe, entice, persuade, provoke, stir up . . . Jezebel walks in dominance, surrounded by bitter envyings and a constant atmosphere of confusion. Jezebel finds it difficult to delegate authority. She gives orders but won't allow them to be carried out without humiliating the other person involved. Then, she

So, You want to do Ekklesia?

takes back the authority. If she delegates, she retracts it, unable to allow others to function in positions of responsibility. She belittles and gossips, operating in bitter envying and strife.

Figure 75 - JEZEBEL VS. ELIJAH - DR. BREE KEYTON

"Jezebel uses anger or silence to control. This is witchcraft. Jezebel tries to control pastors and churches. Some pastors have this spirit, and through it they seek to control their congregations. Some Jezebels manipulate from behind the scenes while others are blatant and in your face. Jezebel won't get along with anyone she can't dominate. When in the presence of a Jezebel spirit, one fervently wishes to be elsewhere. Sometimes a horrible creepy-crawly sensation permeates the atmosphere. When leaving, one just wants to take a shower. Yuk!

"Some people are attracted to Jezebel's company and find amusement through her as she/he ridicules others with her rapier wit. She engages in sarcasm, mocking friend and foe alike. Those who are attracted to her for this should take heed, for she will turn on them as well, like a viper, without pity or feeling.

"Jezebel dominates others by her vanity, hatred, disdain, insecurity and jealousy. She publicly humiliates others, including spouses. With the tongue she wrecks, demeans and destroys. Through character assassination, she makes others fearful of her sharp tongue, willing to compromise in order to avoid the tongue-lashings. Jezebel questions the manhood or ability of others, making them feel small." (***Jezebel vs. Elijah***, by Dr. Bree Keyton, pp. 73-75)

Dr. Keyton's quote above barely scratches the surface to her incredibly mesmerizing text—so clever is the "Jezebel spirit" who "lies in wait to deceive" the seeking soul!

When such a "spirit" manifests in what proposes to be an Ekklesia environment—then it would be wise to do what Paul suggests:

"Now I urge you, brethren, note those who cause divisions and offenses, contrary to the doctrine, which you learned, and avoid them. For those who are such do not serve our Lord Jesus Christ, but their own belly, and by smooth words and flattering speech deceive the hearts of the simple . . . but I want you to be wise in what is good, and simple [lit. "innocent"] *concerning evil"* (Rom. 16:17-19).

Emotional Dependency Works!

I could have titled this section: "Overkill or Too Much of a Good Thing." A true Ekklesia experience IS the manifestation of 1

So, You want to do Ekklesia?

Corinthians 13—the greatest of all these is love. To the point, the love of Christ which constrains, maintains the vibrancy of any Ekklesia—it is the hallmark of gathering around the Lord. That said, a most subtle occurrence known as "emotional transference" to the group, can occur which is NOT spiritually healthy.

This is when deference is shown to one member in hopes that (usually new) member will find, through greater acceptance, emotional dependence upon the group, along with the "group think" that goes with it. Instead of worshiping and exclaiming, *"God is among you of a truth"* the would-be uninformed or unbeliever is overwhelmed by "group love" rather than the Lord Himself. Again, the focus is riveted upon the group, the individual, rather than the Christ, the Son of the Living God.

Figure 76 - WE ARE "DAS VOLK"

One of the distinctive characteristics of Christ vs. the Antichrist or the Lamb of God vs. the Beast in the book of Revelation is as follows:

"... telling those who dwell on the earth to make an image to the beast who was wounded by the sword and lived. He (the False Prophet or Second Beast) *was granted power to give breath to the IMAGE OF THE BEAST, that the image of the beast should both speak and cause as many as would not worship the image of the beast to be killed"* (Rev. 13:14-15).

What's fascinating here is not that they "worshiped the Beast" (which they most definitely did) but that they began to worship the image of the beast—DAS VOLK. Nazi Germany became the reflection or image of the Beast—if you did not worship the people, the Image of the Beast, you were put to death!

How different is the contrast between the worship of the Image of the Beast and the worship of the Image of Christ:

"But we all, with unveiled face, beholding as a mirror the glory of the Lord, are being transformed into the same image from glory to glory, just as by the Spirit of the Lord" (2 Cor. 3:18).

Thus, the saints of the Lord are, by beholding like a mirror beholds an image, are being transformed into the image seen in the mirror—which is the Lord Himself! So, the Image of Christ, is the Ekklesia—the very reflection of Jesus Christ Whom they behold.

Now, at the conclusion of the New Testament—the Revelation—John declares:

"Then I, John, saw the holy city, New Jerusalem, coming down out of heaven from God, prepared as a bride adorned for her husband" (Rev. 21:2)

When Paul speaks of the *"great mystery"* in Eph. 5:32 he speaks of "Christ and the church" and speaks of this great mystery in terms of the wife's relationship to her husband. In this glorious

So, You want to do Ekklesia?

metaphorical expression of "Christ and the Ekklesia" we see "*the husband is head of the wife, as also Christ is head of the Ekklesia; and He is the Savior of the Body . . . therefore, just as the Ekklesia is subject to Christ, so let the wives be to their own husbands in everything*" (Eph. 5:23-24).

What is clearly manifested here, both in Revelation 21 and in Eph. 5, and again in 2 Cor. 3:18, is the very "Image of Christ" is the Bride of Christ who is subject to the her husband in everything—but she is NOT worshiped . . . she, as the Image of Christ only worships her husband, the Head of the Body.

Can you follow me here? Let's put it this way: She only has eyes for Him, none other, and most definitely, not herself; whereas, in the worship of the Image of the Beast, that Image demands to be worshiped.

Let me illustrate: In Nazi Germany "*volk*" were expected not only to attend "Hitler Rallies" but enthusiastically so. If a parade was marching down the street—and you had an apartment overlooking—better hang out the Nazi Banner/Flag. If you didn't, you might get this opportunity: "Herr Schmidt, I see you did not unfurl the Fuhrer's flag. Perhaps you need to attend one of our special re-education seminars? After all, we're all in this together, now, aren't we—or am I missing something here?"

We must be VERY careful NOT to worship the Image of Christ (i.e., the Bride of Christ). How's that? You see it all the time: Wow, what a choir we have! What an incredible gathering we held. Behold our "church building" is magnificent! We have a program for virtually every recovery group imaginable—and something for every age group—we really have our act together—especially, our administration. Our pastor is altogether ascendant—if you want to hear an incredible preacher, then show up at First Glorious Church of Paradise!

Such adoration of the Image of Christ looks a whole lot like the "worship of the Image of the Beast"—as the comedic psychotherapist advised: STOP IT! Heaping "inordinate love" upon any member or group as described borders on the "worship of the Image of Christ"—keep the focus on Christ which isn't easy but the lack thereof is antithetical to what should take place at a real

Ekklesia: The worship of Christ alone! Our ultimate dependence is upon the Lord Himself. As much as the Body of Christ is attractive—she should never replace the Lord Himself!

Each one has a Revelation?

Figure 77 - THE REVELATION OF JESUS CHRIST

"How is it then, brethren? Whenever you come together, each of you has a psalm, has a teaching, has a tongue, has a revelation, has an interpretation" (1 Cor. 14:26).

Strong's Greek word for "revelation" is *apokalupsis* (G#602), when defined: "This word is more comprehensive than *epiphaneia* (2015) and depicts the progressive and immediate unveiling of the otherwise unknown and unknowable God to His church."

The book of Revelation opens with this declaration: *"The Revelation of Jesus Christ"* (Rev. 1:1) . . . which "Revelation" in Greek is *apokalupsis* (Strong's G#602). It's an unveiling of the Person and Work of Jesus Christ—Who He is and what He has done and is doing and will do!

Such revelation in the context of an Ekklesia demonstrates that those participating can "on the spot" receive a revelation . . .

So, You want to do Ekklesia?

and such "revelation" should be in accordance with the unveiling of Jesus Christ to be impactful and edifying; however, what an Ekklesia is NOT is the supposed "hidden wisdom" and "knowledge" which borders on Gnosticism. The Gnostics were banned in the Early Church for claiming they had "hidden wisdom/knowledge" that alone could be achieved by certain training or procedures where novitiates would be brought into the "hidden mysteries" and thereby gain the depths of spirituality not available to most.

Again, a thin line exists between "revelation" vs. "hidden wisdom"—but know this, once a "Christian group" becomes ingrown to the point their "fellowship" is imbued with certain supernatural revelation which "so few have"—lightning arresters arise!

My brother was once in a gathering when a certain "Oracle of God" was speaking and claiming that we must boldly declare that since we are the Body of Christ we must proclaim: I AM CHRIST. Once he said this, literal lightning descended upon the building in which they were meeting and blew out the lights at the evening gathering . . . putting everyone in the dark! Good thing the building had lightning arresters—not good to proclaim one's personal or group deity!

Watch it—once we start proclaiming that we've "seen this or that" to the extent that we commence to delve into some kind of "special knowledge" or "truth"—BEWARE:

> *"Now to you I say, and to the rest in Thyatira, as many as do not have this doctrine, who have not known the DEPTHS OF SATAN"* (Rev. 2:24).

Satan has depths—he has "hidden wisdom" and understanding far and beyond most human effort or genius:

> *"You were the seal of perfection, full of wisdom and perfect in beauty . . . Your heart was lifted up because of your beauty; you corrupted your wisdom for the sake of your splendor"* (Ezk. 28:12, 17).

This is Not an Ekklesia – Part 1

Yes, such hidden wisdom is a beautiful thing—such "revelation" can be a beautiful discovery as well . . . but know this, the one who was adorned with the *"seal of perfection"* was *"full of wisdom and perfect in beauty"* but ultimately became a *"horror!"* (Ezk. 28:19). The Lord may from time to time restore and/or grant us "divine revelation" of His purposes upon this earthly clod; however, don't let it go to your head—He's just as apt to speak through Balaam's ass as He is to speak through a local prophet. Sorry to burst your bubble, but a little humility now and again doesn't hurt—remember:

Figure 78 - SECRET QUEST - THE PATH OF THE CHRISTIAN GNOSTICS

"Knowledge puffs up, but love builds up" (1 Cor. 8:1).

I once knew a most gifted brother who from time to time would head off to the mountains where he had a cabin in which he would be found "alone with God." Then he would descend the mountain (akin to Moses) and speak in terms of: "The Lord revealed to me" or "the Lord told me"—well, anyone who thought otherwise would examine himself: "End of conversation—once the **Lord's anointed** got the message—better affirm it lest I be found challenging God Almighty!"

Better yet—what of those who "dream dreams" or have miraculous visions—normally affecting the immediate sheep under

So, You want to do Ekklesia?

their jurisdiction as in: I had a vision the other evening in which God revealed to me in a dream that you brothers will be used mightily of God "as you stay in fellowship" (with me, no doubt)?

I call this the ministry of "signs, wonders, and cucumbers"— people who incessantly show up in the third heavens are either inhaling smoke or blowing it. I'm not saying they haven't gone there, but most likely, their chances of hallucinating whereby they gain greater control of God's people to do their bidding is nothing more than perpetrating a fraud upon the people of God and should be assiduously avoided!

Summing it up...

These aforementioned "control mechanisms" will manifest themselves even in the most wondrous Ekklesia gatherings. I'm not being a prophet of doom here. When Paul met with the Ephesian elders, his injunctions were a bit foreboding:

> *"Therefore take heed to yourselves and to all the flock, among which the Holy Spirit has made you overseers, to shepherd the church* (lit. *"Ekklesia") of God which He purchased with His own blood. For I know this, that after my departure savage wolves will come in among you, not sparing the flock. Also from among yourselves men will rise up, speaking perverse* (Lit. *"misleading") things, to draw away the disciples after themselves. Therefore watch, and remember that for three years I did not cease to warn everyone night and day with tears"* (Acts 20:28-31).

So much for "positive confession"—that's out there—WARNING, even from our midst those individuals will arise and draw disciples after themselves. Once we commence to elevate brother so-and-so . . . well, it's only a matter of time "such an one" will slowly, but surely, draw disciples to himself and "there goes the Ekklesia." In many cases it's not the fault of the one being elevated but of those doing the elevating!

May the Lord keep us, on the one hand in the *"simplicity and purity in Christ"* (2 Cor. 11:3) but on the other hand, aware of those who would draw disciples after themselves within the Ekklesia of God.

God have mercy on us all . . ..

> For I know this, that after my departing shall grievous wolves enter in among you, not sparing the flock. Also of your own selves shall men arise, speaking perverse things, to draw away disciples after them.
>
> Therefore watch, and remember, that by the space of three years I ceased not to warn everyone night and day with tears.
>
> Acts 20:29-31

Figure 79 - GRIEVOUS WOLVES AMONG THE SHEEP

So, You want to do Ekklesia?

Chapter 13:
This is Not an Ekklesia – Part 2

"Cutting away at your critical thinking skills."

Figure 80 - CUTTING AWAY AT YOUR CRITICAL THINKING SKILLS

WHEN I WAS IN TRAINING IN THE US MILITARY, WE "ENDURED" HOUR AFTER HOUR OF INDOCTRINATION ON SURVIVAL AND HOW TO ELIMINATE (aka "kill") the enemy—an ethnic group I had never met in my life! Since I never was much of a "killer" it became obvious to the management (although I was given a medal as a "sharp shooter"), I'd better serve the "cause" if I were placed behind (at the time) a typewriter, rather than a rifle; although that option remained a present danger for me and all of us.

I was impressed, however, with the overall success of the indoctrination, coupled with the intensity of the schedule—putting it mildly, the US military had it down; they knew what worked and what didn't. Indeed, we were involved in a major "group think" effort that boggled the mind; and, if you from time to time "got out of line," you would quickly be reminded through various

So, You want to do Ekklesia?

activities that put you back on course, lest you forget how, where, when, why and in what manner you should be acting! A somewhat unforgettable experience.

The distinction between one's "ministry" and the Ekklesia experience must be kept in view here. If you would, the "civilian life" is akin to the Ekklesia; whereas military training can be likened to "ministry." I know, a shockingly stark illustration—but it serves the purpose. There is a difference—a somewhat immense difference, come to think of it.

The ministry experienced at a Bible Institute, for example, is done in accordance with the dictum of that school—whereas, the schedule of someone who longs for the experience of Ekklesia should be very different.

If you find yourself grossly involved in what purports to be an Ekklesia, enduring hour after hour of "training" and lectures from the "group's" leadership—you're probably not in an Ekklesia, but engrossed in someone's ministry. Now, if the leadership of said group is clever enough—they will try to align your little Ekklesia experience with that of their ministry's experience.

Let me illustrate: Initially, you find yourself at someone's home gathering; let's say, and after several hours of casual eating, accompanied by fellowship, prayer, worship, along with some Bible study shared by a multiplicity of brethren—then a "ministry hour" is held by an instructor of sorts. There's clearly a demarcation in the timing of said "teaching"—and it is even declared as a time of "ministry" by the brother teaching.

That may certainly take place; however, may I suggest that the proximity to an Ekklesia-style gathering—that is, "ministry" immediately following, by dent of its timing—inadvertently demands those gathering for the Ekklesia wherein all may share "one by one" and where "each one has" are not subjected (if you would) to the singularity of someone's ministry. NOT FAIR! Why do I say this? Because the very purpose of a gathering of the Ekklesia is designed for general participation and contribution—whereas, the purpose of ministry is for (now don't get upset with me here) INDOCTRINATION or, better said, personal edification by a pastor-teacher, evangelist, apostle, and/or even a prophet.

Again, don't get me wrong here. Gifted members of the Body of Christ—apostles, prophets, evangelists, pastors-teachers—or those identified as "workers of miracles" or having "gifts of healing" (1 Cor. 12:29-30) or other manifestations such as "a word of wisdom" or "the word of knowledge" or the manifestation of "faith" or of "tongues and interpretation" (1 Cor. 12:4-11)—such gifts and gifted ones can and should be manifested in part and/or in whole at a gathering of the Ekklesia—but the overall "appearance" of an Ekklesia gathering is not eclipsed by the endeavors of gifted ones nor of any one gift so manifesting! Thus, the proximity of a "minister/ministry" adjacent to an Ekklesia-style gathering should be avoided. God's people need to come to grips with:

> *"For as we have many members in one body, but all the members do not have the same function . . . having then gifts differing according to the grace that is given to us, LET US USE THEM: if PROPHECY, let us prophecy in proportion to our faith; or MINISTRY, let us use it in our ministering; who TEACHES, in teaching; he who EXHORTS, in exhortation; he who GIVES, with liberality; he who LEADS, with diligence; he who shows mercy, with cheerfulness"* (Rom. 12:5-8).

How will the Ekklesia have growing participation if, once again, the "pulpit/pew" becomes the norm? How will God's people learn to FUNCTION if there is not abundant opportunity to do so. The Body of Christ has MANY MEMBERS and they all do NOT have the same function; however, the way things are today one should consider the current expression of the Body is this HUGE MOUTH committed to the pastor/priest-teacher who is given the main platform at all our "services"—services, which we will soon discover in a later chapter, have their roots in Medieval Christianity wherein tradition has bound us all!

Let me clarify: An evangelist does not leave his/her gift at the door upon entering an Ekklesia-style gathering. For example, the ministry of a gifted prophet will from time to time within the context of an Ekklesia manifest his/her gift. I can't imagine that

So, You want to do Ekklesia?

Philip, the Evangelist, and his four virgin daughters ... "*... the house of Philip the evangelist, who was one of the seven, and stayed with him. Now this man had four virgin daughters who prophesied*" (Acts 21:8-9) simply sat around without exercising their gifts of evangelism and prophetic utterance while gathering with the saints in Philip's house? Do you think? I doubt you could shut them up—for these gifted ones would "minister" whenever and wherever they found themselves ... but, again, there's a time and place for such "indoctrination" and/or singularity of the manifestation of a gift.

How About "Deliverance Ministry?"

Incidentally, issues of "deliverance" and of "casting out of demons" within the context of the New Testament experience, aside from the gospels (Matt. 4:23-24; Mark 5; Luke 9-10); and some mentioning in Acts 19:13-20; and although ...

"These signs shall follow them that believe" (Mark 16:17, KJV). *"The Lord working with them and confirming the word with signs following"* (Mark 16:20, KJV).

The deliverance ministry is intended to follow the teaching and preaching of the cross. (I am aware that the validity of the texts just cited is questioned by some, but the principles inherent in them are underlined elsewhere in the Scripture: Acts 8:1-7; 1 Corinthians 2:1-5; Hebrews 2:4.) (From: **"Dangers in the Deliverance Ministry"** by K. Neill Foster of the Alliance World Fellowship) ...

... such "deliverance ministry" is virtually non-existent within the context of an Ekklesia gathering and is certainly not mentioned, *per se*, as one of the "*manifestations of the Spirit*" (1 Cor. 12:7). Tragically, there are some who use Paul's recitation of: "*My preaching was not with enticing words of man's wisdom, but in demonstration of the Spirit and of power*" (1 Corinthians 2:4) to highlight their own abilities; thereby, gaining authority and blatant control over their adherents.

This is Not an Ekklesia – Part 2

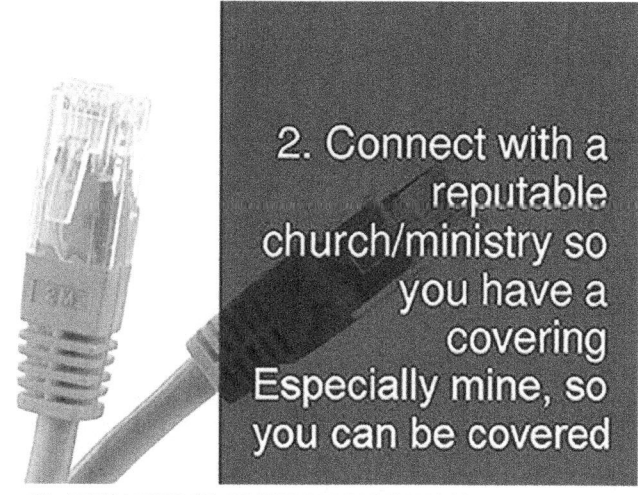

> 2. Connect with a reputable church/ministry so you have a covering Especially mine, so you can be covered

Figure 81 - YOOU NEED TO BE UNDER MY COVERING

The "indoctrination" of "specialized teachings" and "ministry" which draw attention to the gift—not the Giver—borders at times on idolatry whereby just as Simon Magus (Acts 8:9-24) sought to obtain the power of the Holy Spirit akin to Peter's empowerment, and was summarily chastised for such a foolhardy effort, parallels those who justify their own efforts to "*desire spiritual gifts*" (1 Cor. 14:1) not realizing we should "especially" seek after the spiritual gift to "prophesy" (1 Cor. 14:1) for "*he who prophesies speaks edification and exhortation and comfort to men*"—and this is spoken of immediately after Paul's "*more excellent way*" of LOVE in 1 Corinthians 13!

Frankly, if anyone "stands out" at an Ekklesia, it should be inadvertent. ALL CAN PROPHESY—not just an elite few. That smarts with the Simon Magus types and may do some damage to the ego of certain gifted ones—but the "atmosphere" of an Ekklesia IS THE EKKLESIA, not Simon Magus, nor Doug Krieger, nor any one superlative individual with the gift of healing or someone running around prophesying over folks . . . can you follow me? Our attention should be focused upon the Lord Jesus Christ.

I find it a bit disconcerting to behold the "ministry of deliverance" DURING an Ekklesia and the apparent "Special Knowledge" accorded the "exorcist" to perform the exorcism. Whenever such "specialists" show up to exercise their

215

So, You want to do Ekklesia?

spiritual gift, it should be done without fanfare and without drawing attention to either the individual being exorcised and, especially, not to the one(s) involved in the deliverance. Again, if such "manifestations" were accorded such prominence, then why is this "alleged gift" of deliverance wholly omitted from the only abundant example found of an Ekklesia gathering in the New Testament—i.e., 1 Corinthians 11-14? Think about it.

"Once Saved Always Saved" – "Our Little Click"

You can readily tell you're not gathering as an Ekklesia if your big or little group somehow has achieved "exclusive rights" for doling out "salvation tickets." In other words, you can't participate in the "salvation raffle" unless you get a ticket at the door of the gathering—once you get a ticket, you enter into the bliss of our corner on salvation . . . but, once you leave the group by "hook or by crook" you leave your salvation experience. Thus, somehow the "Church saves" you—while all along I thought a Person did!

Some "churches" out there have the uncanny notion that without formal membership in their group—either through "confirmation"—"baptism" or some other methodology—you're not saved, you're not a part of the "chosen few"—because you haven't been initiated into the group—THAT IS ***NOT*** AN EKKLESIA!

I was baptized, confirmed and raised in a Reformational "Church"—but being born in a barn doesn't a cow make . . . I no more had a salvation experience than claims on being that cow; that said, however, it did put a godly, but distant, "fear of the Lord" in me and it certainly didn't damage my psyche.

Some churches actually initiate formal membership as a "covenant procedure" whereby the would-be member undergoes, not only a membership class, but must SIGN a document (virtually in blood) whereby they promise to swear allegiance to that particular church—somehow that church is able to squeeze such a "covenant relationship" out of their Bible's amplified version. I am bemused at Protestants who accord as much, even at times more, significance to the "salvation experience" confined to their church roles—i.e., unless you are a member of "my church" you are not likely to experience heaven's bliss! Face it: A doctrine, a church, a group of individuals did NOT save you, a Person did, and His Name is Jesus, having wrought so great a salvation by giving you the New Birth by the Spirit of Him Who raised Christ from the dead! The "heavenly side" of the "cow barn" illustration is true as well—being "born into the church" does not a Christian make.

It is the Holy Spirit Who anoints and chooses—not the "Church of the Immaculate Perception" nor some "all-seeing Eye." Playing God and determining who is and isn't worthy of salvation is idolatrous. Jeremiah 17:10 still stands today:

"I, the Lord, search the heart, I test the mind, even to give every man according to his ways, according to the fruit of his doings."

We don't determine salvation's gift—*"it is the gift of God, not of works, lest any man should boast"* (Eph. 2:8-9).

Figure 82 - THE CHURCH DOES SAVE YOU - ONLY JESUS CAN

Yet, what is all the more tragic is when you think you have arrived at the real experience of Ekklesia and find when someone "leaves the group" and then is shunned by the group's members or is "distanced" through innuendo or rumor. "Where's brother so-and-so?" "Oh, he had 'issues' and refused to SUBMIT or 'go along with the ministry' of brother so-and-so."

The somewhat slanderous use of 1 John 2:19 is often used out of context:

> *"They went out from us, but they were not of us; for if they had been of us, they would have continued with us; but they went out that they might be made manifest, that none of them were of us."*

The above verse immediately follows:

> *"Little children, it is the last hour; and as you have heard that the Antichrist is coming, even now many antichrists have come, by which we know that it is the last hour"* (1 John 2:19).

Do you see the connection? The ones leaving are directly connected to the spirit of Antichrist. So, why not attach that onerous label upon the person who leaves your "Ekklesia" by insinuating they left because they were ANTICHRIST? Can it get that bad? Yes sir! Any group which has such an "odious exodus" of an individual who finds themselves outside of a given group of believers, aside from overt sin and an unrepentant heart, and is adjudged by the group as some kind of Antichrist, is NOT an Ekklesia!

And, if the group or "church" deigns to place a "curse" on any of its "followers" if they are to fellowship elsewhere or simply "go out into the world"—they have NOT the Spirit of Christ with such derogatory declarations foisted upon ex-members.

Christians Suing Their Brothers and Sisters

We might, at this juncture, for doctrinal reasons, disassociate ourselves as evangelicals from overt "cults" as the Mormons or Jehovah Witnesses but have you ever noticed: They do NOT sue their critics for defamation of their "churches" and/or "organizations?" "Libel" is a difficult thing to prove in a court of law—but Christians who practice and justify clamping down on their critics by going after them via expensive lawsuits of slander (among other issues) to the point of financially breaking those who oppose them—has absolutely nothing to do with Christ and is NOT an Ekklesia in any sense of the word.

We can dance around 1 Corinthians 6 all we want—but the plain text is unequivocal:

> *"Dare any of you, having a matter against another, go to law before the unrighteous, and not before the saints? Do you not know that the saints will judge the world? And if the world will be judged by you, are you unworthy to judge the smallest matters . . . Now therefore, it is already an utter failure for you that you go to law against one another. Why do you not rather accept wrong? Why do you not rather let yourselves be cheated? No, you yourselves do wrong and cheat, and you do these things to your brethren!"* (1 Cor. 6:1-11 excerpts).

If your "Ekklesia experience" is involved in such lawsuits toward other Christians, I suggest you leave posthaste no matter what justifications are used by that group's leadership if they persist in going to court with other believers!

Clump Mentality

If what's keeping your Ekklesia or "group" together is a set of peculiarities, policies and "ways and means" dribbling down from a "council of ecclesiastical brethren"—however they are tagged ("the caring brethren"—"the council of 12"—"the united front"—"the 12 apostles of the church"—the "eldership"—the "board of deacons"—"those in authority"—"the blended brethren"—"the tribunal speaking on behalf of the Trinity")—it's probably NOT an Ekklesia.

A "ministry" may have its oversight board which can justify the anointing of a new member into their ministry—but know this:

> *"But you have an anointing from the Holy One, and YOU ALL KNOW all things . . . but the anointing which you have received from Him abides in you, and you do not need that*

So, You want to do Ekklesia?

anyone teach you; but as the same anointing teaches you concerning all things, and is true, and is not a lie, and just as it has taught you, you abide in Him" (1 John 2:20, 27).

To suggest that the Body of Christ has an anointing—no doubt—but to claim your group or movement has exclusive rights thereto? A picture is worth a thousand words:

Figure 83 - THE MAN WHO DIDN'T "HEIL HITLER"

I would be safe to state, such an *"anointing from the Holy One"* and *YOU ALL KNOW ALL THINGS* is intrinsically connected to the Ekklesia and is NOT consigned to any one ministry. Yes, it is the sole criteria for participation in an Ekklesia.

Now, when Paul and Barnabas got to their impasse over the "profitability for the ministry" concerning John-Mark . . . THAT was a separate matter, having nothing whatsoever to do with the Ekklesia, but having everything to do with a ministry (Acts 15:36-41). John-Mark and Barnabas were NOT "kicked out" of the Ekklesia—*"they departed from them . . . and had not gone with them to the work"* (Acts 15:38). That's as far as it goes—you cannot be removed from the Ekklesia aside from overt sinful practice (1 Cor. 5:1-13).

The Witch Who Broke Up Our Gathering

I once participated in a most wondrous Ekklesia-style gathering of believers which eventually included nigh unto 300 or so brethren who gathered on Thursday mornings in what was called "the Upper Room" at a local business. The gathering grew to such an extent that they had to move the proceedings to a local community hall—meetings were held on Thursday morning and/or evening and then on Saturday evenings. A problem arose in the group—which group truly was an "Ekklesia experience."

A "witch" came into the assembly and would neither repent nor leave the gathering of the saints—in point of fact had joined herself to one of the "worship teams" in the leading of worship, praise, singing, etc. When several prophets and intercessors of the gathering objected to the witch's participation (and she was overtly confronted with her designation and did not deny her affection of the same), a would-be exorcism was held both formally and informally by accomplished brethren known to have such ministry—but to no avail—she would not give up her identification as a witch; nor has she to this day (November, 2019).

Now, something so stark a contrast between "light and darkness" should have been more than apparent . . . it was to some . . . but to others it was seen as both a challenge to the "spiritual prowess" of the Ekklesia, as well as a matter of manifesting the "Lord's patient love" toward the witch in wooing her to the Savior! I know—but you would have had to have been there to understand the "dynamic" taking place among those trying to deal with this "problem" or "challenge"—however you wished to view it.

Tragically, the once vibrant group of nigh 300 discontinued its gatherings; became divided over how to deal with the witch—and everyone went their own way.

You might say, at the same time, that the "internal policies" of the members (there was no formal membership—all who "called upon the Lord" were included and seen as "full members" of this Ekklesia experience) were not administered with a "heavy hand"—liberality was given to all. The leadership of the group was most benign—"rewards and losses" were NOT discriminate—i.e., the more you cooperated with the group, the more you were

So, You want to do Ekklesia?

accorded greater responsibility and position . . . such was NOT the case.

Figure 84 - THE "CHRISTIAN" WITCH

No . . . there was little "manifestation" of an ecclesiastical authority apparent in the group. There were, however, those who appeared to be "genuine" as it declares in 1 Corinthians: *"I hear that there are divisions among you, and in part I believe it. For there must also be factions among you, that those who are genuine* ("approved") *may be manifest among you"* (1 Cor. 11:18-19). Such genuine brethren were most definitely present, but when "push came to shove"—the witch had her way—the saints collapsed under the *"gates of Hades"*—although, some would say otherwise and viewed the disintegration of the experience as naught but a "season" and thus we "moved on."

Now, you might say that a "heavy hand" or "formal authority" is needed in a "Church setting"—you can't have an Ekklesia unless and until you have formal authority controlling the environment or such things as a "witch" coming into a group will blow it up! That, however, is not what the Scriptures suggest when an Ekklesia occurs—no "heavy hand" or "authority" wrought by human instrumentality is to eclipse the gathering. Again, "factions" (not "factious" individuals) are NECESSARY, so that those who are "genuine" or "approved" might be evident, or manifested (1 Cor. 11:19).

If you don't have such factions—then those who are "genuine" have little opportunity to "manifest." In the case of the witch, those who had the capacity to manifest, simply recoiled, and did not do their "genuine" obligation to "keep the unity of the Spirit in the bond of peace" (Eph. 4:3). If we do not "*endeavor*" (lit. Strong's G#4704 "*spoudazo*"—"to make [an] effort, be prompt or earnest—to hasten to do a thing, to exert oneself, endeavor, give diligence")—then you can kiss the "*unity of the Spirit in the bond of peace*" goodbye!

What that means is this: If you come to a gathering and are but an observer—and not a participant—i.e., do not "have a stake" in what's going on . . . then you can simply "stand from afar" and observe the happenings but you're really not all that concerned as to what is happening because you're not making any earnest effort "to hasten to do a thing" nor are you "exerting, endeavoring, nor giving diligence" to affect the situation for a better result. It's like a "Good Samaritan Law" where you see an "accident" or "tragedy" taking place and take a position of "indifference"—walking away from doing anything about it. In certain jurisdictions, if you react in this manner, you can literally be prosecuted by the authorities and be charged for your lack of intervention.

"Clump mentality" is a most dangerous commodity afflicting a would-be Ekklesia experience. We are simply NOT all the same; to wit:

> "*There are diversities* (lit. "allotments or various kinds") *of gifts, but the same Spirit. There are differences of ministries, but the same Lord. And there are diversities of activities, but it is the same God who works all in all. But the manifestation*

of the Spirit is given to each one for the profit of all" (1 Cor. 12:4-6).

Ekklesia Under Strict Eldership Guidelines

There is a genuine desire on the part of some ministers of the gospel—gifted ones—to foster a greater desire for God's people to enjoy Ekklesia-style gatherings. Yes, this should be encouraged; however, the minister(s) must remember and embrace the "equipping of the saints" is for "the work of the ministry . . . for the building up of the body of Christ" (Eph. 4:12). The notion that one is equipping the saints for the "building up of my own ministry" is antithetical to the essence of the functioning position of the gifted ones. May I give a stern, and grossly misunderstood, warning: Leave well-enough alone!

The "ministerial tendency" is to treat the Ekklesia and/or those entering into the experience of true Ekklesia (it's both a "verb" and a "noun") as one's pet who needs training—but even (hate to use the illustration) an animal will not forget its training. Once trained—the dog will more than serve another master . . . are we humans far superior to the animal kingdom? Ministers who keep a tight grip upon "Ekklesia" via "centrality of control" (e.g., an area-wide eldership) are walking on a very thin "Ekklesia-ice shield" apt to cave in at any moment. This is NOT what is in view in the New Testament—rather, a much more fluid expression which meets from house-to-house or wherever allowing God's people to come together "on their own" and at their "own timing" to gather around Christ. Our problem as ministers, pastors-teachers is this: We can't leave well-enough alone—we simply will NOT allow the saints to *"grow up in all things into Him who is the head—Christ . . . to the measure of the stature of the fullness of Christ"* (Eph. 4:15, 13). Instead, we have this idea that the success of any ministry is its multiplication (interior increase), not its duplication (exterior increase).

"Holding the Head" (Eph. 4:15—lit. *"speaking the truth"* means "holding the reality"), even Christ, is one thing . . . holding on to the saints for the sake of "my ministry" is wholly something else. Brethren, we are NOT building "our ministry" we are building "a dwelling place of God in the Spirit"—"a holy temple in the Lord"—upon *"the foundation of the apostles and prophets, Jesus Christ Himself being the chief cornerstone in whom the whole building, being fitted together, grows into a holy temple in the Lord"* (Eph. 2:20-22). Notwithstanding, preacher after preacher is under the erroneous concept that a good shepherd of the sheep must be responsible. True—to a point.

Notwithstanding, isn't it time to grow up as well into Him, Who is the head, IN ALL THINGS? If we cannot entrust His people to the Great Shepherd of the Sheep (Heb. 13:20), we just might be missing the mark. If a minister insists he is to *"Shepherd the flock of God which is among you, serving as overseers* (lit. "caring ones") *not by compulsion but willingly, not for dishonest gain but eagerly; nor as being masters over those entrusted to you, but being examples to the flock"* (1 Peter 5:2-3), then he better well examine his "example to the flock" is not that of a "master" nor is it for "dishonest gain" but is a caring and most willing endeavor—nothing compulsory here (this isn't some "job"). Caring for the flock is not the MASTER over the flock. The best illustration is the growth of one's own family—the kids grow up—they still respect their parents and love being with them . . . but these kids are "on their own" notwithstanding the "extended family" ties. THEY HAVE TO GROW UP—and the parents must allow them to do so.

Holding "tight reigns" over a network of Ekklesia is, in a word, spiritually delimiting. The Ekklesia is NOT like any "social network"—membership is universal and able to "meet and greet" at a moment's notice. It's not the minister's personal "fiefdom." Each "expression of the Body of Christ" wherever it gathers should be under the headship of Christ, the Head of His One Body. The "churches" or "lampstands" of Revelation 2-3 were all different— yet their "communion" was universal—they were all GOLDEN LAMPSTANDS—each with their own approbations and criticisms (5 of the 7) from the Son of Man in their midst. Again, they were all golden—even Thyatira. Attempting to make your "network of Ekklesia" uniform is NOT the model of the New Testament—may be your model but not that of the NT.

So, You want to do Ekklesia?

Conformity and uniformity are NOT the NT model . . . UNITY with DIVERSITY is the model. We are NOT advocating bedlam, but we are advocating "organized chaos"—let me example once more: This is NOT a "controlled burn"—it's a WILDFIRE. We simply cannot "organize the move of the Spirit"—it's a waste of "spiritual energy" to "consolidate" God's people who by very dent of the Lord's declaration were told to EVANGELIZE THE ENTIRE EARTH. If you are somewhat familiar with the lot of the original apostles of the Lamb . . . virtually all were martyred and were scattered to the four winds—especially, after their disbursement from Jerusalem prior to its demise in 70 AD. To say the very least—their "organization skills" were loose. They were too busy keeping the "main thing" the "main thing."

"Get out of your Mind" – "Stop thinking"

"Cognitive Dissonance" is mental discomfort (psychological stress) experienced by a person who holds two or more contradictory beliefs, ideas, or values. To cope with this "disorder" one must compensate by, in the main, avoiding one's normal critical thinking skills which are contrary to the "group think" which has been most likely instilled into the group by the leader or cabal at the helm.

Figure 85 - SHEEP WHO THINK YOU ARE GOD

If you're not thinking the way the group thinks about "spiritual matters"—i.e., "what constitutes spirituality" as explained by the "teachings of the master instructor"—cognitive dissonance will undoubtedly set in . . . you'll have to accommodate, adjust—GET OUT OF YOUR MIND—and start thinking like the group thinks or you'll be ostracized from the group. Such a phenomena is NOT an Ekklesia experience.

I'm not suggesting that we should not be all of the same mind; as in: *"Fulfill my joy by being like-minded, having the same love, being of one accord, of one mind"* . . . but listen to the rest of this admonition:

"Let nothing be done through selfish ambition or conceit, but in lowliness of mind let each esteem others better than himself. Let each of you look out not only for his own interests, but also for the interests of others. LET THIS MIND be in you which was also in Christ Jesus, who, being in the form of God, did not consider it robbery to be equal with God, but made Himself of no reputation, taking the form of a bondservant, and coming in the likeness of men. And being found in appearance as a man, He humbled Himself and became obedient to the point of death, even the death of the cross" (Phil. 2:2-8).

Having the "mind of Christ" is altogether different than the "mindless meanderings" suggested by the phrase: "Get out of your mind." The Bible does NOT encourage mindless adherence to anyone—it does encourage us to have "the mind of Christ" and to THINK SOBERLY as members of the same One Body of Christ:

"For I say, through the grace given to me, to everyone who is among you, not to think of himself more highly than he ought to think, but to think soberly, as God has dealt to each one a measure of faith. For as we have many members in one body, but all the members do not have the same function, so we, being many, are one body in Christ, and individually members of one another . . . having then GIFTS DIFFERING according to the grace that is given to us" (Rom. 12:3-6).

Please notice—*"all the members do not have the same function—individually members of one another—gifts differing."* All this to say we're not a bunch of mindless followers. There is incredible variety in the Body of Christ—we're not all the same in function, not even in the portion of grace given to each member!

So, You want to do Ekklesia?

Don't be shocked if someone enters your Ekklesia experience and is wholly different than you or shares a completely "out of the box" doctrinal leaning. *"Endeavoring to keep the unity of the Spirit in the bond of peace"* does not mean we set aside our mental faculties in order to be "one in the spirit." Thinking soberly suggests we should "sober up" and not act like a bunch of drunks. I've had the distinct privilege of witnessing a "drunken brawl"—no one is in their right mind. Having an opinion during a drunken brawl is NOT occurring in the minds of anyone.

Grief, I sat next to a brother at an Ekklesia gathering the other day, who told us he had "three angels" with whom he was most familiar; and who "ministered" to him from time to time. He was most aware of their ministry. I'm thinking: SAY WHAT!? Then, again, what do I know. My dear shirt-tale relative at age 96 (or was it 97?) just had a glorious salvation experience after our prayers on his behalf nigh fifty years or more. How? Well, two angelic beings showed up in his little home (out building—according to him) up at the ranch near the old farmhouse—he clearly saw them and described them in detail. Although I couldn't tell his story with precise accuracy—suffice it to say, their "message" to him was clear . . . it generated great faith in him to believe the Savior's claims and he accepted Jesus as Savior and Lord—has read nearly all the Bible and written a 50,000-word book on his experience; all the while witnessing to all his relatives and friends of his encounter with the Living God via angelic messengers. So, what do I know?

Talk about "getting out of your mind!" It is one thing to encourage dependence upon the Lord and quite another thing to deny there's a "right and a wrong"—or there is "good and there is evil." Adam and Eve partook of the *"Tree of the Knowledge of Good and Evil"* wherein, like God, they could discern the difference and thereby stay away from the evil and choose the good. Suggesting one's partaking of the "Tree of Life" has nothing to do with "good and evil" is preposterous and can and has led to countless indiscretions where "leaders of the group" inform the unsuspecting lambs to choose LIFE (i.e., the leader's interpretation of what is and what is not life) and to suggest otherwise is nothing but the "Tree of the Knowledge of Good and Evil"—No, no, no—THAT is not an Ekklesia experience!

If someone's ministry participates in "evil" (monetary or moral, for example) and it is overlooked "for the sake of the ministry"—and then attempts to justify such error by stating those who detest such evil—are unable to tolerate it—are IN THEIR MINDS (*ipso facto* partaking of the Tree of the Knowledge of Good and Evil)—such "leadership" is from the pit of hell itself! If you're suffering from such cognitive dissonance, I suggest (a) you FLEE that group or (b) confront the evil within it—and, if the leadership will not hear you, and "turn from their wicked tolerance (i.e., "ways")," then go back to point (a).

"Hit the Road Jack . . . and Don't you come back!"

Dis-fellowship, isolation, shunning of former members of what claims to be His One Body, the Ekklesia, is at variance with the Word of God. The ONLY reason why someone can be dis-fellowshipped from the Ekklesia is overt and unrepentant sin, witchcraft, and obvious divisiveness (they cause brother to turn against brother) . . .

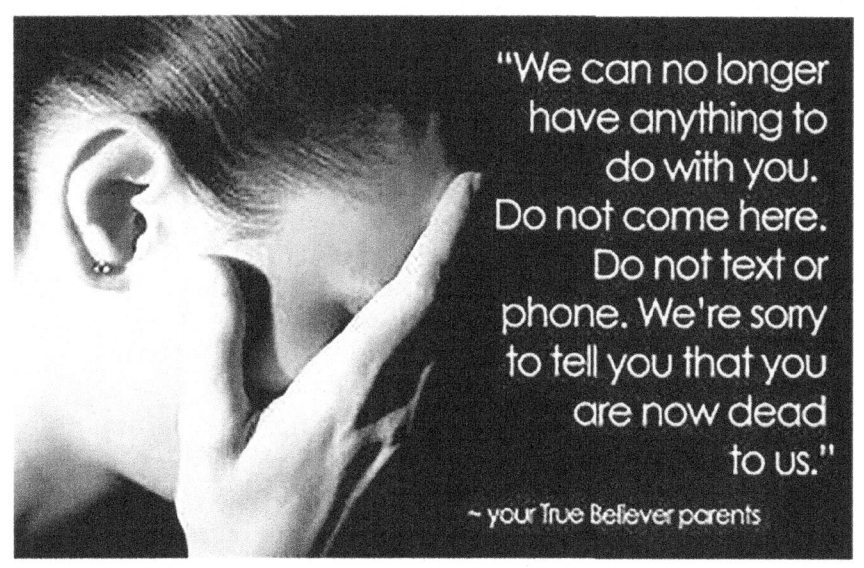

Figure 86 - SHUNNED BY "TRUE BELIEVERS"

"But now I have written to you not to keep company with anyone named a brother, who is sexually immoral, or covetous, or an idolater, or a reviler, or a drunkard, or an extortioner—not even to eat with such a person . . . 'put away from yourselves the evil person'" (1 Cor. 5:11, 13).

But, again, what if this "evil person" repents?

"But if anyone has caused grief, he has not grieved me, but all of you to some extent—not to be too severe. This punishment which was inflicted by the majority is sufficient for such a

So, You want to do Ekklesia?

> man, so that, on the contrary, you ought rather to forgive and comfort him, lest perhaps such a one be swallowed up with too much sorrow. Therefore I urge you to reaffirm your love to him . . . lest Satan should take advantage of us, for we are not ignorant of his devices" (2 Cor. 1:5-11).

Being "ignorant of Satan's devices" has a whole lot to do with excluding a repentant brother for whatever reason; normally, "to teach him a lesson" and "make him an example" to the flock . . . better not do what this brother did or you'll suffer the same fate!

How tenderhearted is that bunch! Instead of *"restoring such a one in the spirit of meekness, considering yourself [lest you also be tempted]"* (Gal. 6:1) you/we, instead, take the attitude of the so-called leadership and exclude the penitent from our fellowship—taking our que from the noble leadership who have discerned the guilt of the former member and deem him altogether unworthy of our presence . . . this is naught but "cruel and unusual punishment" not worthy of any Ekklesia.

Of late, I've had the opportunity and challenge to witness "shunning" by family members of a father who was caught in a moral failure (aka "sin"). Actually, several brothers "caught" in this manner. Certain family members (the more devout as it turns out) and entire churches, have excluded these brothers from their immediate fellowship; although those charged have repented, and have undergone disciplinary action by various brethren who wished to restore them to fellowship. Both brothers have repented—even with tears—to other brothers who "earnestly care for their estate."

The "overtaken in a fault" demands a response—but such a response must be done in accordance with "Scriptural intent." Then, of course, there are those who despite the penitent brother's actions and desire for restoration—refuse to grant restoration because they "sense there is something else" going on . . . so they keep the brother under a form of suspicion, which borders on condemnation. Frankly, brethren who take such a "spiritual attitude" toward their brethren and refuse to embrace them in faith (viz., the brother overtaken in a fault), expose themselves to Satan's devices; they have become IGNORANT of Satan's devices and are now vulnerable to the wiles of the Devil! Why? Because they are NOT accepting the repentant brother at "face value." We are NOT told to accept *"such an one"* at arms' length—but to receive him/her in love, just as God, for Christ's sake, has forgiven us.

What's even worse is when certain brethren embrace the penitent and are then identified as complicit in the penitent's fault—in other words, the REAL PROBLEM are those who "side with the penitent" (even after his repentance) and refuse to "teach him a lesson" concerning faithfulness to the Lord. They are accused of "compromise" because they have genuinely embraced the brother or sought to restore *"such an one"* through diligent fellowship and various forms of discipline—allowing (in the minds of their accusers) additional "undisclosed sin" to fester inside the "evil brother" . . . for with certainty they suppose if there's that much smoke "in there" then surely, secret fires lurk therein—"none dare call it conspiracy!"

Thus, not only is the original one who is "taken in a fault" under cloak of suspicion, but now those who would forgive such an one are worse than the original brother overtaken in the fault. So clever are the devices of the Wicked One.

"Boys will be Boys and Girls will be Girls"

Maybe I should keep these items separate; but they do have common warning signs which are enemies to the gathering of the Ekklesia.

When any group superimposes some restriction above and beyond the roles of male or female, of brother and sister, in a group; well then, there's probably something haywire going on. What do you mean by that?

Ever notice certain groups are altogether enamored with 1 Corinthians 11:3-15 but just don't seem to make it to 1 Corinthians 11:16?

> *"But if anyone seems to be contentious, we have no such custom, nor do the churches of God."*

So, You want to do Ekklesia?

The word "contentious" is taken from the Greek word, *philoneikos* (Strong's G#5380, taken from G#5384 "denoting loved, dear, or friendly" and means: "a quarrel, fond of strife, disputations, contentious"—in other words, "love to quarrel" "fond of strife" and love to involve themselves with "disputations").

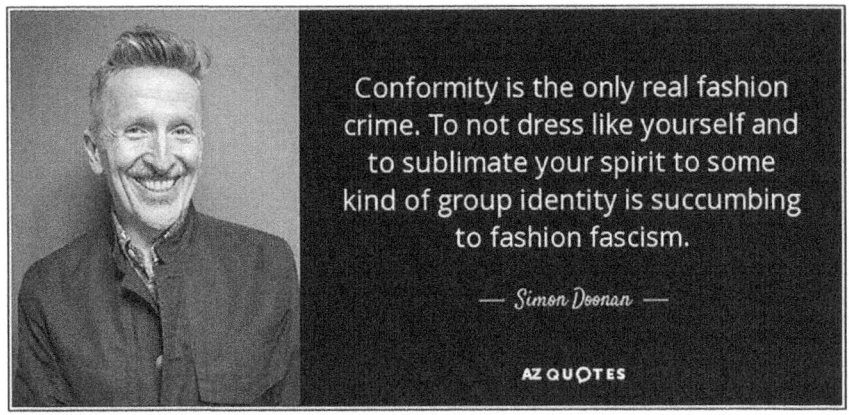

> Conformity is the only real fashion crime. To not dress like yourself and to sublimate your spirit to some kind of group identity is succumbing to fashion fascism.
>
> — *Simon Doonan* —

Figure 87 - CONFORMITY IS THE ONLY REAL FASHION CRIME

Some folks can't stop telling the boys and girls their God-ordained roles in the Ekklesia—be it length of hair, dress, speech, ad nausea, ad infinitute. Could it be they LOVE TO BE CONTENTIOUS? Forbid! Again, I again bring up the Evangelist Philip and his four virgin daughters who are identified as prophesying ([Acts 21:9](#)). Do you think they were spouting off to themselves and "sharing" exclusively at the ladies' home circle? Don't think so. You can read into it what you may but the fact they were all prophesying ought to tell us something about women speaking forth on behalf of the Lord . . . sufficient enough to get themselves written up in the book of the Acts.

What is it we don't get here: ALL CAN PROPHESY (except the women)—EACH ONE HAS (except the women)—"ONE BY ONE" (women excluded)—there are diversities of gifts, ministries, activities (all of which exclude women)—I could go on but I think you get the gist of it.

Sorry (no I'm not), a "male dominated" assembly can so easily lead to "sexual exploitation of women"—of that, there can be little denial—there's just too much "proof" to go around!

And, insofar as everyone looking alike . . . well, allow me to ask what's this business of everyone in the group dressing alike—worse, when we come to a gathering for some inexplicable reason, we have to wear our "Sunday best" to be "in the House of the Lord?" Where did we get that one from? First, we're too casual and expect everyone to dress casual and then we conform to all married men must wear a white shirt and a skinny black tie; and all women married or single must wear doilies atop their heads at the gatherings—and, if they don't, I'm going to get very CONTENTIOUS!

What's bizarre is to see women dressing in prairie garb as if we're living in the Nineteenth Century. Everyone has their notion on what constitutes "modest apparel"—fine, try to keep it to yourself, please. Once we all start looking alike, forbid we deny we're not some denomination.

In point of fact, I am well aware of certain, beloved brethren who vociferously oppose the title of a denomination and go out of their way to deny they are a faction when in reality they all dress the same—men in black and women in "dress blues" just off the prairie, with little bonnets . . . but "we're not a denomination"—oh, really—who knew?

And, what's with the hair? An entire denomination—well beloved—and truly "born from above" demands that the men look just like they got out of a military boot camp—with hair perfectly croft and slicked down so that not one hair is out of place . . . while the women have these little buns affixed to their hair and every time they comb their hair, and some comes out (as is normal), they literally save it and blend it into the bun in the back. Some of the buns are huge—just so you know (I know, too much information here.).

Then the guys are insufferable and look like they just got out of the Pale of Settlement in Eastern Europe somewhere with beards galore. He who doesn't have a beard is "other worldly" when "this worldly" bunch of bearded brethren know who's in and who's out of the group. Utterly noteworthy—right?

If your Ekklesia experience has "a little of this and a little of that"—e.g., some bearded ones, some with cool haircuts, and

So, You want to do Ekklesia?

some bald, some with long dresses, and some with white shirts and ties, and some with sandals, and some who just got back from a wedding—IT DOESN'T MATTER A TWIT! It may be your "custom"—then again it "may not." Whatever it is has little to do with the fellowship of the saints and keeping the "*unity of the Spirit in the uniting bond of peace!*"

Figure 88 - "BEARDED CONFORMITY"

If you, however, think that by "dressing like the elders" makes you a candidate for "greater things than these shall ye do"—let me disabuse you of such grandeur. Playing the part "does not you the part make." In a way, I hate to end these two chapters with these verses . . . but Jesus isn't fooling around when it comes to outward appearances:

> *"Woe to you, scribes and Pharisees, hypocrites! For you cleanse the outside of the cup and dish, but inside they are full of extortion and self-indulgence. Blind Pharisee first cleanse the inside of the cup and dish, that the outside of them may be clean also. Woe to you, scribes and Pharisees, hypocrites! For you are like whitewashed tombs which indeed appear beautiful outwardly, but inside are full of dead men's bones and all uncleanness. Even so you also*

outwardly appear righteous to men, but inside you are full of hypocrisy and lawlessness" (Matt. 23:25-28).

I genuinely hope we can all have a truly wondrous Ekklesia experience—for we are the Body of Christ and MEMBERS IN PARTICULAR... NOT PARTICULAR MEMBERS. Got it? Hope so.

So, You want to do Ekklesia?

Chapter 14:
Lord's Supper – Division in the Camp?

Figure 89 - The Body - The Blood - Communion

WHY IS IT THAT WHAT WAS DIVINELY INSTITUTED—THE LORD'S SUPPER (AKA, THE "HOLY COMMUNION" – LORD'S TABLE – EUCHARIST)—has become one of the most divisive issues within the Body of Christ, among believers in Yeshua/Jesus? You'd think that *"discerning the Lord's Body"* would be the keynote in bringing and expressing our oneness we have in Christ—but it has become a lightning rod for Christians to divide from one another—more so than baptism!

Even the phrase: "Let's break bread"—gives us a sense of peace; of gathering as one without contention and separation . . . ALAS! We're so factious to the point we have no idea how separated we really are!

This segment on EKKLESIA is not easy to transcribe—for swirling around in my cranium are a myriad of ways to approach this theological imbroglio. Unraveling the meaning and practice of this expression of Christian Oneness and its myriad practices

So, You want to do Ekklesia?

and those divisions which ensue from the how, when, why, where and what it all means to believers today is no small fete.

This brevity would be preposterous to advance the notion we can summarize the manifold issues which surround this topic in one setting—so, consider this a 40,000-ft. high overview of the Grand Canyon, AZ on the left side of the plane (hardly an in-depth look at this immense site). Let's try to approach it from an "Ekklesia" point of view, as well as touch on some major theological issues surrounding this most sacred, yet divisive (sad to say), experience.

Alas! It turns out that this may be one of the longest chapters of what has become a book on the topic of Ekklesia. Unfortunately, some have "tabled" the Table because of its tendency to "ceremony" and sundry methodologies and acute theological contentions. So sad this has happened when such a celebration of our Lord can be a joyous experience for all believers!

We'll consider the following:

(1) Major traditional theological issues relative to the Lord's Table.
(2) New Testament occurrences, descriptions of the Lord's Supper.
(3) New Covenant and New Commandment implications
(4) The "Ekklesia" implications regarding "Breaking of Bread"

Traditional Theological Issues on Communion

Again, this practice and/or experience of the "Communion Table" is one of the most "separating" issues within the Body of Christ—What is its essence? What really takes place when it occurs? Who can participate? What so-called qualifications are necessary to "partake"? How is the "Lord's Table" administered (and who can serve it)? When should it occur? Why should we do it in the first place? All these considerations afflict the Body of Christ and cause enumerable division and separation from one another—tragic as it is. Keeping a blind eye to the myriad of division abounding in the Body of Christ over this issue could readily be observed as someone in unintended denial!

Virtually all of Christendom (Catholic, Orthodox, Protestants, non-affiliated Christians) consider the Lord's Table to be a "sacrament" or "ordinance"—with all agreeing that baptism is the other "main sacrament" or ordinance (at least these two sacraments are accepted by virtually all of Christendom—other so-called sacraments like "marriage" would be considered on an equal par with these two main ones—but, again, all of Christianity embraces these two practices as sacraments (i.e., "sacred" to the Christian experience and practice—and directly ordained by the Lord). Duly noted, however, are our Quaker/Friends and Salvation Army brethren who consider both such "sacraments" unnecessary for "holy living" (shocking—but "live with it"—their conviction: Such practices do not assure anyone of "holy living").[1] (Note: All Endnotes at end of Chapter 14)

Figure 90 - The Last Supper - Leonardo Da Vinci

"Holy Communion" (again, I waft back and forth on these expressions which all mean "the same object of our discussion" but are spoken of by sundry segments of Christianity in different ways—Lord's Table, Holy Communion, the Lord's Supper, Eucharist, Blessed Sacrament, the Breaking of Bread, the Bread and the Cup, the Love Feast, Memorial, Remembrance, "The Lord's Evening Meal' (Jehovah Witnesses), even "the Mass" in the Catholic

So, You want to do Ekklesia?

Church, etc.) yet, even from these expressions, one can tell we are obviously deeply embedded in the Christian practice of the "Table." Incidentally, the term "Eucharist" is derived from the following (original links in quotes kept for viewing in printed editions):

> The Greek noun εὐχαριστία (*eucharistia* [from whence Eucharist]), meaning "thanksgiving", appears fifteen times in the New Testament[10] but is not used as an official name for the rite;[11] however, the related verb is found in New Testament accounts of the Last Supper,[12][13][14] including the earliest such account:[11]

> *"For I received from the Lord what I also delivered to you, that the Lord Jesus on the night when he was betrayed took bread, and when he had given **thanks** (εὐχαριστήσας), he broke it, and said, 'This is my body which is for you. Do this in remembrance of me'"* (1 Corinthians 11:23–24).

> The Lord's Supper, in Greek Κυριακὸν δεῖπνον (*Kyriakon deipnon*), was in use in the early '50s of the 1st century,[11][12] as witnessed by the First Epistle to the Corinthians (11:20–21):

> *When you come together, it is not **the Lord's Supper** you eat, for as you eat, each of you goes ahead without waiting for anybody else. One remains hungry, another gets drunk.*[2]

You can see from all these descriptions of this Passover Preparation Feast (Nisan 13) which took place in the Upper Room (prior to Passover Day on Nisan 14 when He was buried) by our Lord and His disciples, just how many "divisions" have resulted from what was clearly the Lord's effort in gathering together His disciples/friends, coupled with His "Upper Room Discourse" and prayer for the ONENESS of His followers (John chapters 12-17). For such a brief moment in time and space—can you imagine how many practices and intense divisions within Christendom have resulted! Dare you read the entire article in Wikipedia on this, you will be exhausted—as in: How could something so simple become so incredibly complicated and ultimately, so divisive? (See Endnote #**10** at end of this chapter 14)

The THREE **traditional** views on the essence of the practice of the Lord's Supper (i.e., "What's IN the bread and cup?") include:

(1) **Transubstantiation** -

(Latin: *transsubstantiatio*; Greek: μετουσίωσις *metousiosis*) is, according to the teaching of the Roman Catholic Church, the change of substance or essence by which the bread and wine offered in the sacrifice of the sacrament of the Eucharist during the Mass, become, in reality, the body and blood of Jesus Christ. In this teaching, the notions of substance and transubstantiation are not linked with any particular theory of metaphysics.[3]

(2) **Consubstantiation** or "Sacramental Union" (Note: There is a difference.) This is much more elaborate than meets the less astute theological eye; to wit:

In the sacramental union the consecrated bread is united with the body of Christ and the consecrated wine is united with the blood of Christ by virtue of Christ's original institution with the result that anyone eating and drinking these "elements"— the consecrated bread and wine—really eats and drinks the physical body and blood of Christ as well. Lutherans maintain that what they believe to be the biblical doctrine of the *manducatio indignorum* ("eating of the unworthy") supports this doctrine as well as any other doctrine affirming the Real Presence. The *manducatio indignorum* is the contention that even unbelievers eating and drinking in the Eucharist really eat and drink the body and blood of Christ.[3] This view was put forward by Martin Luther in his 1528 Confession Concerning Christ's Supper.

AND

So, You want to do Ekklesia?

For the reason why, in addition to the expressions of Christ and St. Paul (the bread in the Supper is the body of Christ or the communion of the body of Christ), also the forms: under the bread, with the bread, in the bread [the body of Christ is present and offered], are employed, is that by means of them the papistical transubstantiation may be rejected and the sacramental union of the unchanged essence of the bread and of the body of Christ indicated.[5][4]

(3) **Memorialism**/Remembrance Only: These three categories (Transubstantiation, Sacramental Union, and Memorialism) are exceedingly broadly based and have scores of theological derivations. However, this so stated, the "Remembrance/Memorial" view is as follows (and it's a mouthful):

Memorialism: Is the belief held by some Christian denominations that the elements of bread and wine (or juice) in the Eucharist (more often referred to as The Lord's Supper by memorialists) are **purely symbolic representations of the body and blood of Jesus**, the feast being established only or primarily as a commemorative ceremony. The term comes from Luke 22:19: "This do in memory of me" and the attendant interpretation that the Lord's Supper's chief purpose is to help the participant *remember* Jesus and his sacrifice on the Cross.

Yes – Divisions in the Body

This viewpoint is commonly held by Baptists,[1][2] Anabaptists,[3] the Plymouth Brethren, [3] Jehovah's Witnesses, [4][5][6][7] segments of the Restoration Movement[3] and some non-denominational Churches, [8] as well as those identifying with liberal Christianity, but it is rejected by most branches of Christianity, including the Roman Catholic Church, the Eastern Orthodox Church, the Oriental Orthodox Church, Independent Catholic Churches, the Church of the East, Lutherans, Presbyterians and other traditional Calvinists, as well as the vast majority

242

of *Anglicans* and *Methodists, who variously affirm the doctrine of the* real presence.⁵

I know, it's exhausting . . . but moving on here . . .

NT Occurrences and Descriptions

It is of keen interest to this writer that the "Last Supper" is described with the "bread and the cup" in the so-called synoptic gospels (Matthew 26:26-30; Mark 14:22-26; Luke 22:14-20). Prominent in these accounts; however, the Gospel of John has no mention (at best "veiled allusions") to the "bread and the cup" (John 13:1-30); but instead, elaborates upon "foot washing"—absolutely, NOTHING is given concerning the **New Covenant** nor anything about the sequence and administration of the "bread of His Body" and the "cup of redemption in His blood" nor the inauguration of the New Covenant . . . but the **New Commandment** is most definitely mentioned (John 13:31-35; 14:15, 21, 23; 15:12-15).

Likewise, in John's gospel Jesus goes into great detail regarding the Promise of the Spirit in His Upper Room discourse—more so than in any of the synoptic gospels (i.e., by His "going, He is coming to us"—John 14)—He speaks of His Indwelling us; of the Father and the Son through the Spirit of Promise (John 14:19-31) abiding in us.

Furthermore, John speaks of the "abiding life" wherein Jesus is the vine and we are the branches (John 15); and then of the "interior work of the Holy Spirit" in the lives of the believers in John 16, culminating in His High Priestly prayer found in John 17 and offered at the conclusion of the Last Supper before His disciples/friends in that same Upper Room.

No, nothing is said about the New Covenant with the bread and the wine but a whole lot is said in John's gospel concerning the intimacy and indwelling of the Spirit of Life in Christ Who would, through His death, be sent from the Father to indwell all of His believers!

Notwithstanding, the allusions to the "breaking of bread" are recorded in Acts 2:46 and, most definitely, in 1 Corinthians 11:17-

So, You want to do Ekklesia?

34—we will discuss this in some detail in item #4 on the implications of the practice of Ekklesia within the context of the Lord's Supper.

I find it most remarkable that the synoptic gospels are riveted upon the "bread and the wine" but the gospel of John is focused on the subjective impact of the Holy Spirit's life within believers and of the oneness of the Body of Christ resulting in the Promise of the Spirit—along with the New Commandment given to "*love one another AS I have loved you—that you also love one another*"—for it is this that produces the Oneness of His people including the gifts given to us in John 17 of a common **Life** (the Life of the Father—for we are all His children—John 17:2-3—the **Truth**—John 17:8, 14, 17 [for His "word is truth"]—and His **Glory**, John 17:22-24 that we might manifest this glory to the world around us).[6]

The expression of the GLORY is based upon the common Life of the Father and the Truth of His Word (Christ is the "Word made flesh") and the Spirit of God is expressed in the Spirit of Promise enabling us to share in the LOVE that the Father and the Son share (John 17:22-24) . . . without the New Commandment (i.e., the "Love Commandment") the world will not be able to see how the Father loved and still loves the Son "*before the foundation of the world*" (John 17:24). John 17 clearly reveals that through the giving up of His Life we now would be brought into the very fellowship of the Triune God wherein we share in the same love and fellowship the Son and the Father have always had before the foundation of the world! This is truly amazing!

New Covenant & New Commandment - Implications

I would like to expand upon how the New Covenant and the New Commandment are one in the same—with separate emphases. We at ONE BODY LIFE MINISTRY, on whose board I currently serve, has had the privilege of serving/teaming-up in ministry with our beloved brother in Christ, Gaylord Enns of LOVE REVOLUTION NOW.[7] Gaylord's THE LOVE REVOLUTION[8] embodies the vision and practice of this most dynamic discovery—

even revelation (aka, "illumination" by the Holy Spirit)—of such a doctrine and practice.

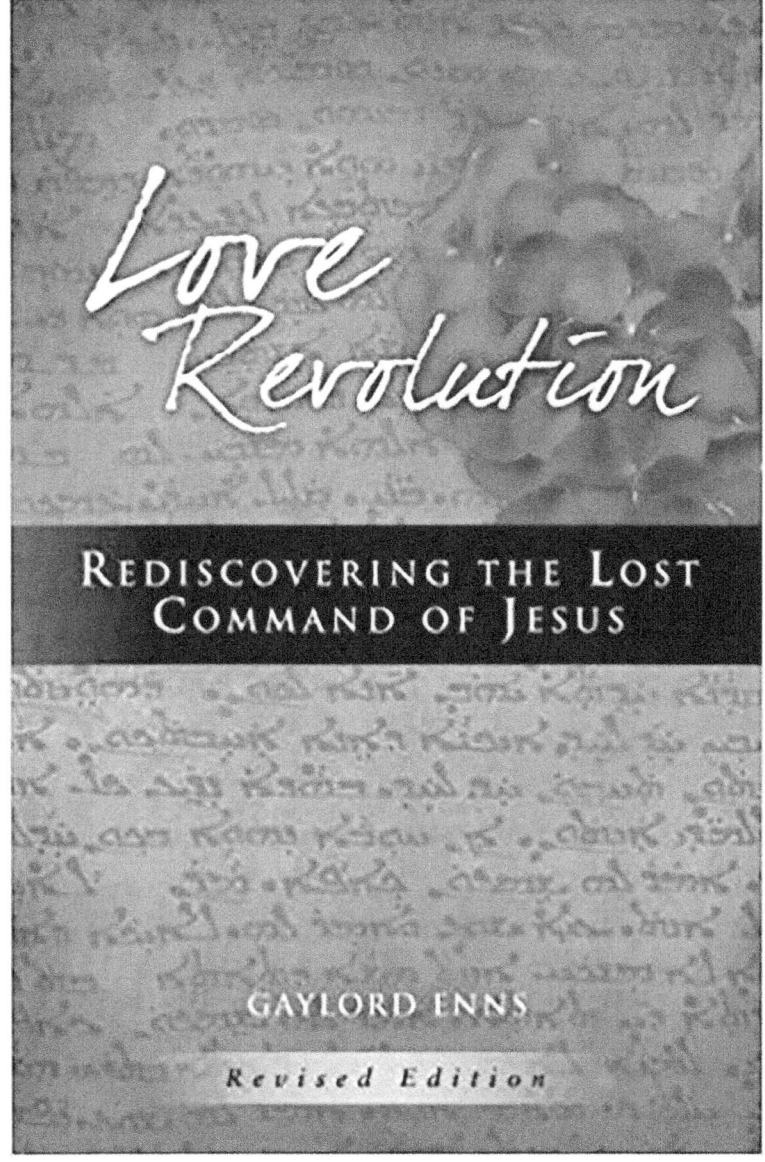

Figure 91 - "LOVE REVOLUTION NOW" - BY GAYLORD ENNS

The "Great Commandment" is contrasted by the "New Commandment" by brother Enns. In essence:

The **Great Commandment** (or **Greatest Commandment**)[1] is a name used in the New Testament to describe

So, You want to do Ekklesia?

the first of two commandments cited by Jesus in Matthew 22:35–40, Mark 12:28–34, and Luke 10:27a.

In Mark, when asked *"which is the great commandment in the law?"*, the Greek New Testament reports that Jesus answered, *"Hear, O Israel! The Lord Our God, The Lord is One; Thou shalt love thy Lord, thy God with all thy heart, and with all thy soul, and with all thy mind"*,[2] before also referring to a second commandment, *"And the second is like unto it, thou shalt love thy neighbor as thyself."*[3] Most Christian denominations consider these two commandments to be the core of correct Christian lifestyle.[4][9]

Yet, even in this Wikipedia disclosure, the New Commandment given in John's gospel is obfuscated. Observe the statement: "Most Christian denominations consider these two commandments to be the core of correct Christian lifestyle." Enns brings out that in his research into Church history over the last 2,000 years, scarcely any recognition to the importance of the New Commandment—nor of LOVE itself—is mentioned by Christian scholars, Early Church Fathers, theologians, pastors or teachers. This historical absence of content regarding the New Commandment, juxtaposed to the Great Commandment, is a striking discovery made by Enns and something wholly significant (viz., its absence) from Christian teaching.

According to Enns, its omission from Christian theology is both revealing and tantamount to a complete exposure as to why division persists within wide swaths of Christendom. There is little (if any) emphasis upon the New Commandment with the empowerment of the "abiding Life" needed to love as the Lord has loved us by His "resurrection love" poured into the believer when Jesus in resurrection breathed INTO the disciples the HOLY BREATH (viz., the Spirit of Life) and poured out (i.e., "clothed") that same Spirit of Power upon the early disciples at Pentecost!

The Great Commandment puts the emphasis upon the believer doing the love; whereas the New Commandment places the emphasis to love one another upon the very love of Christ which would abide in us upon His death, resurrection and impartation of the Spirit of Life into us—viz., we can love one another because He is loving through us!

Brother Gaylord's BREAKTHROUGH on this topic is invigorating the Body of Christ at this very season and bringing an emphasis so terribly neglected; yea, nigh for the past 2,000 years!

At a recent conference held here in Sacramento (Fall, 2019), I broached the question to Gaylord:

> Can we say that the New Commandment found only in John's Gospel is the working out—nigh, the actual MANIFESTATION—of the New Covenant? That is, Jesus' washing of the feet of the disciples, and speaking of the Promise of the Spirit, and of the abiding Life of Christ in the believer (viz., "*I am the vine you are the branches*") and the subsequent repetition of the Love Commandment—the New Commandment ([John 13:34]; [15:12-14]—after He speaks of the Vine/Branches and the abiding life of His believers) being the very manifestation of the New Covenant—for by ingesting His body (the bread) and drinking from the cup of His redemption (His blood) are we not living by His very Life under the New Covenant?

Most certainly we are because John's gospel makes this impeccable reality known to us all:

> "*Most assuredly, I say to you, he who believes in Me has everlasting life. I am the bread of life. Your fathers ate the manna in the wilderness, and are dead. This is the bread which comes down from heaven, that one may eat of it and not die. I am the living bread which came down from heaven. If anyone eats of this bread, he will live forever; and the bread that I shall give is My flesh, which I shall give for the life of the world.*"

> "*The Jews therefore quarreled among themselves, saying, 'How can this Man give us His flesh to eat?'*"

> "*Then Jesus said to them, 'Most assuredly, I say to you, unless you eat the flesh of the Son of Man and drink His blood,*

So, You want to do Ekklesia?

you have no life in you. Whoever eats My flesh and drinks My blood has eternal life, and I will raise him up at the last day. For My flesh is food indeed, and My blood is drink indeed. He who eats My flesh and drinks My blood abides in Me, and I in him. As the living Father sent Me, and I live because of the Father, so he who feeds on Me will live because of Me. This is the bread which came down from heaven—not as your fathers ate the manna, and are dead. He who eats this bread will live forever" (John 6:47-58).

One might deem me, in certain evangelical circles, involved in some form of Catholic heresy, however, does this not speak not only of the "abiding life" but of the "assimilated life" we share in his body and blood? It is by eating His bread (body) and drinking His cup (blood) that we enjoy Him as our Life (bread) and as our Redemption (blood)—and by His Body and Blood we now live out **the New Commandment . . . the very expression of the New Covenant.**

There's more—MUCH MORE—but should this not be all-sufficient? Why would the Lord enjoin us to practice this "supper" over and over for the last 2,000 years? Surely, we are not to "crucify the Lord of Glory" afresh? No, but in that He died once, He is NOT to be sacrificed over and over again:

"So Christ was once offered to bear the sins of many; and unto them that look for him shall he appear the second time without sin unto salvation" (Heb. 9:28).

More so:

"But this Man, after He had offered one sacrifice for sins forever, sat down at the right hand of God . . . For by one offering He has perfected forever those who are being sanctified. But the Holy Spirit also witnesses to us; for after He had said before, 'This is the covenant that I will make with them after those days, says the LORD: I will put My laws into their hearts, and in their minds I will write them,' then He adds,

'Their sins and their lawless deeds I will remember no more'" (Hebrews 10:12-17).

I'm leading up to something here. The writer of Hebrews is drawing our attention to the "once and for all sacrifice" of the spotless Lamb of God, thereby inaugurating the NEW COVENANT—for, *"This is the covenant"* is taken right out of Jeremiah 31:31-34 whereupon the SPIRIT OF GOD is to write His laws upon the fleshy tablets of our hearts.

This is NOT some far off, prior to the commencement of the literal 1,000-year Millennium, New Covenant exclusively and prophetically reserved for the Jews (viz., Judah); no, it IS the very New Covenant promised in Jeremiah 31:33-34 and inaugurated in the Upper Room by the "bread of His body" and the "cup of His blood" given to both Jew and Gentile with the Promise of the Spirit: *BUT THE HOLY SPIRIT ALSO WITNESSES TO US.* We are empowered to embrace the outworking of the New Covenant via the New Commandment to love one another AS HE LOVED US!

> *"Behold, the days are coming, says the LORD, when I will make a **new covenant with the house of Israel and with the house of Judah**—not according to the covenant that I made with their fathers in the day that I took them by the hand to lead them out of the land of Egypt, My covenant which they broke, though I was a husband to them, says the LORD. But this is the covenant that I will make with the house of Israel (both with Ephraim and with Judah) after those days, says the LORD: I will put My law in their minds, and write it on their hearts; and I will be their God, and they shall be My people. No more shall every man teach his neighbor, and every man his brother, saying, 'Know the LORD,' for they all shall know Me, from the least of them to the greatest of them, says the LORD. For I will forgive their iniquity, and their sin I will remember no more"* (Jeremiah 31:31-34).

Brethren, there is but ONE NEW COVENANT—its origins are in Jeremiah and its inauguration is in that Upper

So, You want to do Ekklesia?

Room. Likewise, there is but ONE NEW COMMANDMENT and it is intrinsically connected to the working out by the Spirit of God based upon that same New Covenant written upon the fleshly tables of our hearts . . . time to pay attention:

"You are our epistle written in our hearts, known and read by all men; clearly you are an epistle of Christ, ministered by us, written not with ink but by the Spirit of the living God, not on tablets of stone but on tablets of flesh, that is, of the heart. And we have such trust through Christ toward God. Not that we are sufficient of ourselves to think of anything as being from ourselves, but our sufficiency is from God, who also made us sufficient as ministers of the NEW COVENANT, not of the letter but of the Spirit; for the letter kills, but the Spirit gives life" (2 Cor. 3:1-6)

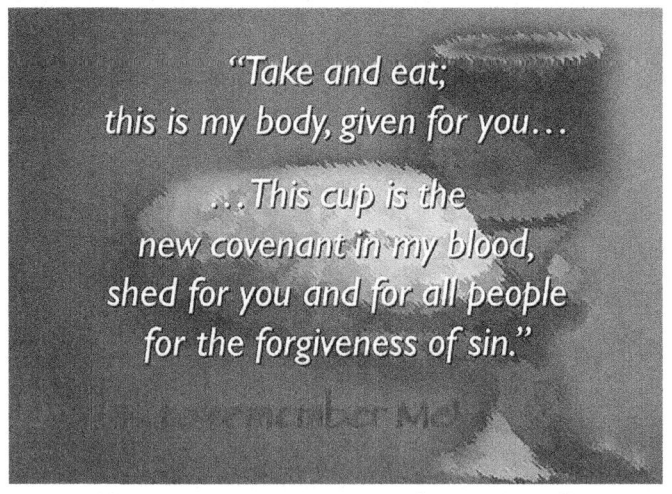

Figure 92 - THE NEW COVENANT "IN MY BLOOD"

The very GLORY of the New Covenant bursts forth in 2 Corinthians 3:7-18 culminating in this glory:

"Nevertheless when one turns to the Lord, the veil is taken away. Now the Lord is the Spirit; and where the Spirit of the Lord is, there is liberty. But we all, with unveiled face, beholding as in a mirror the glory of the Lord, are being

transformed into the same image from glory to glory, just as from the Lord, the Spirit" (2 Cor. 3:16-18).

In other words—the expression of the New Covenant not only transforms believers in Christ—into the Image of Christ, the Messiah, but enables them under the banner of the New Commandment to love one another as He first loved us.

Yes, the emphasis of the New Commandment is the empowerment to love one another by the Spirit of the Lord working and writing upon the fleshy tables of our hearts—for His commands are not grievous—AND, all of this partaking, transformation, and loving one another has a glorious result: THE ANSWER TO OUR LORD'S PRAYER IN JOHN 17—the ONENESS of His One Body!

It is through the blood of His cross—the very expression of His everlasting Life in the person and work of our Lord Jesus Christ that He has made of the two (Jew and Gentile) ONE NEW MAN – SO MAKING PEACE (Eph. 2). Now, we are enjoined to practice the "truth of the gospel" (Galatians 2:5, 14—Jewish believers in Yeshua should eat with Gentile believers in Jesus)—living out the New Covenant/New Commandment—all within the context of: *I WILL BUILD MY EKKLESIA*. This brings us to our fourth and final discussion regarding the Lord's Table:

"Ekklesia" Implications at the "Lord's Table"

I Corinthians 11:17-34 is broken down into three segments:

1. Conduct at the Lord's Supper (1 Cor. 11:17-22).
2. Institution of the Lord's Supper (1 Cor. 11:23-26).
3. Discerning the Lord's Body (1 Cor. 11:27-34).

I purposefully used the phrase "discerning the Lord's Body" juxtaposed, over against the phrase "Examination of Yourself" for that is precisely NOT the emphasis found at the Lord's Supper—it has everything to do with "discerning the Lord's Body"—not discerning what a wretched sinner you are!

Allow me some latitude to explain myself. I will NOT magnify the sordid divisions resulting from the institution of this

So, You want to do Ekklesia?

partaking with its myriad of theological differences. Suffice it to say there is ONE BODY/BREAD and ONE CUP/BLOOD and it is predicated upon and inaugurated as the NEW COVENANT (the fulfillment of Jeremiah 31) so recognized as *"often as you drink it, in remembrance of Me"* (1 Cor. 11:25).

How we go about doing this is somewhat irrelevant—so is our frequency thereof . . . *"For as often as you eat this bread and drink this cup, you proclaim the Lord's death till He comes"* (1 Cor. 11:26). Indeed, whether you use the "fruit of the vine" or water—it's the SAME CUP which we share! Good grief, Krieger, you're off the reservation now!

What concerns me is the DIVISION so amplified at Corinth among the brethren. Apparently, the wealthy were gorging themselves by taking their own supper ahead of others (at the very Love Feast) while those with little (the poor) were going hungry. This wasn't much of a "Love Feast" as much as it was an apparent "feeding frenzy" taking place, leading to drunkenness by some of the wealthier brethren (hard to visualize this environment)—how inconsiderate of them! For: *"Do you despise the ekklesia of God and shame the poor who have nothing"* (Free translation of 1 Cor. 11:22).

This puts a new twist on the phrase: *"Whose God is their belly!"* Imagine, the Ekklesia at Corinth was an expression of economic inequality on display. Of course, we in the West and/or those following our example, would never delight in such a separation of the poor vs. the wealthy in a "Church setting." Go figure—there appears to be a pernicious tendency of such in certain congregations and among even house gatherings where those of a certain economic affluence find it far more comfortable to "table" with those of equal enhancement—while the poor of the congregation/gathering are viewed with contempt. It ought not so to be among us!

At issue in Corinth was a division of the wealthy vs. the poor; consequently, this division spewed over, if you would, into this:

*"Therefore whoever eats this bread or drinks this cup of the Lord in an UNWORTHY manner will be guilty of the body and blood of the Lord. But let a man **EXAMINE*** (Strong's

Greek #1381 – *dokimazo*) *himself, and so let him eat of the bread and drink of the cup. For he who eats and drinks in an unworthy manner eats and drinks judgment to himself, not discerning the Lord's body"* (1 Cor. 11:27-29).

We have the notion that this kind of self-examination has everything to do with our own sinful condition—and that somehow we must confess our wretched condition, our sins, by reflecting not only upon them but, on the affirmative side whereby we both confess and apply the blood of Jesus afresh, by asking Him to forgive us of our sins. THAT, dear friend is NOT the injunction so given here—sorry to disappoint—for I know that most of us, including yours truly, find this occasion a blessed time to reflect upon the Lord's forgiveness of my/our sin(s).

Nor is the understanding of "*he who eats and drinks in an unworthy manner*" well positioned in our thinking—it has little or nothing to do with coming to the Table with unconfessed sin but everything to do with these divisions aforementioned . . . it's not "How's it going with me?" but "How's it going with me and the brethren?" "*Not discerning the Lord's Body*" is grossly misunderstood!

Let me explain what IS going on here (not to sound "too presumptuous"). The word *dokimazo* (translated *examine*) is derived from the Greek word *dokimos* (Strong's Greek #1384 meaning "acceptable" or "approved") and is used in 1 Corinthians 11:19:

*"For there must also be factions among you, that those who are **APPROVED** (dokimos) may be recognized* (i.e., "manifested") *among you."*

In other words, "*But let a man **EXAMINE** (dokimazo) himself*" in 1 Corinthians 11:28 is derived from the same Greek word found in 1 Corinthians 11:19; to wit: "*That those who are **APPROVED** (dokimos) may be recognized among you.*"

The necessity of factions (NOT *heresies*) found in 1 Corinthians 11:19 are there in the Ekklesia so that those who are "examined" or "approved" or "acceptable" will be manifested.

So, You want to do Ekklesia?

Obviously, these are mature brethren who keep the "*Unity of the Spirit in the uniting bond of peace*" amongst the sundry, but necessary factions—for there is wide diversity among the brethren—we are NOT a homogeneous group (although we "like our own" who think and act like us and even look like us and practice the Faith as we do—but that is NOT what's going on here).

In order to overcome this disunity in Corinth, the brethren were challenged by Paul to examine themselves (**approve** themselves)—to be those brethren who keep the unity among the factions which most certainly will be there—for some in Corinth were of Paul, some of Apollos, some of Peter and some, even, of Christ (1 Cor. 1:11-14; 3:4-9). We're all affected by various ministers/ministries—"factions" (in a good way)—but we praise God for those "approved" brethren . . . in point of fact, all the brethren should seek such APPROVED CONDITION and, thus, embrace the unity of the Body of Christ . . . ridding ourselves of such disunity among the factions . . . ending factious disputations!

What is "unworthily" here is not your sinful condition . . . well, yes, it is in one way . . . but what's at stake here is our disunity we may have in the Ekklesia, the Body of Christ. It has everything to do with DISCERNING—*CONTENDING* for the Lord's Body. The Corinthian Christians were NOT discerning the Lord's One Body but holding to their factions—either to various ministry leaders or to their own economic differences. DISCERNING in the Greek (Strong's #1252 – *diakrino*) literally means to "discern" or "contend" as per the Lord's One Body—i.e., one who is approved (examined) is one who contends for the Lord's One Body and is wholly opposed to separation of that One Body due to anything which would keep the brethren apart from one another (viz., a factious spirit).

The Lord's Supper is, yes, DO THIS IN REMEMBRANCE OF ME . . . but ME has everything to do with MY ONE BODY! You may be thinking our brother Doug borders on the sacrilegious in that he takes away from this expression of our celebration of the person of Christ Himself Who has forgiven us all our sins and has committed to us His very Life that we may live in His presence forevermore! Surely, He has so forgiven us and given to us His Eternal Life—but THAT'S NOT WHAT IS GOING ON HERE nor

Lord's Supper – Division in the Camp?

is such an emphasis exclusively celebrated each time we come to the Table of the Lord. Yes, remember Him, but know this: He's remembering, if you would, His One Body . . . and so should we!

What is going on here—and the reason why some of God's children at Corinth were getting sick, even unto death (1 Cor. 11:30)—has to do with the divisions among them/us. Why does Paul then say:

> ***"For if we would judge ourselves, we would not be judged****. But when we are judged, we are chastened by the Lord, that we may not be condemned with the world. Therefore, my brethren, when you come together to eat, wait for one another. But if anyone is hungry, let him eat at home, lest you come together for judgment . . ."* (1 Cor. 11:31-34).

Can you follow me here? Paul's concern was for the Oneness of the Ekklesia—not for how we examine our sinful condition and then rehearse how He forgives us of our sins. Although we should keep short accounts with the Almighty . . . but again, that's NOT the emphasis displayed at the Communion Table. It has everything to do with the Oneness of His One Body and our relationship thereto. Imagine, someone of Catholic persuasion partaking in this manner with a view that he or she is truly One Body with their Orthodox brethren—and the same goes for Protestants, Evangelicals and unaffiliated brethren. Our "gaze" should not be on our "Roman Catholic Communion" of parishioners but upon the whole Body of Christ! We're not just one with all Baptists or Protestants but one with all who call upon the Name of the Lord!

Yes, it sure sounds like when the Love Feast took place in Corinth folks had lots of food brought in by the brethren—yet, some were "more equal than others" . . . meaning, they (the rich) were hogging the goodies and stuffing themselves with the very own food they brought . . . better to eat at home than to display such selfish behavior. You come to this Table to declare there is but ONE BODY—One Bread—One Cup—but you act like there are a multitude of such entities (aka, DIVISIONS gone DIVISIVE, factions gone factious). Paul's not asking them to drop all their factions and divisions or economic differences—but he's sure appealing to them to stop with the divisive and factious behavior—let alone the outworking of their economic differences. Better for those to manifest who are approved; to examine yourself to see if you are contending for the Ekklesia, and NOT contending for your own belly!

The best way to do this in *"remembrance of Me"* is to be at peace, at Oneness with all God's children and to *"love one another as I have loved you that you also love one another."* If you come to celebrate the Lord through a corporate meal—remember, you're NOT the only one at the table—others are there to eat as well . . . it's called *sharing*. We share the bread and the cup—but there is one bread so broken and one cup so shared. Indeed, if you're that hungry, better to eat at home than to come to a Love Feast to gorge yourself! How practical is that? Very!

What appears to have been taking place as the "whole assembly came together" were these clusters of wealthy believers huddling off in one direction serving themselves their scrumptious meal, all the while the poor were off to the side viewing this spectacle and pondering their impoverished state of affairs . . . and asking themselves: "Why aren't our brothers and sisters not sharing their abundance with us?"

I hope this little study on the Breaking of Bread has been helpful. We find in 1 Corinthians 11:17 through I Corinthians 14 one of the rarest glimpses of the Ekklesia's gathering. Though it is but a brief window into how, what, when, why, and even where the Ekklesia comes together, it is simply a marvelous account of how brethren can experience Christ and bring the riches of their experience of Him to His One Body—SHARING in the "Table of His Love"—pouring out our love to Him and to one another through the love wherewith He first loved us!

Dividing the Cup in Luke's Gospel?

I find it most fascinating how only in Luke's gospel we read of the "passing of the cup" prior to the breaking of the bread and Jesus' comment: "This cup is the New Covenant in My blood" being shared:

> *"Then He said to them, 'With fervent desire I have desired to eat this Passover with you before I suffer; for I say to you, I will no longer eat of it until it is fulfilled in the kingdom of God.'* **then He took the cup, and gave thanks, and said, 'Take this and divide it among yourselves**; *for I say to you, I will not drink of the fruit of the vine until the kingdom of God comes"* (Luke 22:15-18)

It is only after these comments in Luke that we hear:

> *"He took bread, gave thanks and broke it, and gave it to them, saying, 'this is My body which is given for you; do this in remembrance of Me.' Likewise He also took the cup after supper, saying, 'This cup is the new covenant in My blood, which is shed for you.'"* (Luke 22:19-20).

I am not concerned with the Passover practice of sundry cups prior to the bread and the wine (interesting though that may be); however, I am fixated upon Jesus' behavior in Luke's gospel to *"take this (i.e., the cup) and divide it among yourselves."* Why? The singularity of this recording by Luke is theologically impressive!

Does this suggest prior to the taking of the bread, the cup of His blood was shared? The other gospels do NOT indicate this sequence. God's original intention was for humanity/mankind to partake of the Tree of Life in the Garden of God/Eden—to enjoy and be sustained by His Eternal Life; however, that intention was disrupted by rebellion, deception, and disobedience. So, we partake of the BREAD OF LIFE first and then, due to the fall of man, we partake of His Redemption, which brings us back, if you would, to the Tree of Life.

But here, in Luke's gospel we have the "passing around of the cup"—the cup whereof He said: *"Take this and divide it among yourselves."* Paul certainly places the "bread before the cup" in 1 Corinthians 11:24-26. So, why is the cup being passed around and divided among the disciples prior to the bread and the cup?

So, You want to do Ekklesia?

Be aware of the fact that Luke does share the "sequence" of the bread (Luke 22:19) and then the "cup" (Luke 22:10). But is this simply (viz., Luke 22:17) a forethought or emphasis by Luke of what was going to take place in Luke 22:19 (i.e., the bread comes first and then the cup). In other words, Luke is just giving us a little foretaste prior to the actual sequence of events? Or, is there a more profound meaning going on here? The other gospels do NOT record this "prior sharing of the cup" in this manner.

Could this be a glimpse of how the Body of Messiah would participate in ONE CUP of Blessing to be SHARED among them? It wasn't Jesus serving each one of them the cup—they were dividing the cup (sharing the cup) among themselves . . . from disciple to disciple with the express intent that each would be able to drink therefrom . . . and not that anyone of them would drink it all; leaving nothing for the others.

Furthermore, I find it implausible that the "dividing of the initial cup" was empty—i.e., passing around an empty cup. That would be very peculiar—thus, it was filled with a liquid; no doubt wine as well. But that initial cup had not been designated as the "blood of the New Covenant." It wasn't multiple cups but one cup that was divided among the disciples.

Could it be the sharing of this cup expressed the equality they would all have under the immediate pending of *"This cup is the New Covenant in My Blood"* (Luke 22:20)? That's the imagery one derives from these statements. Likewise, perhaps it was indicative—as they passed the initial cup around—that it contained the blood (the fruit of the vine), not yet shed, wherein the disciples had participated in our Lord's initial earthly ministry which would culminate in the actual shedding of His blood and the inauguration of the New Covenant? I think so.

There appears to be an immediate reflection of His One Cup being shared by each of the disciples—they were doing the sharing under His injunction: DIVIDE IT AMONG YOURSELVES. Fascinating, when the cup is mentioned after the bread in Luke 22:20, He doesn't tell them to drink it (nor record their drinking of the cup) as in Matthew 26:27; Mark 14:23-24; nor, for that matter Paul's sequence of drinking from the cup found in 1 Corinthians 11:25.

Lord's Supper – Division in the Camp?

You may consider that I'm making "something out of nothing"—however, the Scriptures are inspired by the Holy Spirit—this is no *faux pas* on Luke's part. Jesus fully intended them to mutually participate in this sharing of this cup PRIOR TO the bread and the cup being shared. The emphasis here is upon the disciples' participation—what He has given to them, they are to share it with one another!

When we do celebrate His Supper—we do so with the profound awareness we are One Body, at peace with all God's people . . . and, if we have ought against any member, we should DISCERN, **contend** against such factious attitudes and divisive spirits within "ourselves" (aka, "let a man ***examine/approve*** himself"). Indeed, could these not be the "approved ones" who manifest when the "whole Ekklesia comes together?" May we earnestly seek to be those approved of God, who stand against our "own belly"—pass the cup brethren—and share in the love and joy given to us in Christ under the New Covenant by living out the New Commandment in answer to our Lord's prayer in John 17: THAT THEY ALL MAY BE PERFECTED INTO ONE!

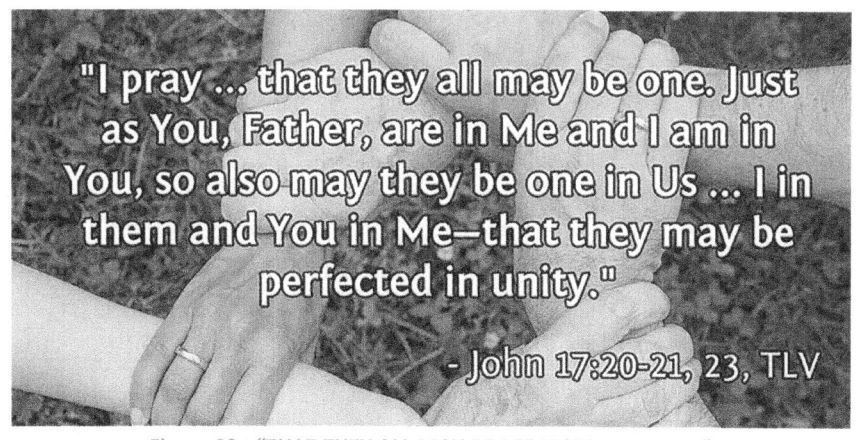

"I pray ... that they all may be one. Just as You, Father, are in Me and I am in You, so also may they be one in Us ... I in them and You in Me—that they may be perfected in unity."

- John 17:20-21, 23, TLV

Figure 93 - "THAT THEY ALL MAY BE PERFECTED IN UNITY"

Endnotes to Chapter 14:

1. https://en.wikipedia.org/wiki/Eucharist (retrieved on 11/11/2019)
2. Ibid.

So, You want to do Ekklesia?

3. https://en.wikipedia.org/wiki/Transubstantiation (retrieved on 11/11/2019)
4. https://en.wikipedia.org/wiki/Sacramental_union (retrieved on 11/11/2019)
5. https://en.wikipedia.org/wiki/Memorialism (retrieved on 11/11/2019)
6. Henry Hon's three books, with similar entitlements: **One Ekklesia, One Truth, One Life & Glory** illuminate the message of John 17 @ https://www.amazon.com/Henry-Hon/e/B07GK3T3W6%3Fref=dbs_a_mng_rwt_scns_share (retrieved on 11/11/2019)
7. https://www.loverevolutionnow.org/ (retrieved on 11/11/2019)
8. https://www.loverevolutionnow.org/shop (retrieved on 11/11/2019)
9. https://en.wikipedia.org/wiki/Great_Commandment (retrieved on 11/11/2019)
10. Please note that the Last Supper took place on Nisan 13 (Passover Preparation Day) when the lamb is slain [for Jesus was crucified on this very day—the slaying of the Pascal Lamb] but the bodies of the crucified were taken from the crosses prior to the actual Passover Day [when the lamb is eaten] commencing on Nisan 14 at 6 p.m. that "same day" of His crucifixion; for the Hebrew calendar begins a "new day" in the evening/morning sequence from 6:00 p.m. to 6:00 p.m. the "next 24-hour time frame." Therefore, He was buried on the Passover (Nisan 14) in the tomb of Joseph of Arimathea (Luke 23:50-56)—the "Sabbath" being considered a "high holy day" on Passover in the "middle of the week" or Wednesday/Thursday (Nisan 13/14) based on the Julian Calendar, not the Gregorian calendar.

Chapter 15:
The 24 Axioms of Ekklesia

> Ye are our epistle written in our hearts, known and read of all men: Forasmuch as ye are manifestly declared to be the epistle of Christ ministered by us, written not with ink, but with the Spirit of the living God; not in tables of stone, but in fleshy tables of the heart.
>
> 2 Corinthians 3:2-3

Figure 94 - 2 CORINTHIANS 3:2-3

WITH SOME HESITATION I APPROACH THIS FINAL CHAPTER BECAUSE OF ITS APPARENT LEGALISTIC TONE—I MEAN, REALLY, A BIT OVER THE TOP to conclude this final chapter with my own Ten Commandments concerning: **So, You want to do Ekklesia?** Therefore, to avoid this appearance, I have, instead, sought to frame these summations using mathematical or scientific/logical terms. You'd think such conclusions should be reached only by the Lord Himself—i.e., He doesn't need my help; since He said: "*I will build My Ekklesia*"!

Know this about an Axiom:

Basically, anything declared to be true and accepted, but does **not have** any proof or **has** some practical way of proving it, is an **axiom**. It is also sometimes referred to as a postulate, or an assumption. A **theorem**, by definition, is a statement proven based on **axioms**, other **theorems**, and some set of logical connectives. (Definitions/Google search)

Therefore, an axiom may or may not have proof—it can be proven that its "proof" is either invalid or valid. Either way the "negative" or "positive" is legitimate whose action corollaries

So, You want to do Ekklesia?

evolve into sundry theorems which are expressed in "some set of logical connectives." The axiom is taken as overtly true.

The "set of logical connectives" (viz., theorems) are what we're talking about derived from the stated axioms converted as they are by this author into tangible proofs—in other words, the "proof is in the pudding". . . that's how we know these postulates are workable, tangible, convincing, and as close to **absolute** as the word indicates. Simply put: If you stand out in the rain you will get wet (axiom)—you stood out in the rain and, sure enough, you got wet (theorem).

Translated: If you grasp the vision and general practice of Ekklesia as presented in these inscriptions, you will manifest the essence of Ekklesia which, hopefully, will resemble the fullness of the meaning of our Lord's assertion and confirmed by His high priestly prayer; to wit: *"I will build my Ekklesia and the Gates of Hades will not prevail against it* . . . AND . . . *"that they all may be one, as You, Father, are in Me, and I in You; that they also may be one in Us, that the world may believe that You sent me . . . I in them, and You in Me; that they may be perfected into one, and that the world may know that You have sent Me, and have loved them as You have loved Me."* (Matt. 16:18; John 17:21, 23)

Thus, Jesus' statement that He would build His Ekklesia (the verbal objective) results in the Gates of Hades being thwarted (a classical theorem).

Moreover, such a simple register of these fourteen chapters (originally presented as blog articles), thus far, augers for some kind of a conclusion—perhaps, if you're like me—in which you go to the back of the book feverishly looking for "What's this book all about?" thereby making an immediate judgment if it's worth reading, then you just might proceed to read the whole text.

Could I be a bit presumptuous as Paul regarding his recommendations regarding marriage when he concluded his remarks on the topic: *"And I think I also have the Spirit of God"* (1 Cor. 7:40)? I know, one can read this as somewhat equivocating or Paul's identification with Christ was profoundly substantial, he could relay his convictions on matters considered socially

The 24 Axioms of Ekklesia

consequential by announcing his conclusions in terms of the Spirit's validation.

The purpose of this writing is simply the view of an author whose attention to this topic is both theological (viz., ecclesiology) and pragmatic over the course of over sixty years of Christian experience. My obvious prejudices must be weighed in the context of the "arguments" raised herein which I feel honor the Lord's quest to answer His Own prayer in John 17 . . . I have attempted to interpret the Scripture with appropriate hermeneutic in securing both the "spiritual sense" and any cultural implications of the text and how these two integrate into the vision and practice of His Ekklesia.

Again, my deep appreciations to those listed in the ACKNOWLEDGEMENT section of this tome—this writing is severely colored by their influence. It's within this framework that our focus upon the words of our Lord—"*I will build My EKKLESIA*"—is open-ended . . . what does Ekklesia look like? We are not here to suggest we precisely know just how He is about doing that. We can account what we do know, framing our interpretations in "spiritual hyperbole" but when the dust clears—only He, along with the other writings of the apostles based upon the "prophetic Scriptures" (Rom. 16:26), knows how He's going about building His Ekklesia. I've tried to give a composite of what it does and does not look like. "*Let each be fully convinced in his own mind*" (Rom. 14:5).

With that background (i.e., **justification** for writing these conclusions), let me be perfectly clear. The authors of the testaments have given us both prophetic and in real time descriptions depicting God's eternal plan and purpose—i.e., why humanity was created in the first place. These include, the One New Man, the Body (of Messiah/Christ), the Bride, the Dwelling Place, the Father's House, the Temple of the LORD, the Holy City, the New Jerusalem, the Holy District, the New Creation, the Commonwealth of Israel, the United Kingdom of David/Tabernacle of David, The Two Olive Trees/One Olive Tree, the Two Sticks/One Stick, the Household of God/Faith, the Elect of God, the Mystery of Messiah/Christ, the Woman of Revelation 12, the Mighty Army/Army of God, the Kingdom of our God, the Image of Christ—and many more.

The advantage we have in the New Testament is limited to the rather concise accounts primarily from the Ekklesia in Corinth and sundry writings scattered throughout the remainder of the NT but most vividly in Romans; and that ensconced within the final eight chapters of Paul's letter—predicated upon Jesus' original statement in Matthew 16:18 and, of course, His prayer in John 17, but as well, the extrapolation of the prophecy made by John concerning the high priest Caiaphas:

> *"Now this he did not say on his own authority; but being high priest that year he prophesied that Jesus would die for the nation, and not for that nation only, but also that **He would gather together in one the children of God** who were scattered abroad"* (John 11:51-52).

All the aforementioned disclosures or descriptions must yield their amplifications to His goal: My EKKLESIA—for without this ultimate reflection both as a noun and as a verb—we are missing the imperative of His original statement.

Yes, He is the Messiah, the Son of the Living God—it is upon this revelation of His Person and Work that He can, through the pinnacle of His creation, humanity, build His Ekklesia and thereby crush . . . utterly defeat His enemy—the very Gates of Hades and all it entails.

This is all the more reinforced by Paul's finality in Romans 16:20 that it would be through the saints who follow the injunctions set forth in the first fifteen chapters of Romans and, most definitely, the "meet and greet" final chapter sixteen that *"The God of peace will crush Satan under your feet shortly."*

The 24 Axioms of Ekklesia

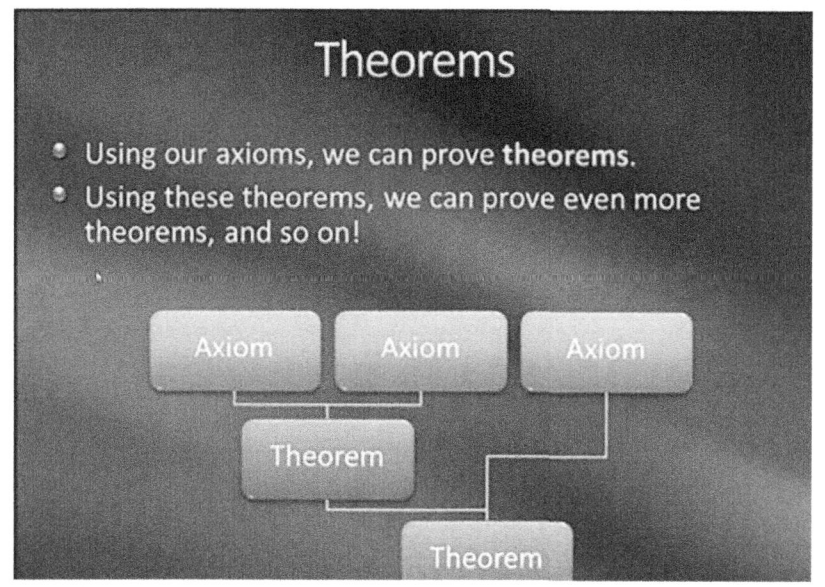

Figure 95 - THE 24 AXIOMS OF EKKLESIA

**THE 24 AXIOMS & THEOREMS OF EKKLESIA
(Note: If it works—then it's a Theorem—
not in order of priority)**

1. The EKKLESIA is not an organization or "religious institution"—it is based upon the Spirit's revelation of the Person and Work of the Messiah, the Son of the Living God (Matt. 16:15-18; John 1:47-51; Rom. 16:25-26) and comprised of living witnesses to that revelation; therefore, it is at its core: organic, spiritual, yet revealed to "spiritual powers" (Eph. 6:10-18) and "earthly kingdoms" as His Kingdom on this earth . . . the "Centrality of Christ/the Messiah" is at the nexus of any Ekklesia.
2. The EKKLESIA is the very "Kingdom of God"—This statement summarizes the Kingdom of God juxtaposed to the "kingdoms of this world." For the EKKLESIA to manifest the Kingdom of God (Acts 28:31) she must be "*teaching*

the things which concern the Lord Jesus Christ with all confidence." She is the Life of Jesus reflecting His Image through the power of the Indwelling Spirit of God as His EKKLESIA—she is literally the very Body of Christ on visible display to the heavens and to the earth. Regarding earthly authorities, in Romans 13 we are enjoined not to "resist the authorities" lest we be found resisting the ordinance of God, bringing judgment on ourselves (Rom 13:2) and to *"render therefore to all their due: taxes to whom taxes are due, customs to whom customs, fear to whom fear, honor to whom honor"* —regarding these matters Paul eventually found himself in Rome under Nero's rule (having cir. 56 A.D. written his epistle to the Christians in Rome during Nero's reign) and in 68 A.D. was beheaded perhaps in the same month (June) in which Nero committed suicide. The Ekklesia is "salt and light" and "a city set on a hill"—she cannot be hid! (Matt. 5:13-16).

3. The EKKLESIA is comprised by all (her membership) who *"Call upon the Name of the Lord"*—both Jew and Gentile (Rom. 10:6-13); entry into this reality is wrought by the Holy Spirit of Promise, NOT by man's manipulation nor human criteria.

4. Exclusion from the EKKLESIA: Reasons for disfellowship of a believer from any Ekklesia assembly is not casual but persistent and unrepentant sinful behavior toward others, obvious and incriminating division coupled with refusal to accept the discipline of entreating brethren—a divisive spirit left unchecked or a "controlling-style spirit" akin to that of a "Jezebel/Ahab spirit", witchcraft, drunkenness, and fornication/adultery directly impacting the Ekklesia— these are grounds for exclusion; likewise we are enjoined to do the following: *"Now I urge you, brethren, note those who cause divisions and offenses, contrary to the doctrine which you learned, and avoid them . . . For those who are such do not serve our Lord Jesus Christ, but their own belly"* (Rom. 16:17-18).

The 24 Axioms of Ekklesia

5. The EKKLESIA enjoins its members to resolve offenses/sins or "faults" between one another by addressing such issues directly between one another—*"go and tell him his fault between you and him"* (Matt. 18:15); then if *"he will not hear, take with you one or two more"* (Matt. 18:16); and if *"he refuses to hear them, tell it to the Ekklesia"* and then, stage four, if he fails to hear the Ekklesia— *"let him be to you like a heathen and a tax collector"* (Matt. 18:17). However, regarding disputes/contentions within any given ministry (see below) the resolution of these issues is committed to the operation of that particular ministry and does not directly involve the Ekklesia—although, those in such ministries are part of the Ekklesia (Acts 15:36-41).

6. The EKKLESIA is best expressed through "brethren" who consistently assemble (Heb. 10:24-25) to uplift the Lord Jesus Christ through manifold expressions based on biblical text found primarily in the books of the Acts, Romans, the Corinthians and the Epistles—writings of Paul, Peter, James and John and confirmed by the gospels, while substantiated by the "prophetic Scriptures" (Rom. 16:26)—in other words: The *"whole counsel of God."*

7. The EKKLESIA's members are all essential with deference given to those who appear "less significant"—its members are all equal in significance—all are needed and all loved without prejudice nor discretion—the New Commandment, the expression of the New Covenant—is at the heart of Ekklesia expression (We love one another as He loved us.). Its membership is "heavenly" and bears no prejudice (Gal. 3:28-29; Eph. 2:11-22; Col. 3:10-11) and it is diverse on many levels—each member has a "portion of Christ" to be shared with others of His One Body (1 Cor. 12:12-27). Each member's portion is his/her "produce of the Good Land"—having entered His rest (Hebrews 4:1-11). The main expression of the EKKLESIA is testifying/prophesying (1 Cor. 14:29-32, 39).

8. EKKLESIA is NOT under anyone's control. No one person or group of people should in appearance or practice

So, You want to do Ekklesia?

attempt to "control" any manifestation of the Ekklesia—nor should its members tolerate anyone manifesting such control (overt, overbearing in time and space)—"control" can be manifested in monopolizing time or technique in any gathering. *"But one and the same Spirit works all these things, distributing to each one individually as HE WILLS."* (Ref. 1 Cor. 12:4-11)

9. EKKLESIA "meeting and greeting"—Romans 16 is given by Paul as a command to practice the integration of the One Body, His Ekklesia. Such "house to house" visitation by the saints is NOT optional or a simple suggestion as a "good idea" but a prerequisite for qualifying as a viable and vibrant EKKLESIA as a verb form! It is the antithesis of exclusivity, isolation and prideful activity. Such "meeting and greeting" of the saints is the anecdote for avoiding division within His One Body.

10. EKKLESIA and Ministers: Ministers or gifted members of His Body do not leave their gift at the door of a gathering; however, they should "tone it down" to allow others to manifest their portion, gifts and ministry. Clearly, 1 Cor. 11-14 does NOT exclude the participation of such gifted members (1 Cor. 12:27-31) but in the affirmative leads us to the expression of "the more excellent way"—LOVE—1 Corinthians 13 to be manifested among all the brethren so gathered for the expression of the EKKLESIA. This "love chapter" is not random—it is specifically related to the inter-relationships within the EKKLESIA.

11. The EKKLESIA is a "corporate offering" unto the Lord. Just as Romans 12 in reference to the "mercies of God" is related to the previous chapters in Romans 9-11 regarding the "inclusion" of us all in "disobedience that He might have mercy on us all" (Rom. 11:31); even so, by these same mercies of God we should present our bodies to be His One Body, a singular sacrifice, *"holy, acceptable to God"* not conformed to the religious systems of this world with their divisive and factious spirit and practice (Rom. 12:1-2).

The 24 Axioms of Ekklesia

12. EKKLESIA is constituted by *"diversities of gifts"*—*"differences of ministries"*—and *"diversities of activities"*—*"but the same Spirit/Lord/God"* (1 Cor. 12:4-7). The overarching expression of any Ekklesia-style gathering is *"each of you has"* and *"one by one"* (1 Cor. 14:26, 31) wherein *"Let all things be done for building up/edification"*—the propensity to "control a gathering" is wrong... for *"the spirits of the prophets are subject to the prophets"*—not to any one prophet or cabal of brethren (1 Cor. 14:32).

13. EKKLESIA "time environments"—Avoid manipulating "time" or "technique" so that *"all may prophesy one by one... that all may be edified"* (1 Cor. 14:31). Finally, such gatherings are not "out of control" participations but are done *"decently and in order"* (1 Cor. 14:40). Grace, mercy and love must be the practice of the Ekklesia—Romans 14 allows for a wide-variety of practice and "manifested grace"—*"Let each be fully convinced in his own mind"* (Rom. 14:6).

14. There are "gifted ones" in the EKKLESIA—Apostles, prophets, evangelists, pastor-teachers (1 Cor. 12:27-31; Eph. 4:11-13)—their primary "ministry" is to "equip" the saints for the "work of the ministry"—not to build up their own ministry (only) but to release others to replicate their own in the building up of the Ekklesia.

15. EKKLESIA leadership: "Leadership" in any Ekklesia is most benign and is NOT formal nor is it under the gifted members of His One Body (the so-called "five-fold ministry")... 1 Corinthians 11:18-19; 1 Peter 5:1-4) depicts "elders" as mature brethren who *"serve willingly, not for dishonest gain"* and are *"examples to the flock"*—none of which appears as an expression of "overlords" (1 Peter 5:3). Such "approved ones" manifest within the Ekklesia on an "as needed" basis—in particular, when the unity within the Ekklesia is put at risk.

16. Within the EKKLESIA there is the *"endeavoring to keep the unity of the Spirit in the bond of peace"* (Eph. 4:3). This endeavoring is maintained by those brethren who are "genuine" or "approved"—Ekklesia must have various

factions who are not factious or divisive; if so, then those who are genuine/approved will manifest (1 Cor. 11:19; 11:28).

17. Each member of an EKKLESIA at the Lord's Table is called to "*examine*" himself (same word for "*approve*" as found in 1 Cor. 11:19 is found in 1 Cor. 11:28) at the Lord's Supper whereby "discerning the Lord's Body" is in view and is the responsibility of everyone attending the assembly to contend for the One Body—to be at peace with all members of the Ekklesia, locally and throughout the world and to encourage all in the assembly to do the same.

18. EKKLESIA is not someone's "ministry." There is a distinction between the Ministry on behalf of the Ekklesia and the Ekklesia itself—neither should "control" and/or "administer" the other. Disputes/contentions within a ministry should be resolved by that ministry—it does not concern the diversity within an Ekklesia. John-Mark (who wrote the Gospel of Mark) became unprofitable for the ministry of Paul but was not disfellowshipped from the Ekklesia and later became profitable for Paul's ministry—none of these affiliations/issues were "brought to the Ekklesia" (Matt. 18:15-20; Acts 15:36-41; 2 Tim. 4:11).

19. The EKKLESIA's Communion Table is open to all who call upon the Lord—it's practice and meaning purposefully varies, as does baptism. It may take place during a "Love Feast" (an actual meal). Unbelievers or the uninformed may be found at such a gathering (1 Cor. 14:23-24).

20. The practice of EKKLESIA tends toward "traditionalized" Christian practice—this is inevitable; however, to avoid falling into a "rut" believers should be versatile and spontaneous in their practice but as "unto the Lord." Likewise, they should welcome diversity (factions but not the factious) AND practice "meeting and greeting" (Romans 16) other brethren in their homes, places of business, education to discover the "riches of Christ" throughout the Ekklesia—keeping in mind and spirit: "You're not the only game in town!"

The 24 Axioms of Ekklesia

21. "Doctrine" within the EKKLESIA—Keep in view that there is "eternal truth" (doctrine) that is well-founded and other doctrine which is available as "healthy teaching" but greatly varies in practice and conviction—doctrine should NOT divide the Body of Christ if the Person and Work of Christ is proclaimed in the Ekklesia—*"We would see Jesus"* (John 12:21). *"The Word was made flesh"* (John 1:14)—*"full of grace and TRUTH"* . . . *"You pore over the Scriptures because you presume that by them you possess eternal life. These are the very words that testify about Me, yet you refuse to come to Me to have life"* (John 5:39-40)—it is in this sense that the Scriptures in and of themselves do not constitute truth—only when mixed with grace can the Word of Life (Christ) be considered eternal truth.

22. A true Minister or Work of the Lord will seek to collaborate/team-up with other Ministers and/or Works building up the Ekklesia (Phil. 1:27). Equippers/ministers of sundry ministries who cannot collaborate with other ministries dedicated to the building up of the Ekklesia run the risk of going solo and are apt to find themselves with an overweening sense of their own propriety—it should be encouraged to "team-up" with one's peers—not federate via ever-expanding organizational systems but seek to "strive together for the faith of the gospel."

23. The EKKLESIA should not be federated aside from the "spiritual definition" wherein Christ is Head of His One Body (Eph. 1:22; 4:15); neither should sundry ministries for the equipping of the saints be federated aside from the mutuality of the fellowship and "teaming up" for the faith of the gospel. (See the differences among the seven ekklesia of Asia in Revelation 2-3.) and the differentiation of the various workers (1 Cor. 1:12-17; 3:5-10). No federation but visitation and fellowship (meeting and greeting other brethren outside our immediate Ekklesia experience) should be the practice of all Ekklesia; however, it goes beyond "meeting and greeting" insofar as ministries concern—ministries should team up with other ministries

So, You want to do Ekklesia?

      which advances the victorious Christian experience; to wit: *"Not in any way terrified by your adversaries, which is to them a proof of perdition, but to you of salvation, and that from God"* (Phil. 1:28).

24. The gospel is comprised of the "*Gospel of the Grace of God*" unto salvation (Acts 20:24) and the "*Gospel of Peace*" between peoples (Rom. 10:11-15)—together they constitute the *Completion Gospel of Christ* (Rom. 15:29) which is the Kingdom of God concerning those things pertaining to "*the Lord Jesus Christ*" (Acts 28:31). Peace with God (personal) must be coupled by "the other side of the same coin"—Peace with others (corporate)—Salvation is personal but "peace through the blood of the cross" involves "*He is our peace, Who has made both one, and has broken down the middle wall of separation . . . so as to create in Himself One New Man from the two, thus making peace . . . He might reconcile them both to God in one body through the cross*" (Eph. 2:14-18).

May the Lord use these feeble efforts to encourage God's people to both see the vision and the practice of His Ekklesia.

                                                    Doug Krieger
                                                   November 2019

ENDNOTES & INDEXES & PUBLICATIONS

Author's Introduction

---

[1] "The religious landscape of the United States continues to change at a rapid clip. In Pew Research Center telephone surveys conducted in 2018 and 2019, 65% of American adults describe themselves as Christians when asked about their religion, down 12 percentage points over the past decade. Meanwhile, the religiously unaffiliated share of the population, consisting of people who describe their religious identity as atheist, agnostic or "nothing in particular," now stands at 26%, up from 17% in 2009. Both Protestantism and Catholicism are experiencing losses of population share. Currently, 43% of U.S. adults identify with Protestantism, down from 51% in 2009. And one-in-five adults (20%) are Catholic, down from 23% in 2009. Meanwhile, all subsets of the religiously unaffiliated population – a group also known as religious "nones" – have seen their numbers swell. Self-described atheists now account for 4% of U.S. adults, up modestly but significantly from 2% in 2009; agnostics make up 5% of U.S. adults, up from 3% a decade ago; and 17% of Americans now describe their religion as "nothing in particular," up from 12% in 2009. Members of non-Christian religions also have grown modestly as a share of the adult population." (Pew Research Center—Religion & Public Life—An update on America's changing religious landscape @ https://www.pewforum.org/2019/10/17/in-u-s-decline-of-christianity-continues-at-rapid-pace/ retrieved on 11.15.2019.

[2] Yet as the Monitor reported in a recent cover story ("Why religion still matters," Oct. 12), religion is still flourishing in the United States, especially within many conservative denominations. While fewer people may now affiliate themselves with a particular religion, more than 3 in 4 Americans still do, and many of them are becoming more committed and active within their houses of worship, according to the Pew Research Center. But not included in this group are what sociologists are now identifying as the "dones." **Roughly 30 million Americans are former churchgoers who nevertheless maintain their faith in God and their Christian identity, according to Professor Packard, who coined the term. According to his research, another 7 million are "almost done" with institutional religion.** (Why these Americans are 'done' with church, but not with God; Christian Science Monitor, December 19, 2015 @ https://www.csmonitor.com/USA/Society/2015/1219/Why-these-Americans-are-done-with-church-but-not-with-God - retrieved on 11.15.2019.

Note: By 2020 the figure in the USA has in all probability exceeded upwards of 40 million "dones" (opinion of this researcher—Doug Krieger).

[3] Although the following article is some five years old—it, nevertheless, follows a demographic trend which can be validated by numerous resources which project the growth of Christianity in all forms throughout nations outside the immediate West (i.e., USA/Canada and Western Europe/Australia); to wit:

> "While Christianity may be on the decline in the United States, the world is becoming more religious, not less. While rising numbers of "nones" — those who claim no religious affiliation when asked — claim the attention of religious pundits, the world tells a different story. Religious convictions are growing and shifting geographically in several dramatic ways.

So, You want to do Ekklesia?

The center of Christianity has shifted from Europe to the global South.
The religious landscape is particularly changing for the world's Christians. A century ago, 80 percent lived in North America and Europe, compared with just 40 percent today. In 1980, more Christians were found in the global South than the North for the first time in 1,000 years. Today, the Christian community in Latin America and Africa, alone, account for 1 billion people. Over the past 100 years, Christians grew from less than 10 percent of Africa's population to its nearly 500 million today. One out of four Christians in the world presently is an Africa (sic.), and the Pew Research Center estimates that will grow to 40 percent by 2030. Asia is also experiencing growth as world Christianity's center has moved not only South, but also East. In the last century, Christianity grew at twice the rate of population in that continent. Asia's Christian population of 350 million is projected to grow to 460 million by 2025. The global religious wildcard is China. Even today, demographers estimate that more Christian believers are found worshipping in China on any given Sunday than in the United States. Future trends, while difficult to predict because so much is below the religious radar, could dramatically drive down the world's religious "nones."

In Latin America, the massive Christian population is becoming more Pentecostal or Charismatic.

The growth of Pentecostalism in Latin America is estimated to be at three times the rate of Catholic growth. Non-Catholic believers now account for 2 percent of Latin America's 550 million Christians. Today, Brazil not only has more Catholics than any other country, but also more Pentecostals, reflecting Pentecostalism's astonishing global growth. Tracing its roots to the Azusa Street revival in 1910, and comprising 5 percent of Christians in 1970, today one of four Christians is Pentecostal or Charismatic. Or think of it this way: one out of 12 people alive today has a Pentecostal form of Christian faith. (Think Christianity is dying? No, Christianity is shifting dramatically; By Wes Granberg-Michaelson, May 20, 2015, The Washington Post)

[4] Other knowledgeable writers on this topic who have addressed the "organic" and/or "house church" phenomenon taking place not only in the West but elsewhere throughout the world, include: Richard Jacobson (***Unchurching: Christianity without Churchianity***—July, 2016); Steve Simms: ***The Joy of Early Christianity and Beyond Church...The Lost Word of the Bible--Ekklesia***—2018; Francis Chan: **Letters to the Church** & Author's Page @ https://www.amazon.com/Francis-Chan/e/B00LLWURSG; Henry Hon: ***One Ekklesia***; ***One Truth***; ***One in Life and Glory***; and the book: ***ONE*** @ www.onebody.life; Ed Silvoso—***Ekklesia: Rediscovering God's Instrument for Global Transformation***; Keith Giles: ***JESUS UNVEILED—Forsaking Church as we know it for Ekklesia as God intended***—(Kindle – 2018); John Zens: From Building to Body Transitioning from Institutional to Organic Church (Web site and resources @ www.searchingtogether.org

INDEX OF PROPER NAMES

(Note: Biblical names, dates, places are NOT placed in this index because of their abundance.)

A

Abraham, Ola. xxiii
Adebayo, Femi (Churchman). xxiii
Allegorical. 127
Alliance World Fellowship. 214
Anabaptist. 48, 51, 242
Anglicanism. 51
Anglicans. 25, 108, 242
Antiochus IV Epiphanes. 157-160, 162, 172
Assemblies of God. 97
Azusa Street Revival. 274

B

Baptists. 51, 93, 108, 242
Barna, George. xvii
Bartleman, Frank. 48-49
Bikers for Christ. 26
Bonito, G. 143
Brace, Kendra. xxiii
Brace, Rod. xxiii

C

Caesar, Julius. 17
California State U. Los Angeles. xv
California State U. Sacramento. xv
Calvary Chapel (Denomination). 52
Calvinists. 242
Campus Crusade for Christ. 97
Cessationism. 127
Chan, Francis. 274
Charismatics. 51

Christian Church (Denomination). 51
Christian Science Monitor. 273
Christian World Liberation Front. 97
Church of Christ (Denomination). 51
Church of the East. 242
Church, J. R. 167
Clarke's Commentary on the Bible. 7
Commonwealth of Israel Foundation. xv
Commonwealth Theology (Blog). 144, 147, 153
Confessional Concerning Christ's Supper (Luther). 241
Conservapedia. 157
Constantine, Emperor. 48, 145, 152
Council of Laodicea. 93, 145, 152
Council of Nicaea. 145, 152

D

Dark Ages. 48
Dangers in the Deliverance Ministries (Foster). 214
Daniel – The Key to Prophetic Revelation (Dr. John Walvoord). 157-160, 162
Daniel Reveals the Bloodline of the Antichrist (J. R. Church). 167
Denver 2019 Convocation. xv
Dispensationalism. 127, 157
DONES. 89-90, 108, 138
Doonan, Simon. 232

E

Early Church Fathers. 246
Early Church/Fathers. 206
Eastern Orthodox Church. 242
Edison, Tom. xx
Edwards, Gene. Xix
Ekklesia: Rediscovering God's Instrument for Global Transformation (Ed Salviso). 274
Enns, Gaylor. 244-247
Evangelicals. 255

F

Fall of Trebizond. 20
Finley, Dr. Gavin. xxiii
Foster, K. Neill. 214
From Building to Body Transitioning from Institutional to Organic Church (John Zens). 274
Further Talks on the Church Life (Watchman Nee). 98, 100

G

Giles, Keith. 274
Gladiator, The (film). 18
Gnosticism (Gnostics). 206
Gospel Outreach (Ministry). 52
Granberg-Michaelson. 274
Great Commandment. 245-246
Gregorian Calendar. 147-148, 151, 260

H

Hamp, Dr. Doug. xxiii
Hebrew Sacred Calendar. 147-152, 185
Hitler, Adolf. 34, 204, 220
Hon, Henry. xiii, xv, 16, 27, 41, 55-56, 274
Hon, Sylvia. xiii

I

Independent Catholic Churches. 242

J

Jacobson, Richard. 274
Jehovah Witnesses. 101, 157, 218, 239, 242
Jesus Movement. xv, 51-53, 97
Jesus People. 52
Jesus Unveiled—Forsaking Church as we know it for Ekklesia as God intended (Keith Geiles). 274
Jezebel vs. Elijah - Dr. Bree Keyton. 199-201

Julian Calendar. 260

K

Keyton, Dr. Bree M. 199-201
Krieger, April. xiii
Krieger, Deborah. xiii, xv
Krieger, Eric. xiii
Krieger, Geoffrey. xiii

L

Laodiceans (ism). 92
Letters to the Church (Francis Chan). 274
Liberal Christianity. 242
Lion's Club. 195
Love Revolution Now (Gaylord Enns). 244
Ludwig's Fountain (UC Berkeley). 97
Luther, Martin. 48, 57, 101, 241
Lutheran State Church(es). 48
Lutheranism. 51, 241-242

M

Maccabean(ees) or Judas M.. 157, 162
Mao, Chairman. 34
Masonic Lodge. 195
McCarroll, Scott. xxiii
McGriff, Carol. xxiii
McGriff, Dene. xv, xxiii
Mein Kampf (Adolf Hitler). 34
Mensa International. 26
Methodism. 51, 242
Mormon. 101, 157, 218
Murray, Andrew. 33

N

Nazi Germany. 203-204
Nee, Watchman. 98
Nero, Emperor. 18, 139, 266
New Commandment. 83, 243-249, 251, 267
New Covenant. 57, 77-78, 81, 83, 243-244, 248-252, 256, 258, 267
Nicolaitanism. 90-91, 93
Non-Denominational Churches. 242
NONES. 273-274

O

ONE (by Henry Hon). 73
One Body Life, Inc. xv, 244
ONE EKKLESIA (By Henry Hon). 55, 274
ONE IN LIFE & GLORY (By Henry Hon). 55, 274
ONE TRUTH (By Henry Hon). 55, 58, 71-72, 274
Oriental Orthodox Church. 242
Orthodox. 239, 255

P

Packard, Professor. 273
Pale of Settlement. 233
Pentecostals (ism). 25, 51, 97, 108, 116, 274
Pew Research Center. 273-274
Plymouth Brethren. 51, 242
Polli, John. xxiii
Presbyterianism. 51, 93, 242
Protestants. 239, 255, 274

R

Red Book (*Little Red Book* by Mao). 34
Redeemer Church of God, Nigeria. 25, 108, 120
Renner. 91
Restoration Movements. 242

Resurrection City (Berkeley, CA). 97
Rodriquez, Milt. xvii xviii-xix
Roman Catholic Church. 38, 46, 48, 95, 100-101, 103, 108, 114, 239, 241, 255, 273-274
Roman Empire. 43
Romulus. 20
Russian Orthodox. 46

S

Salvation Army. 239
Schafer, Chad. Xv
Scientology. 101
Seder Olam Rabbah (Jewish Calendar). 167
Seventh Day Adventist. 108, 157, 162
Shakespeare, William. 17
Shearer, Douglas R. xxiii
Shearer, Sita (Margo). Xxiii
Signs in the Heaven and On The Earth...Man's Days are Numbered and he is Measured (By Doug Krieger). 162
Silvoso, Ed. 274
Simms, Steve. 274
Southern Baptist. 138
Spiritual Counterfeits Project (SCP). 97
Sproul Plaza (Berkeley, CA). 97
St. Peter's Basilica. 25
Steinle, Chris. xxiii

T

The Joy of Early Christianity and Beyond Church (Steve Simms). 274
Titanic (The). 89
Titus, Arch of. xv
Tobih, Dr. xxiii
Townsend. xxiii

U

Unchurching: Christianity without Churchianity (Richard Jacobson). 274
Union Gospel Rescue Mission. 134
Upper Room (Loomis, CA). 122, 221
Urban Hope Alliance. xv
Ussher, Bishop James. 167

V

Viola, Frank. xvii

W

Walvoord, Dr. John. 157-159
Washington Post. 274
White, Ellen G. 162
Woodward, S. Douglas. xv (2x)

Z

Zens, John. 274

INDEX OF SCRIPTURE REFERENCES

Genesis

1:5. *148, 151, 159*
8:4. *150*
25:26. *168*
26:1-6. *168*

Exodus

3:8. *187*
12. *150*
12:1-14. *151*
12:14-15. *151*
12:15-20. *151*
12:40-41. *168*
13:3-10. *151*
23:16. *151(2x)*
34:22. *151(2x)*

Leviticus

4:6-8. *151*
16. *151*
23:4-5. *151*
23:9-14. *151 (2X)*
23:15-21. *151*
23:26-32. *151*
23:34. *154*
23:34-36. *156*
23:33-36, 39-43. *151*
25:8. *164*
26:11-12. *172*

Numbers

9:1-14. *151*
14:7-9. *187*
22-24. *91*
28:16. *151*
28:17-25. *151*
28:26. *151*
28:26-31. *151*
29:7-11. *151*
19:12-38. *151*

Deuteronomy

8:7. *187*

16:1-7. *151*
16:3-4, 8. *15*
16:9-12. *151*
16:13-15. *151*

Joshua

4:19. *185*
5:11-12. *187*

Judges

17:1-18:31. *123*

2 Samuel

5:4-5. *165*

1 Kings

6:1. *155, 175*
6:37-38. *155, 175*
6:38. *167*
7:23. *166*
8:1. *154*
21:26. *199*

2 Chronicles

3:2. *175*
5:2. *154*
7:8-10. *154*
7:9-10. *156*

Ezra

6:15. *157*

Isaiah

25:6. *76*

Jeremiah

17:10. *217*
29:10. *164*
31. *252*
31:31-34. *249*
31:33. *172*
31:33-34. *249*

Ezekiel

28:12, 17. *206*
28:19. *207*
34:30-31. *172*
37:27-28. *172*
40-48. *169, 172, 186 (2X)*
40:1-2. *185*

Daniel

7:25. *160*
8. *vii, 157*
8:1-14. *158*
8:13. *159*
8:13-14. *157*
8:14. *157, 161*
8:15, 17. *159*
8:26. *160, 162*
9:24. *173*
9:24-27. *159, 164*
9:27. *160, 162*
11:31. *160*
12. *160(2x)*
12:7. *160(2x)*
12:11. *160(2x), 161, 162(2x)*

Joel

2:28-32. *43*

Amos

9. *xxiii*

Haggai

1:6-8. *163*
1:14. *164*
2. *167, 172, 177*
2:1. *156*

282

2:4. *169*	16. *61*	10:1. *164*
2:6. *182*	16:12. *65*	10:27. *246*
2:6-7. *171*	16:15-18. *265*	15:4. *165*
2:6-9. *156(2x), 170*	16:16, 18. *188*	19-20. *186*
2:7. *185*	16:18. *3, 14, 43, 45, 262,*	22:3. *174, 176*
1:9. *iv, 1*	*264*	22:10. *258*
2:9. *iv, 1, 172, 178,*	16:27. *152*	22:14-20. *243*
179(2x), 181	17. *61*	22:15-18. *257*
2:10. *163*	18:12. *165*	22:17. *258*
2:10, 18, 20. *157*	18:15. *267*	22:19. *242, 258*
2:10-23. *148*	18:15-17. *126*	22:19-20. *257*
2:10-14. *178*	18:15-20. *270*	22:20. *258(2x)*
2:14. *178*	18:16. *267*	23:50-56. *260*
2:15. *179*	18:17. *267*	
2:15-19. *179*	18:21-22. *164*	**John**
2:18. *179*	21-22. *186*	1:1, 14. *57*
2:18-19. *180*	22:14. *195*	1:9. *55*
2:20-23. *182*	22:35-40. *246*	1:11-14. *254*
2:22-23. *182, 186*	23:25-28. *235*	1:14. *271*
	23:39. *152*	1:17. *61*
Zechariah	24:15. *163*	1:29. *152*
	24:21. *152*	1:47-51. *265*
4. *184*	24:27. *152*	2:18. *21*
6:11-14. *183*	24:30. *152*	3:4-9. *254*
6:12-13. *185*	24:31. *152*	5:39-40. *56, 271*
9. *189*	24:44. *152*	6:47-58. *248*
9:9. *189*	25:23. *152*	7. *148, 176*
9:9-10. *186(2x), 189*	26:26-30. *243*	7:2-39. *152, 175*
9:10. *189*	26:27. *258*	7:14. *177*
14:6. *146*	27:45-50. *44*	7:14, 37-39. *175*
14:16-21. *151*		7:37-39. *176*
	Mark	7:38. *177*
Malachi		7:39. *177*
	5. *214*	7:40. *263*
4:5. *41*	11-12. *186*	10. *148*
	12:28-34. *246*	10:22-24. *173*
Matthew	13:14. *163*	10:22-42. *173*
	14:22-26. *243*	10:30. *173*
4:23-24. *214*	14:23-24. *258*	10:33. *173*
5:13-16. *266*	16:17. *214*	10:38. *173*
5:23-24. *79*	16:20. *214*	11. *174*
6:16. *68*		11-14. *268*
9:37-38. *122*	**Luke**	11:9. *186*
10:36. *50*		11:19. *270(2x)*
12:38. *21(2x)*	4:32. *65*	11:28. *270(2x)*
15. *68*	9-10. *214*	
15:9. *67*		

So, You want to do Ekklesia?

11:30. *255*	2:13. *43*	**Romans**
11:31-34. *255*	2:15. *43*	
11:51-52. *264*	2:42. *65*	1-8. *18*
12. *186(2x)*	2:46. *243*	1:7. *18*
12-17. *240*	3.20. *41*	6:4. *152*
12:4-7. *269*	3:25. *45*	8. *18*
12:4-11. *268*	5:28. *65*	8:38-39. *18*
12:12-27. *267*	6:5. *91*	9-11. *24, 268*
12:21. *271*	8:1-7. *214*	9-16. *19*
12:27-31. *268-269*	8:9-24. *215*	10:6-13. *266*
13:1-30. *243*	10:12. *44*	10:11-15. *272*
13:31-35. *243*	10:28. *34-36*	10:12. *26, 45*
13:34. *247*	10:30. *44*	10:15-16. *22*
14. *243*	10:34-36. *45*	11:31. *269*
14:6. *56-57*	10:44-45. *46*	12. *268*
14:15, 21, 23. *243*	11:17. *45*	12:1-2. *269*
14:17. *57*	13. *99*	12:5. *79*
14:19-31. *243*	13:1-4. *99*	12:5-8. *213*
14:23-24. *270*	13:2. *101*	13. *266*
14:26, 31. *269*	13:2-3. *68*	13:1-14. *18*
14:29-32, 39. *268*	13:3. *101*	13:2. *266*
14:31. *269*	13:4. *101*	14. *25, 123, 145*
14:32. *269*	13:14. *99*	14:1. *144*
14:40. *269*	14:1. *99*	14:5. *263*
15. *243*	14:8. *99*	14:5, 1. *82*
15:1-8. *188*	14:21. *99*	14:5-6. *153*
15:12-14. *247*	14:23. *68, 99*	14:6. *269*
15:12-15. *243*	15. *xxiii*	14:17-19. *26*
15:26. *57*	15:23. *94*	15:4. *66*
16. *243*	15:30-41. *94*	15:5-6. *26*
16:13. *57*	15:36-41. *127, 220,*	15:7. *16*
16:13-15. *57*	*267, 270*	15:7-13. *16*
17. *xx, 59, 243-244,*	15:37-40. *126*	15:16, 19-20, 29. *22*
259-260, 263-264	15:38. *220*	15:29. *22, 272*
17:2-3. *244*	17:19-20. *21*	15:29-33. *22*
17:8, 14, 17. *244*	17:21. *21*	16. *268, 271*
17:21, 23. *262*	17:32. *21*	16:1-5. *16*
17:22-24. *244(3x)*	19:9-10. *111*	16:1-27. *16, 17(2x)*
17:23. *xxi*	19:13-20. *214*	16:5. *79*
17:24. *244*	20:9. *34*	16:5, 23. *134*
	20:17-38. *135*	16:15. *16*
Acts	20:24. *45, 272*	16:17. *66*
	20:28-31. *208*	16:17-18. *125, 267*
2:1-4. *152*	21:8-9. *214*	16:17-19. *201*
2:4. *42*	21:9. *232*	16:20. *14, 87, 264*
	28:31. *266, 272*	

16:23. *7-8*	11:25. *252, 258*	14:29-30. *117*
16:25. *16, 22*	11:26. *252*	14:29-32, 39. *268*
16:25-26. *265*	11:27-29. *253*	14:31. *9, 75, 269*
16:26. *19, 263, 267*	11:27-34. *251*	14:32. *75, 269*
1 Corinthians	11:28. *253, 270(2x)*	14:32-33. *11*
	11:29-30. *79*	14:33. *83*
1:11-14. *254*	11:30. *255*	14:36. *109*
1:12. *xix, 32, 34*	11:31-34. *255*	14:40. *41, 269*
1:12-17. *272*	12:4-6. *224*	14:40, 33. *83*
1:22. *21-22*	12:4-7. *5, 83, 269*	15:20-23. *152*
3:4-9. *254*	12:4-11. *213, 268*	15:52. *152*
3:5-10. *272*	12:7. *115, 214*	
3:11. *179*	12:7-11. *113*	**2 Corinthians**
2:4. *214*	12:8. *84*	
2:12-30. *111*	12:8-10. *85*	1:5-11. *230*
5:1-13. *220*	12:9-31. *118*	3:1-6. *250*
5:7. *152*	12:11. *85, 195*	3:2-3. *261*
5:8. *152*	12:12-13. *152*	3:4-6. *39*
5:11, 13. *229*	12:12-27. *267*	3:7-18. *250*
6. *219*	12:13. *26*	3:16-18. *251*
6:1-11. *219*	12:14. *117*	3:18. *203-204*
7:1, 8, 32. *68*	12:26, 31. *269*	10:12. *196*
7:40. *263*	12:27. *111, 152*	11:3. *208*
8:1. *207*	12:27-31. *268-269*	
9:16. *xxi*	12:28. *10*	**Galatians**
11-14. *4-6, 10-11, 80,*	12:28-30. *111*	
107-108, 111-113,	12:29-30. *85, 213*	2:5, 14. *251*
119(2x), 120, 216,	12:31. *111*	2:6. *45*
268	13. *268*	3:15-18. *168*
11:3-15. *231*	13:1-13. *111*	3:28. *26*
11:16. *231*	13. *10-11, 14, 119(3x),*	3:28-29. *267*
11:17-18. *29*	*201-202, 215*	6:1. *230*
11:17-22. *251*	13:12. *39*	
11:17-34. *243-244, 251*	14:1. *215(2x)*	**Ephesians**
11:17-chap. 14. *256*	14:6. *66*	
11:18-19. *128, 269*	14:23-24. *270*	1:13. *57*
11:19. *6-7, 22(2x), 25,*	14:23, 26. *73*	1:14-18. *17*
113, 222-223,	14:23. *45, 74*	1:21. *271*
253(3x), 270(2x)	14:23-24. *270*	2. *251*
11:20-22. *77*	14:23-25. *107*	2:8-9. *64, 217*
11:22. *77, 252*	14:25. *106*	2:11-22. *267*
11:23-24. *240*	14:26. *30, 75, 84, 108,*	2:12. *xxiii*
11:23-26. *251*	*205*	2:14-15. *xiii*
11:24-26. *257*	14:26, 31. *269*	2:14-18. *45(2x), 81, 272*
	14:26-33. *5(2x)*	

So, You want to do Ekklesia?

2:14-22. *171*	2:16-17. *143, 153*	**Hebrews**
2:15. *57*	2:19-23. *146*	
2:20-22. *180, 225*	3:10-11. *267*	2:4. *214*
3:1-12. *181*	3:11. *26*	3:11, 18. *187*
3:1-20. *181*		4:1, 3, 5, 8-11. *187*
3:21. *177, 181*	**1 Thessalonians**	4:1-11. *187, 268*
4:3. *xxi, 7, 56, 103, 223,*		5:12-13. *136*
270	4:16. *152*	6:1. *55*
4:3-5. *87*		7:1-3. *184*
4:4-7. *87*	**2 Thessalonians**	9:11-12. *152*
4:11-12. *94*		9:28. *248*
4:11-13. *269*	1:10. *177*	10:12-17. *249*
4:11-14. *194*	2. *172*	10:24-25. *267*
4:11-15. *105*	2:3-4. *175*	12:26-29. *171*
4:12. *35, 73, 106, 224*	2:3-10. *174*	13:9. *65*
4:13. *xxi, 71, 197*	2:3-12. *163*	13:20. *225*
4:14. *67-68*		
4:15. *224, 271*		**James**
4:15, 13. *224*	**1 Timothy**	
4:21. *57*	1:10. *66*	2:20. *64*
4:24. *58*	2:4. *58*	
4:32. *14*	3:1-13. *94*	**1 Peter**
5. *204*	4:1-3. *68*	
5:21. *193*		1:17. *45*
5:23-24. *204*	**2 Timothy**	2:9. *195*
5:25-27. *xxiii*		3:18-22. *150*
5:32. *203*	2:2. *110, 136*	5:1-4. *269*
6. *189*	2:15. *94*	5:2-3. *225*
6:9. *45*	2:16-18. *140*	5:3. *269*
6:10-18. *265*	2:25. *58*	
	3:5. *48*	**1 John**
Philippians	3:7. *58*	
	3:10. *66*	2:19. *218(2x)*
1:1. *35, 94*	3:16. *66, 147*	2:20, 27. *220*
1:27. *35(2x), 53, 271*	4:2-4. *136*	4:6. *57*
1:28. *45, 272*	4:3. *66-67*	5:6. *57*
2:1-8. *38*	4:5. *110, 136*	**2 John**
2:2-8. *227*	4:10-11, 14. *140*	
2:12. *69*	4:11. *127, 270*	1:2. *58*
3:8-15. *63*	4:17. *139-140*	1:9. *55*
4:2. *35*		1:9-10. *65*
	Titus	
Colossians		**3 John**
	1:9. *67*	
2:9. *57*	2:1. *67*	1:4. *57*

286

Revelation

1. *184*
1:1. *205*
2-3. *92, 225, 271*
2:6. *90*
2:14. *65*
2:14-15. *91*
2:15. *65*
2:24. *65, 206*
3:16. *92*
3:17. *92*
6:12-17. *152*
7. *165*
8-9. *152*
9:11. *163*
11. *vi, 49(2x)*
11:15-18. *152(2x)*
12. *264*
12:7-17. *163*
12:14. *160*
13. *177*
13:1-18. *163*
13:14-15. *203*
14. *122, 165*
14:14-16. *42(2x)*
14:17-20. *42*
17:8-11. *42*
19:11. *183*
21. *50, 169, 204*
21:2. *203*
21:3, 22. *172*
21:16. *165-166*
21:16-17. *165*
21:17. *167*

So, You want to do Ekklesia?

PUBLICATIONS BY DOUG KRIEGER & ASSOCIATE AUTHORS

Doug Krieger's Author Page @ Amazon:

NEWER PUBLICATIONS

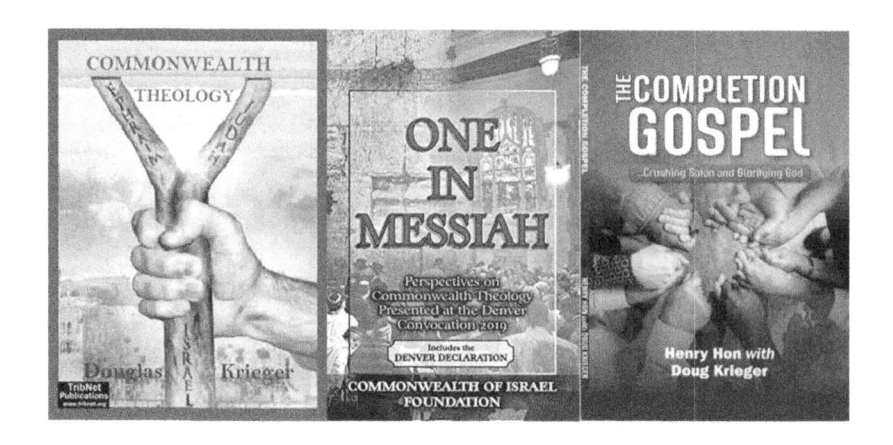

DOUGLAS W. KRIEGER – AUTHOR'S PAGE

Newest Release – Summer, 2020:

COMMONWEALTH THEOLOGY ESSENTIALS

Douglas Krieger   Dr. Douglas Hamp
Dr. Gavin Finley   Chris Steinle

Made in the USA
Monee, IL
29 December 2020